The
Economics
of Public Issues

The Economics of Public Issues

FIFTEENTH EDITION

Roger LeRoy Miller
Institute for University Studies, Arlington, Texas

Daniel K. Benjamin
Clemson University and PERC, Bozeman, Montana

Douglass C. North
Washington University, St. Louis, Missouri

Boston San Francisco New York
London Toronto Sydney Tokyo Singapore Madrid
Mexico City Munich Paris Cape Town Hong Kong Montreal

Publisher: Greg Tobin
Editor in Chief: Denise Clinton
Sponsoring Editor: Noel Kamm
Director of Development: Kay Ueno
Assistant Development Editor: Sara Holliday
Editorial Assistant: Courtney Schinke
Managing Editor: Nancy H. Fenton
Senior Production Supervisor: Kathryn Dinovo
Supplements Coordinator: Heather McNally
Senior Marketing Manager: Roxanne Hoch
Senior Prepress Supervisor: Caroline Fell
Senior Manufacturing Buyer: Carol Melville
Cover Design: Gina Hagen Kolenda
Text Design: Gina Hagen Kolenda
Production Coordination: Orr Book Services
Composition: Nesbitt Graphics, Inc.

Cover photograph: Copyright © Heather Forcier

Library of Congress Cataloging-in-Publication Data
Miller, Roger LeRoy.
    The economics of public issues / Roger LeRoy Miller, Daniel K. Benjamin,
Douglass C. North. — Fifteenth ed.
        p. cm.
    Includes bibliographical references and index.
    ISBN 978-0-321-41610-0
    1. Economics. 2. Industrial policy. 3. Economic policy. I. Benjamin, Daniel K.
II. North, Douglass Cecil. III. Title.
    HB171.M544 2008
    330.973'0931--dc22
                                        2007019536

ISBN-13: 978-0-321-41610-0
ISBN-10: 0-321-41610-4

1 2 3 4 5 6 7 8 9 10—DOC—11 10 09 08 07

To Larry Mayle,
The man who puts economics to work.
Thanks for your friendship.

—R.L.M

To Scott Ryerson Benjamin,
An outstanding addition to the crew.

—D.K.B.

Contents

Suggestions for Use

At the request of our readers, we include the following table to help you incorporate the chapters of this book into your syllabus. Depending on the breadth of your course, you may also want to consult the companion paperback, *The Economics of Macro Issues*, 3rd Edition, which features macroeconomic topics and a similar table in its preface.

Economics Topics	Recommended Chapters in *The Economics of Public Issues*, 15th Edition
Introduction to Economics	1, 3, 4, 23
Opportunity Costs and Scarcity	1, 2, 26
Demand and Supply	5, 6, 7
Demand and Supply Applications	5, 6, 7, 8, 9, 10, 12, 16, 21, 28
The Public Sector and Public Choice	1, 20, 21, 22, 23, 24, 25, 27, 28
Taxes, Transfers, and Public Spending	22, 23, 24, 25
Consumer Behavior	1, 3, 5, 7, 9, 10
Elasticity of Demand and Supply	2, 3, 5, 7, 9, 11, 18, 21
Rents, Profits, and the Financial Environment of Business	10, 13, 15, 16, 20
Firm Production and Cost	1, 3, 10, 15, 16
Perfect Competition	21
Monopoly	16, 17, 20
Monopolistic Competition	15, 17, 18, 19
Oligopoly	16, 22
Regulation and Antitrust	3, 15, 17, 20
Unions and the Labor Market	12, 13, 14, 17
Income, Poverty, and Health Care	4, 13, 14, 15, 24
Environmental Economics	1, 2, 7, 26, 27, 28, 29
International Trade	14, 30, 31, 32
International Finance	32

Preface

This book is about some issues of our times. Several of these issues are usually thought of as being inherently noneconomic. Others provide classic illustrations of the core of economic science. Many are controversial and thus are likely to evoke noneconomic reactions to what we have to say. In our view, however, the one feature that ties all of the issues together is that they illustrate the power of economics in explaining the world around us. And, we might add, we hope all of them illustrate that economics can be entertaining as well as informative.

Over the years, we have sought to select issues for this book that, in addition to the attributes just noted, possess a sense of immediacy. We hope you will find that the issues we have added for this edition meet this criterion. The new issues include the following:

- Death by Bureaucrat *(when bureaucratic choices mean life for some people—and death for others)*
- Ethanol Madness *(how one government policy illustrates the nature of all government policy)*
- (Why) Are Women Paid Less? *(why are women paid less while men are working less?)*
- Immigration, Superstars, and Poverty *(are the rich getting richer and the poor getting poorer—and if not, why does it look that way?)*
- Monopsony and Competition in Health Care *(insurance makes health care expensive, but it also makes it good)*
- Big Oil, Big Oil Prices? *(does ExxonMobil really decide how much we pay at the pump?)*
- College Costs (. . . and Costs and Costs) *(college costs have tripled, but the quality of the product hasn't; what's going on?)*

Also new for this edition is a greater emphasis throughout on the interplay between economics and the process of making the policies that address (or create) the public issues we analyze. In numerous chapters, for example, we show that the **rational ignorance** that results from the diffuse costs of many government policies helps explain why those programs are able to concentrate so many benefits in the hands of so few. One classic example of this is found in America's program of farm subsidies, but other illustrations abound, and we make the common threads of all of them clear to the reader.

This edition also continues two features that seem universally appreciated by students and faculty: a Glossary and a list of Selected References, both at the back of the book. The glossary terms are set in boldface in the text the first time they are used, and the terms are arranged alphabetically in the Glossary, with a succinct definition for each. The Selected References only scratch the surface of the rich literature we have drawn upon in preparing this book, but the interested reader will be able to use them as a springboard for as much research as he or she wishes to undertake.

Longtime users will recognize that the book has been reorganized to bring back "Labor Markets" as Part Three. Because today's students soon will be facing the rigors of full-time participation in the workforce, we believe it is important for them to build their knowledge of some of the public issues that will confront them there.

We also have substantially expanded Part Four ("Market Structures") to reflect the growing importance in the economy of markets that cannot be considered purely competitive. Indeed, three entirely new chapters are included in this part of the book, and they embody ways of thinking about public issues that we think readers will find both novel and exciting.

All of the other chapters in this edition have been partly or completely rewritten, and every chapter is as up-to-date as we can make it. What you will consistently find is a straightforward application of economic principles as they are taught in virtually all courses in economics, public policy, and the social sciences. This book can be understood by readers who have taken a course in economics, are taking a course in economics, or have never taken a course in economics: We have made it as self-contained and as accessible as possible.

The chapters are organized into seven parts. Part One examines the foundations of all economic analysis, including the concepts of scarcity, trade-offs, opportunity cost, marginal analysis, and the like. In a sense, the four chapters in this introductory part set the stage for the remaining twenty-eight chapters. Parts Two through Six cover the topics—demand and supply, labor markets, imperfect competition, environmental issues, and the impact of government policies—that are integral to virtually every course in which economics plays a role. Finally, Part Seven examines global affairs because these matters are an essential part of the public issues of today.

Every part has an introduction that prepares the reader for the material that is included in the chapters in that part. These part openers summarize and tie together the relevant issues, thus serving as launchpads for the analyses that follow. Students would be well advised to read these part openers before they embark on any of the chapters they precede.

Every instructor will want to access the *Instructor's Manual* that accompanies *The Economics of Public Issues*. It is available online to all adopters of the book at the Instructor Resource Center, a secure and password-protected Web site (www.aw-bc.com/irc). In writing this manual, we have tried to incorporate the very best of the teaching aids that we use when we teach from *The Economics of Public Issues*. For each chapter, the manual provides the following:

- A synopsis that cuts to the core of the economic issues involved in the chapter.
- A concise exposition of the "behind the scenes" economic analysis on which the discussion in the text is based. In almost all cases, this exposition is supplemented with one or more diagrams that we have found to be particularly useful as teaching tools.
- Answers to the Discussion Questions posed at the end of the chapter—answers that further develop the basic economic analysis of the chapter and almost always suggest new avenues of discussion.

The world of public issues continues to evolve. By the time you read these words, we will be working on the next edition. If you have any particular subjects you would like included in the future, let us know by writing us in care of Pearson Addison Wesley.

Several chapters in this edition draw on the "Tangents" column that Daniel Benjamin writes for *PERC Reports*. We are grateful to the Property and Environment Research Center (PERC) for permission to use that material. In addition, literally dozens of kind users of the last edition of this book, as well as several extremely diligent and thoughtful reviewers, offered suggestions for the current edition, including

Timothy Fuerst, Bowling Green State University
John Horowitz, Ball State University
Jim Hubert, Seattle Central Community College

Richard Marcus, University of Wisconsin, Milwaukee
Cyril Morong, San Antonio College
Ray Pepin, Stonehill College
Valerie Ramey, University of California, San Diego
David Schweikhardt, Michigan State University

Scarcity of space precluded us from adopting all of their recommendations, but we believe they will be able to identify the impact they each had on this edition. To them and to our users who wrote to us we offer our sincere thanks and hope that the end result was worthy of their time and concern. We also thank Noel Kamm and Sara Holliday for shepherding the project, Sue Jasin for her expert manuscript preparation, and Robbie Benjamin, whose editorial skills once again have improved the final product. All errors remain, of course, solely our own.

R.L.M.
D.K.B.
D.C.N.

PART ONE

The Foundations of Economic Analysis

Introduction

Our world is one of **scarcity;** we want more than we have. The reason is simple. Although we live in a world of limited **resources,** we have unlimited wants. This does not mean we all live and breathe solely to drive the fastest cars or wear the latest clothes. It means that we all want the right to make decisions about how resources are used—even if what we want to do with those resources is to feed starving children in developing nations.

Given the existence of scarcity, we must make choices; we cannot have more of everything, so to get more of some things, we must give up other things. Economists express this simple idea by saying that we face **trade-offs.** For example, a student who wants higher grades generally must devote more time to studying and less time to, say, going to the movies; the trade-off in this instance is between grades and entertainment.

The concept of a trade-off is one of the (surprisingly few) basic principles you must grasp to understand the economics of public issues. We illustrate the simplicity of these principles with Chapter 1, "Death by Bureaucrat," which examines a behind-the-scenes trade-off made every day on our behalf by the U.S. Food and Drug Administration (FDA). This federal government agency is charged with ensuring that new prescription medicines are both safe and effective. In carrying out its duties, the FDA requires pharmaceutical companies to subject proposed new drugs to extensive testing. Additional exhaustive testing improves the chances that a drug will be both safe and effective, but it also slows the approval of new drugs, thus depriving some individuals of the ability to use the drugs to treat their illnesses.

The drug-approval process undoubtedly reduces pain and suffering for some people and even saves the lives of others because it lowers the chances that an unsafe or ineffective drug will reach the market. Yet because the process also slows the rate at which drugs reach the market (and may even prevent some safe and effective drugs from ever being introduced), the pain and suffering of other individuals are increased. Indeed, some people die as a result. This, then, is the terrible trade-off we face in Chapter 1: Who shall live and who shall die?

As Chapter 1 suggests, there are times when government bureaucrats don't always make the choices we would expect and may not even make the choices we would prefer. We explore the reasons behind such decisions in Chapter 2, "Ethanol Madness," where we answer this simple query: If the **biofuel** ethanol doesn't protect the environment or conserve resources, why do we mandate its use as a gasoline additive and subsidize its production? The answer lies at the heart of **political economy,** the use of economics to study the causes and consequences of political decision making. It is true (as we emphasize in Chapter 4) that a critical function of government is to provide the institutional structure necessary for the creation and retention of our total wealth, broadly construed. Nevertheless, the essence of much government policymaking has nothing to do with making the economic pie larger. Instead, many government policies are directed at dividing up the pie in new ways, so that one group gets more resources at the expense of some other group. To do this successfully, politicians must be adept at exploiting the **rational ignorance** of voters, concentrating the benefits of policies among a few favored recipients while dispersing the costs of those policies across a large number of disfavored individuals. In the case of ethanol, we see that members of Congress do this in ways that enrich farmers and large ethanol producers at the expense of motorists and taxpayers.

All public issues compel us to face the question of how to make the best choices. Economists argue that doing so requires the use of what we call **marginal analysis.** The term *marginal* in this context means incremental or additional. All choices involve costs and benefits—we give up something for anything that we get. As we engage in more of any activity (eating, studying, or sleeping, for example), the **marginal benefits** of that activity eventually decline: The *additional* benefits associated with an *additional* unit of the activity get lower. In contrast, the **marginal costs** of an activity eventually rise as we engage in more and more of it. The best choices are made when we equate the marginal benefits and marginal costs of activity; that is, we try to determine whether engaging in any more of a given activity would produce additional costs in excess of the additional benefits.

In Chapter 3, "Flying the Friendly Skies?" we apply the principles of marginal analysis to the issue of airline safety. How safe is it to travel at 600 miles per hour 7 miles above the ground? How safe *should* it be? The answers to these and other questions can be explored using marginal analysis. One of the conclusions we reach is that *perfect* safety is simply not in the cards. Every time you step into an airplane (or even across the street), there is some risk that your journey will end unhappily. As disconcerting as this might sound at first, we think you will find after reading this chapter that once the costs and benefits are taken into account, you would have it no other way.

Every choice we make entails a **cost:** in a world of scarcity, something must be given up to obtain anything of value. Costs, combined with the benefits of our choices, comprise the **incentives** that ultimately inform and guide our decisions. That these decisions—and thus the incentives—have real and lasting consequences is nowhere more evident than in Chapter 4, "The Mystery of Wealth." Here we seek to answer a simple but profound question: Why are the citizens of some nations rich while the inhabitants of others are poor? Your initial answer might be "Because of differences in the **natural-resource endowments** of the nations." It is true that ample endowments of energy, timber, and fertile land all help raise wealth. But it turns out that natural resources are only a very small part of the answer.

Far more important in determining the wealth of the citizenry are the fundamental political and legal **institutions** of a nation. Institutions such as political stability, secure private property rights, and legal systems based on the **rule of law** create the incentives that encourage people to make long-term investments in improving land and in all forms of **physical** and **human capital.** These investments raise the

capital stock, which in turn provides for more growth long into the future. And the cumulative effects of this growth over time eventually yield much higher standards of living: They make us rich. Thus incentives, comprising both costs and benefits, turn out to be an integral component of the foundations of economic analysis, as well as the foundations of society.

Death by Bureaucrat

How would you rather die? From a lethal reaction to a drug prescribed by your doctor? Or because your doctor failed to prescribe a drug that would have saved your life? If this choice sounds like one you would rather not make, consider this: Employees of the Food and Drug Administration (FDA) make that decision on behalf of millions of Americans many times each year. More precisely, FDA bureaucrats decide whether or not new medicines (prescription drugs) should be allowed to go on sale in the United States. If the FDA rules against a drug, physicians in America may not legally prescribe it, even if thousands of lives are being saved by the drug each year in other countries.

The FDA's authority to make such decisions dates back to the passage of the Food and Drug Safety Act of 1906. That law required that medicines be correctly labeled as to their contents and that they not contain any substances harmful to the health of consumers. Due to this legislation, Dr. Hostatter's Stomach Bitters and Kickapoo Indian Sagwa, along with numerous rum-laden concoctions, cocaine-based potions, and supposed anticancer remedies, disappeared from druggists' shelves. The law was expanded in 1938 with the passage of the Food, Drug, and Cosmetic Act, which forced manufacturers to demonstrate the safety of new drugs before being allowed to offer them for sale. (This law was prompted by the deaths of 107 people who had taken Elixir Sulfanilamide, an antibiotic that contained poisonous diethylene glycol, a chemical cousin of antifreeze.)

The next step in U.S. drug regulation came after a rash of severe birth defects among infants whose mothers during pregnancy had taken a sleep aid known as thalidomide. When these birth defects first became apparent, the drug already was widely used in Europe and Canada, and the FDA was nearing approval for its use in America. In fact, about 2.5 million thalidomide tablets were already in the hands of U.S. physicians as samples. The FDA ordered all of the samples destroyed and

we must give up other things. Although FDA review of drugs saves lives by preventing the introduction of unsafe or ineffective drugs, the cost is billions of dollars of added expenses, plus delayed availability of safe and efficacious drugs, resulting in the deaths of hundreds of thousands of people.

2. *The cost of an action is the alternative that is sacrificed.* Economists often express costs (and benefits) in terms of dollars because this is a simple means of accounting for and measuring them. But that doesn't mean that costs have to be monetary, nor does it mean that economics is incapable of analyzing costs and benefits that are quite human. The costs that led to the 1938 and 1962 amendments were the very visible deaths caused by sulfanilamide and the terrible birth defects due to thalidomide. Subsequent revisions to the FDA process for reviewing drugs, as with AZT and Taxol, have been in response to the adverse effects caused by the regulation-induced drug lag.

3. *The relevant costs and benefits are the marginal (incremental) ones.* The relevant question is not whether safety is good or bad; it is instead how much safety we want—which can only be answered by looking at the added (marginal) benefits of more safety compared to the added (marginal) costs. One possible response to the sulfanilamide poisonings or thalidomide was to have outlawed new drugs altogether. That would guarantee that no more people would be harmed by new drugs. But surely this "solution" would not be sensible, because the marginal cost (due to higher Type II errors) would exceed the marginal benefit (caused by reduced Type I errors).

4. *People respond to incentives.* And this is true whether we are talking about consumers, suppliers, or government bureaucrats. Here the incentive to amend the law in 1938 and 1962 was the very visible death and disfigurement of individuals. The eventual FDA decision to speed up the review process was prompted by intense lobbying by individuals who believed (correctly, as it turned out) that they might be benefited by drugs not yet approved.

5. *Things aren't always as they seem.* Many analyses of the effects of government policies take an approach that doesn't fully recognize the actions that people would otherwise have taken. Thus official pronouncements about the effects of policies routinely misrepresent their impact—not because there is necessarily any attempt to deceive but because it is often difficult to know what would have happened otherwise. Pharmaceutical manufacturers, for example,

have strong incentives to avoid introducing drugs that are unsafe or ineffective because the companies are subject to loss of reputation and to lawsuits. For similar reasons, physicians have strong incentives to avoid prescribing such drugs for their patients. Even without FDA regulation, there would thus be extensive testing of new drugs before their introduction. Hence it is incorrect to ascribe the generally safe and effective nature of modern drugs entirely to FDA protection. The flip side, however, is that the drug development process is inherently long, complicated, and costly. Even without FDA oversight, some people would die waiting for new drugs because self-interested manufacturers would insist on some testing and cautious physicians would proceed slowly in prescribing new drugs.

The people who work at the FDA (and members of Congress) are publicly castigated when they "allow" a Type I error to occur— especially when it is a drug that kills people. Thus FDA bureaucrats have a strong incentive to avoid such errors. But when testing delays cause a Type II error—as with Septra—it is almost impossible to point to specific people who died because the drug was delayed. As a result, officials at the FDA are rarely attacked directly for such delays. Because the costs of Type II errors are much more difficult to discern than the costs of Type I errors, many observers believe that there is an inherent bias at the FDA in favor of being "safe rather than sorry"—in other words, excessive testing.

6. *Policies always have unintended consequences, and as a result, their net benefits are almost always less than anticipated.* In the case of government regulations, balancing incremental costs and benefits (see principle 3) fails to make good headlines. Instead, what gets politicians reelected and regulators promoted are *absolute* notions such as safety (and motherhood and apple pie). Thus if a little safety is good, more must be better, so why not simply mandate that drug testing "guarantee" that everyone is free of risk from dangerous drugs. Eventually, the reality of principle 3 sinks in, but in this case not before the drug lag had killed many people.

As is often true with important public issues, our story has one more interesting twist. Thalidomide is back on the market. In 1998, it was approved by the FDA for use in treating Hansen's disease (leprosy), and in 2006, the FDA gave physicians the OK to use it in treating bone marrow cancer. In each instance, there are strong protections to prevent pregnant women from taking the drug. And so perhaps the very drug that brought us the deadly drug lag will turn out to be a lifesaver for a new generation of patients.

DISCUSSION QUESTIONS

1. Does the structure of the drug industry have any bearing on the types of errors that drug firms are likely to make? That is, would a drug industry made up of numerous highly competitive firms be more or less likely to introduce unsafe drugs than an industry consisting of a few large firms?

2. How could the incentives facing the people at the FDA be changed to reduce the incidence of Type II errors? (*Hint:* Is it possible to compare the FDA approval process with the drug-approval process in other nations?)

3. What would be the advantages and disadvantages of a regulatory system in which, rather than having the FDA permit or prohibit new drugs, the FDA merely published its opinions about the safety and efficacy of drugs and then allowed physicians to make their own decisions about whether or not to prescribe the drugs for their patients?

4. Suppose, for simplicity, that Type I and Type II errors resulted in deaths only. Keeping in mind that too little caution produces Type I errors and too much caution produces Type II errors, what would be the best mix of Type I and Type II errors?

Ethanol Madness

Henry Ford built his first automobile in 1896 to run on pure ethanol. If Congress has its way, the cars of the future will be built the same way. But what made good economic sense in the late nineteenth century doesn't necessarily make economic sense in the early twenty-first century—although it does make for good politics. Indeed, the ethanol story is a classic illustration of how good politics routinely trumps good economics to yield bad policies.

Ethanol is made in the Midwest just like moonshine whiskey is made in Appalachia: Corn and water are mixed into a mash, enzymes turn starch to sugar, yeast is added, and heat ferments the brew. Once this is distilled, the liquid portion is ethanol and the solids are used as a high-protein animal food. The high-proof ethanol is combustible but yields far less energy per gallon than gasoline does. Despite this inefficiency, the Energy Policy Act of 2005 requires that ethanol be added to gasoline, in increasing amounts through 2012. This requirement is supposed to conserve resources and improve the environment. It does neither. Instead, it lines the pockets of American corn farmers and ethanol makers and incidentally enriches some Brazilian sugarcane farmers along the way.

Federal law has both encouraged and subsidized ethanol as a so-called alternative fuel for more than thirty years. But it was not until 2005 that ethanol really achieved national prominence. The use mandates of the Energy Policy Act, combined with surging gas prices and an existing 51-cent-per-gallon federal ethanol subsidy, created a boom in ethanol production. By 2006, ethanol refineries were springing up all over the Midwest, and imports of ethanol from Brazil reached record-high levels.

Three factors are typically used to justify federal use mandates and subsidies for ethanol. First, it is claimed that adding ethanol to gasoline reduces air pollution and so yields environmental benefits. That may have been true fifteen or twenty years ago, but even the Environmental Protection Agency acknowledges that ethanol offers no environmental advantages over other modern methods of making reformulated gasoline. Hence neither the congressional mandate to add ethanol nor the 51-cent-per-gallon subsidy for its use as a fuel additive can be justified on environmental grounds.

A second argument advanced on behalf of ethanol is that it is "renewable," in that fields on which corn is grown to produce ethanol this year can be replanted with more corn next year. This is true enough, but we are in little danger of running out of "nonrenewable" crude oil any time in the next century. Indeed, proven reserves of oil are at record-high levels, and the price of oil would have to exceed $80 per barrel to match the inflation-adjusted level of twenty-five years ago. Perhaps more to the point, the production of ethanol uses so much fossil fuel and other resources that under most circumstances, its production actually *wastes* resources overall compared to gasoline. In part, this is because ethanol is about 25 percent less efficient than gasoline as a source of energy. But it is also because the corn used to make ethanol in the United States has a high **opportunity cost:** If it were not being used to make fuel, it would be used to feed humans and livestock. Moreover, because ethanol production is most efficiently conducted on a relatively small scale, it must be transported by truck or rail, which is far more costly than the pipelines used for gasoline.

The third supposed advantage of ethanol is that its use reduces our dependence on imports of oil. In principle, this argument is correct, but its impact is tiny, and the likely consequences are not what you might expect. Total consumption of all **biofuels** in the United States amounts to less than 3 percent of gasoline usage. To replace the oil we import from the Persian Gulf with corn-based ethanol, at least *50 percent* of the nation's total farmland would have to be devoted to corn for fuel. Moreover, any cuts in oil imports will likely *not* come from Persian Gulf sources. Canada and Mexico are the two biggest suppliers of crude oil to the United States, and both countries send almost 100 percent of their exports to the U.S. market.

All of this raises an interesting question: If ethanol doesn't protect the environment, conserve resources, or have any compelling foreign policy advantages, why do we mandate its use and subsidize its production? The answer lies at the heart of **political economy,** the use of economics to study the causes and consequences of political decision making. It is true that a critical component of what the government does (such as providing for national defense and law enforcement) provides an institutional structure necessary for the creation and retention of our total wealth. Nevertheless, the essence of much government policy-making has nothing to do with making the size of the economic pie larger than it otherwise would be. Instead, many government policies are directed at dividing up the pie in new ways so that one group gets more resources at the expense of some other group. To do this successfully, politicians must be adept at concentrating the benefits of policies among a few favored recipients while dispersing the costs of those policies across a large number of disfavored individuals.

At first blush, such an approach sounds completely at odds with the essence of democracy. After all, under the principle of "one person, one vote," it seems like benefits should be widely spread (to gain votes from many grateful beneficiaries), and costs should be concentrated (so that only the votes of a few disfavored constituents are lost). The concept of **rational ignorance** explains what is really going on. It is costly for individuals to keep track of exactly how the decisions of their elected representatives affect them. When the consequences of political decisions are large enough to outweigh the **monitoring costs,** voters swiftly and surely express their pleasure or displeasure, both in the voting booth and in their campaign contributions. But when the consequences to each of them individually are small relative to the monitoring costs, people quite sensibly don't bother to keep track of them—they remain "rationally ignorant."

In the case of ethanol, almost one-fourth of all ethanol for fuel is made by one company: Archer Daniels Midland (ADM). Clearly, even small changes in the price of ethanol are important to ADM. Because federal use mandates and the federal ethanol subsidy both increase the profitability of making ethanol, ADM has strong incentives to ensure that members of Congress are aware of the benefits (to ADM) of such policies. Similarly, corn farmers derive most of their income from sales of corn. Federal ethanol policies increase the demand for corn and thus increase its price; again, because the resulting benefits are highly concentrated on corn farmers, each has a strong incentive to ensure that his or her members of Congress understand the benefits (to the farmer) of such policies.

Contrast this with the typical taxpayer or consumer of gasoline. It is true that the $3 billion or so spent on ethanol subsidies each year must come out of taxpayers' pockets. Nevertheless, this amount is spread thinly across tens of millions of federal taxpayers. Similarly, although the mandated use of ethanol in gasoline is estimated to raise the cost of gas by about 8 cents per gallon, this amounts to no more than $50 per year for the typical driver. Neither taxpayer nor motorist is likely to spend much time complaining to his or her senator.

Thus it is that farmers and ethanol producers are quite rationally willing to lobby hard for use mandates and subsidies at the same time that taxpayers and drivers put up little effective resistance to having their pockets picked. It may make for bad economics, but it is classic politics. And for the producers, farmers, and politicians involved, it just as surely turns corn into "yellow gold."

DISCUSSION QUESTIONS

1. Brazilian ethanol producers (who make ethanol from sugarcane) have lower production costs than U.S. producers. Indeed, even though it costs 16 cents per gallon to transport ethanol from Brazil to the United States, which also imposes an **import tariff** of nearly 60 cents per gallon on Brazilian ethanol, the United States still imports about 60 million gallons of ethanol per year from Brazil. If Congress really cares about protecting the environment and reducing our reliance on foreign crude oil, why do you suppose we have a large import tariff on ethanol?

2. If imports of Brazilian ethanol begin to rise sharply in the future, what do you predict will happen to the size of the import tariff levied on this good?

3. Why do you suppose it is owners of fertile farmland who are given special treatment by the federal government, rather than, say, automobile mechanics?

4. Use the theory of rational ignorance to explain why the ethanol subsidy is only 51 cents per gallon rather than, say, $5 per gallon.

CHAPTER THREE

Flying the Friendly Skies?

Most of us hop into our car with little thought for our personal safety, beyond perhaps the act of putting on seat belts. Yet even though travel on scheduled, commercial airlines is safer than driving to work or to the grocery store, many people approach air travel with a sense of foreboding, if not downright fear.

If we were to think carefully about the wisdom of traveling 600 miles per hour in an aluminum tube 7 miles above the earth, several questions might come to mind: How safe is this? How safe should it be? Because the people who operate airlines are not in it for fun, does their interest in making a buck ignore our interest in making it home in one piece? Is some form of government regulation the only way to ensure safety in the skies?

The science of economics begins with one simple principle: We live in a world of **scarcity,** which implies that to get more of any good, we must sacrifice some of other goods. This is just as true of safety as it is of pizzas or haircuts or works of art. Safety confers benefits (we live longer and more enjoyably), but achieving it also entails **costs** (we must give up something to obtain that safety).

As the degree of safety rises, the total benefits of safety rise, but the marginal (or incremental) benefits of additional safety decline. Consider a simple example: Adding exit doors to an airplane increases the number of people who can escape in the event of an emergency evacuation. Nevertheless, each *additional* door adds less in safety benefits than the previous one; if the fourth door enables, say, an extra ten people to escape, the fifth may enable only an extra six to escape. (If this sounds implausible, imagine having a door for each person; the last door added will enable at most one more person to escape.) So we say that the marginal (or incremental) benefit of safety declines as the amount of safety increases.

Let's look now at the other side of the equation: As the amount of safety increases, both the total and the marginal (incremental) costs of providing safety rise. Having a fuel gauge on the plane's instrument panel clearly enhances safety, because it reduces the chance that the plane will run out of fuel while in flight.[1] It is always possible that a fuel gauge will malfunction, so having a backup fuel gauge also adds to safety. Because having two gauges is more costly than having just one, the total costs of safety rise as safety increases. It is also clear, however, that while the cost of the second gauge is (at least) as great as the cost of the first, the second gauge has a smaller positive impact on safety. Thus the cost per unit of additional (incremental) safety is higher for the second fuel gauge than for the first.

How much safety should we have? For an economist, the answer to such a question is generally expressed in terms of **marginal benefits** and **marginal costs.** The economically *efficient* level of safety occurs when the marginal cost of increasing safety just equals the marginal benefit of that increased safety. Put somewhat differently, if the marginal benefits of adding (or keeping) a safety feature exceed the marginal costs of doing so, then the feature is worthwhile. But if the added benefits of a safety device do *not* exceed the added costs, we should refrain from installing the device. Note there are two related issues here: How safe should we *be,* and how should we *achieve* that level of safety?

Both of these issues took on added urgency on the morning of September 11, 2001, when terrorists hijacked and crashed four U.S. commercial jetliners. This episode revealed that air travel was far less safe than previously believed. Immediately, it was clear that we should devote additional resources to airline safety; what was not clear was how *much* additional resources should be thus devoted and precisely *what* changes should be made. For example, almost everyone agreed that more careful screening of passengers and baggage at airports would produce important safety benefits. But how should we achieve this? Should carry-on bags be prohibited or just examined more carefully? How thoroughly should checked luggage be screened for bombs? Even now, our answers to these questions are evolving as we learn more about the extent of the threat and the costs of alternative

---

[1]Notice that we say "reduces" rather than "eliminates." In 1978, a United Air Lines pilot preoccupied with a malfunctioning landing gear evidently failed to pay sufficient attention to his cockpit gauges. When the plane was forced to crash-land after running out of fuel, eight people died.

responses to it. Nevertheless, throughout the process, economic principles can help us make the most sensible decisions.

In general, the efficient level of safety will not be perfect safety, because perfection is simply too costly to achieve. For example, to be absolutely certain that no one is ever killed or injured in an airplane crash, we would have to prevent all travel in airplanes—an unrealistic and impractible prospect. This means that if we wish to enjoy the advantages of flying, we must be willing to accept *some* risk—a conclusion that each of us implicitly accepts every time we step aboard an airplane.

Changes in circumstances can alter the efficient level of safety. For example, if a technological change reduces the costs of bomb-scanning equipment, the marginal costs of preventing terrorist bomb attacks will be lower. It will be efficient to have more airports install the machines and to have extra machines at large airports to speed the screening process. Air travel will become safer because of the technological change. Similarly, if the marginal benefits of safety rise for some reason—perhaps because the president of the United States is on board—it could be efficient to take more precautions, resulting in safer air travel. Given the factors that determine the benefits and costs of safety, the result of a change in circumstances will be some determinate level of safety that generally will be associated with some risk of death or injury.

Airplanes are complex systems, and an amazing number of things can go wrong with them. Over the century that humans have been flying, airplane manufacturers and airlines have studied every one of the things that has gone wrong thus far and have put into place design changes and operating procedures aimed at preventing recurring error. Of course, consumers have the greatest incentive to ensure that air travel is safe, and if information were free, we could assert with some confidence that the actual level of safety supplied by firms was the efficient level of safety. Consumers would simply observe the safety offered by different airlines, the prices they charge, and select the degrees of safety that best suited their preferences and budgets, just as with other goods. But of course, information is not free; it is a **scarce good,** costly to obtain. As a result, passengers may be unaware of the safety record of various airlines or the competency of the pilots and the maintenance procedures of an airline's mechanics. Indeed, even the airlines themselves may be uncertain about the efficient level of safety, perhaps because they have no way of estimating the true threat of terrorist attacks, for example. Such possibilities have been used to argue that the federal government should mandate certain minimum levels of safety, as it does today through the operation of the Federal Aviation Administration (FAA). Let's look at this issue in some detail.

One argument in favor of government safety standards rests on the presumption that, left to their own devices, airlines would provide less safety than passengers want. This might happen, for example, if customers could not tell (at a reasonable cost) whether the equipment, training, and procedures employed by an airline are safe. If passengers cannot cheaply gauge the level of safety, they will not be willing to reward airlines for being safe or punish them for being unsafe. If safety is costly to provide and consumers are unwilling to pay for it because they cannot accurately measure it, airlines will provide too little of it. The conclusion is that government experts—such as the FAA—should set safety standards for the industry.

This conclusion seems plausible, but it ignores two simple points. First, how is the government to know the efficient level of safety? Even if the FAA is fully knowledgeable regarding the costs of all possible safety measures, it still does not have enough information to set efficient safety standards because it does not know the value that people place on safety. Without such information, the FAA has no way of assessing the benefits of additional safety and hence no means of knowing whether those benefits are greater or less than the added costs.

The second point is that people want to reach their destinations safely. Even if they cannot observe whether an airline hires good pilots or bad pilots, they can observe whether that airline's planes land safely or crash. If it is *safety* that is important to consumers—and not the obscure, costly-to-measure set of reasons for that safety—the fact that consumers cannot easily measure metal fatigue in jet engines may be totally irrelevant to the process of achieving the efficient level of safety.

Interestingly, evidence shows that consumers are indeed cognizant of the safety performance of airlines, and that they "punish" airlines that perform in an unsafe manner. Researchers have found that when an airline is found to be at fault in a fatal plane crash, consumers appear to downgrade their safety rating of the airline (that is, they revise upward their estimates of the likelihood of future fatal crashes). As a result, the offending airline suffers substantial adverse financial consequences over and above the costs of losing the plane and being sued on behalf of the victims. These findings suggest a striking degree of safety awareness on the part of supposedly ignorant consumers.

Of course, this discussion leaves open the issue of how to handle safety threats posed by terrorists and other miscreants. For example, much of the information that goes into assessing terrorist threats is classified as secret, and its revelation to airlines or consumers might compromise key sources of the data. Hence there could be an advantage to having the government try to approximate the efficient safety outcome by mandating certain screening provisions without revealing exactly why they are being chosen. Similarly, because airlines are connected in networks (so that people and baggage move from one airline to another in the course of a trip), one might argue that achieving the efficient level of safety requires a common set of screening rules for all airlines. Even so, this does not inform us whether the government should impose those rules or the airlines should come to a voluntary joint agreement on them.

We began this chapter with the commonplace observation that airlines are safer than cars. Yet many people still worry for their safety every time they get on an airplane. Are they being irrational? Well, the answer, it seems, is in the eye of the beholder. Measured in terms of fatalities per mile traveled, airplanes are some 15 times safer than cars (and 176 times safer than walking, we might add). But this number masks the fact that 68 percent of aircraft accidents happen on takeoff and landing, and these operations occupy only 6 percent of flight time. It is presumably this fact that quite sensibly makes people nervous whenever they find themselves approaching an airport.

DISCUSSION QUESTIONS

1. Is it possible to be too safe? Explain what you mean by "too safe."

2. Many automobile manufacturers routinely advertise the safety of their cars, yet airlines generally do not even mention safety in their advertising. Can you suggest an explanation for this difference?

3. Many economists would argue that private companies are likely to be more efficient than the government at operating airlines. Yet

many economists would also argue that there is a valid reason for government to regulate the safety of those same airlines. Can you explain why the government might be good at ensuring safety, even though it might not be good at operating the airlines?

4. Professional football teams sometimes charter airplanes to take them to their "away" games. Would you feel safer riding on a United Air Lines plane that had been chartered by the Washington Redskins than on a regularly scheduled United Air Lines flight?

CHAPTER FOUR

The Mystery of Wealth

Why are the citizens of some nations rich while the inhabitants of others are poor? Your initial answer might be "Because of differences in the **natural-resource endowments** of the nations." It is true that ample endowments of energy, timber, and fertile land all help raise wealth. But natural resources can be only a very small part of the answer, as witnessed by many counterexamples. Switzerland and Luxembourg, for example, are nearly devoid of key natural resources, yet the real incomes of citizens of those lands are among the world's highest. Similarly, Hong Kong, which consists of but a few square miles of rock and hillside, is one of the economic miracles of the twentieth century, while in Russia, a land amply endowed with vast quantities of virtually every important resource, most people remain mired in economic misery.

A number of studies have begun to unravel the mystery of **economic growth.** Repeatedly, they have found that it is the fundamental political and legal **institutions** of society that are conducive to growth. Of these, political stability, secure private property rights, and legal systems based on the **rule of law** are among the most important. Such institutions encourage people to make long-term investments in improving land and in all forms of **physical capital** and **human capital.** These investments raise the **capital stock,** which in turn provides for more growth long into the future. And the cumulative effects of this growth over time eventually yield much higher standards of living.

Consider first the contrasting effects of different legal systems on economic growth. Many legal systems around the world today are based on one of two basic models: the English **common law system** and the French **civil law system.** Common law systems reflect a conscious decision in favor of a limited role for government and emphasize the importance of the judiciary in constraining the power of the executive and legislative branches of government. In contrast, civil law systems favor the creation of a strong centralized government in which the

TABLE 4-1 Differing Legal Systems	
Common Law Nations	*Civil Law Nations*
Australia	Brazil
Canada	Egypt
India	France
Israel	Greece
New Zealand	Italy
United Kingdom	Mexico
United States	Sweden

legislature and the executive branches have the power to grant preferential treatment to special interests. Table 4–1 shows a sampling of common law and civil law countries.

Research reveals that the security of **property rights** is much stronger in common law systems, such as observed in Britain and its former colonies, including the United States. In nations such as France and its former colonies, the civil law systems are much more likely to yield unpredictable changes in the rules of the game—the structure of **property and contract rights.** This unpredictability makes people reluctant to make long-term fixed investments, a fact that ultimately slows the economic growth of these nations and lowers the standard of living for their citizens.

The reasoning here is simple. If you know that the police will not help you protect your rights to a home or a car, you are less likely to acquire those assets. Similarly, if you cannot easily enforce business or employment contracts that you make, you are less likely to make those contracts—and hence less likely to produce as many goods or services. And if you cannot plan for the future because you don't know what the rules of the game will be in ten years or perhaps even one year from now, you are less likely to make the kinds of productive long-term investments that take years to pay off. Common law systems seem to do a better job at enforcing contracts and securing property rights and so would be expected to promote economic activity now and economic growth over time.

Research into the economic performance of nations around the world from 1960 until the 1990s found that economic growth was one-third higher in the common law nations, with their strong property rights, than in civil law nations. Over the more than three decades covered, the standard of living—measured by real **per capita income**—increased more than 20 percent in common law nations compared to civil law nations. If such a pattern persisted over the span of a century, it would produce a staggering 80 percent real per capita income differential in favor of nations with secure property rights.

Other research has taken a much broader view, both across time and across institutions, in assessing economic growth. Institutions such as political stability, protection against violence or theft, security of contracts, and freedom from regulatory burdens all contribute to sustained economic growth. Indeed, it is key institutions such as these, rather than natural-resource endowments, that explain long-term differences in economic growth and thus present-day differences in levels of real income. To illustrate the powerful effect of institutions, consider the contrast between Mexico, with per capita real income of about $10,000 today, and the United States, with a per capita real income of about $42,000. Had Mexico developed with the same political and legal institutions that the United States has enjoyed, per capita income in Mexico would today be *equal* to that in the United States.

Given the great importance of such institutions in determining long-term growth, one might ask another important question: How have countries gotten the political and legal institutions they have today? The answer has to do with disease, of all things. An examination of more than seventy former European colonies reveals that a variety of strategies were pursued. In Australia, New Zealand, and North America, the colonists found geography and climates that were conducive to good health. Permanent settlement was attractive, so colonists created institutions to protect private property and curb the power of the state. But when Europeans arrived in Africa and South America, they encountered tropical diseases, such as malaria and yellow fever, that produced high mortality rates. This discouraged permanent settlement and encouraged a mentality focused on extracting metals, cash crops, and other resources. As a result, there were few **incentives** to promote democratic institutions or stable long-term property rights systems. The differing initial institutions helped shape economic growth over the years and, because of the broad persistence of those institutions, continue to shape the political and legal character and the standard of living in these nations today.

Recent events also illustrate that the effects of political and legal institutions can be drastically accelerated—in either direction. Consider China, which in 1979 began to change its institutions in two key ways. First, as we discuss more fully in Chapter 32, on a very limited basis China began to experiment with private property rights for a few of its citizens, under narrow circumstances. (This experiment even included amending its constitution to strengthen private property protections.) Second, the Chinese government began to clear away obstacles to foreign investment, making China a more secure place for Western companies to do business. Although the institutional changes have been modest, their combined effects have been substantial. Over the years since, economic growth in China has accelerated, averaging better than 6 percent per year. And if that doesn't sound like much, keep in mind that it has been enough over that period to raise real per capita income in China by a factor of 5.

For an example of the potential *destructive* impact of institutional change, we need look no further than Zimbabwe. When that country won its independence from Britain in 1980, it was one of the most prosperous nations in Africa. Soon after taking power as Zimbabwe's first (and so far only) president, Robert Mugabe began disassembling that nation's rule of law, tearing apart the institutions that had helped it grow rich. He reduced the security of property rights in land and eventually confiscated those rights altogether. Mugabe has also gradually taken control of the prices of most goods and services in his nation and even controls the price of its national currency, at least the price at which Zimbabweans are allowed to trade it. Moreover, the Mugabe government has confiscated large stocks of food and much of anything of value that might be exported out of or imported into Zimbabwe. In short, anything that is produced or saved has become subject to confiscation, so the incentives to do either are—to put it mildly—reduced.

As a result, between 1980 and 1996, real per capita income in Zimbabwe fell by one-third, and since 1996, it has fallen by an additional third. Unemployment is rampant, investment is nonexistent, and the annual inflation rate reached 1,000 percent in recent years. In less than thirty years, the fruit of many decades of labor and capital investment has been destroyed, because the institutions that made that fruit possible have been eliminated. It is a lesson we ignore at our peril.

DISCUSSION QUESTIONS

1. Consider two countries, A and B, and suppose that both have identical *physical* endowments of, say, iron ore. But suppose that in country A, any profits that are made from mining the ore are subject to confiscation by the government, while in country B, there is no such risk. How does the risk of expropriation affect the *economic* endowment of the two nations? In which nation are people richer?

2. In light of your answer to question 1, how do you explain the fact that in some countries there is widespread political support for government policies that expropriate resources from some groups for the purpose of handing them out to other groups?

3. If the crucial factor determining a country's low standard of living is the adverse set of legal and cultural institutions it possesses, can you offer suggestions for how the other nations of the world might help in permanently raising that country's standard of living?

Supply and Demand

Introduction

The tools of **demand** and **supply** are the most basic and useful elements of the economist's kit. Indeed, many economists would argue that the **law of demand**—the lower the price of a good, the greater the quantity of that good demanded by purchasers—is the single most powerful proposition in all of economics. Simply stated, the law of demand has the capacity, unmatched by any other proposition in economics, to explain an incredibly diverse range of human behaviors. For example, the law of demand explains why buildings are taller in downtown areas than in outlying suburbs, and also why people are willing to sit in the upper deck of football stadiums even though lower-deck seats are clearly superior. The great explanatory power of the law of demand is almost matched by that of the **law of supply,** which states that the higher the price of a good, the greater will be the quantity of that good supplied by producers. The law of supply helps us understand why people receive a premium wage when they work overtime, as well as why parking places at the beach are so much more expensive during the summer months than during the winter.

When the laws of demand and supply are combined, they illuminate the enormous **gains from trade** that arise from voluntary exchange. In Chapter 5, "Sex, Booze, and Drugs," we examine what happens when the government attempts to prohibit the exchanges that give rise to these gains. The consequences are often surprising, always costly, and—sadly—sometimes tragic. We find, for example, that when the federal government made alcoholic beverages illegal during the era known as Prohibition, Americans responded by switching from beer to hard liquor and by getting drunk a larger proportion of the times when they drank. We also show that the government's ongoing efforts to prevent individuals from using drugs such as marijuana and cocaine cause the drive-by shootings that occur in many major cities and also encourage drug overdoses among users. Finally, we explain why laws against prostitution help foster the spread of AIDS.

Sometimes, as illustrated in Chapter 6, "Expanding Waistlines," we have to examine both demand and supply to understand a public issue. Obesity is rising in the United States, chiefly as a result of three separate economic forces. First, wages paid in sedentary occupations have risen relative to those in physically demanding jobs, inducing people to spend more of their time exercising their brains on the job rather than their muscles. An even more important factor, however, is that the entry of women into the workforce has increased the demand for prepackaged prepared foods—which have been gladly supplied by producers. This has sharply reduced the **full cost** of eating (especially the full cost of snacks) and so increased the amount of food consumed. Finally, higher taxes and limits on smoking in public have raised the full cost of consuming cigarettes in recent decades. This cost increase has induced people to substitute food for cigarettes. Because expanding waistlines today will almost surely generate adverse health effects in the future, we can expect this issue to become a widely debated one in the years to come.

In Chapter 7, "Is Water Different?" we dispel the myth that the consumption of some goods does not conform to the law of demand. Here we examine the demand for water, that "most necessary of all necessities," and find that—lo and behold—when the price of water is raised, people consume less of it—exactly as predicted by the law of demand. We also see that the law of supply applies to water. One important conclusion of this chapter is that the water shortages and water crises that afflict various parts of the nation are not the result of droughts but in fact are caused by government officials who are unwilling or unable to accept the reality of the laws of demand and supply.

It is distasteful to think in terms of the supply and demand for human beings, yet that is what developments half a world away compel us to do in Chapter 8, "Slave Redemption in Sudan." Nearly a century after human slavery was abolished there by the British, the slave trade reemerged in Sudan, the largest nation in Africa. Following in the tracks of the slave raiders are slave redemptionists, who seek to alleviate the human suffering in Sudan by purchasing freedom for thousands of enslaved individuals. Yet the efforts of these well-intentioned individuals are having unintended consequences. Indeed, attempts to reduce slavery in Sudan have actually encouraged the slave trade and may even have resulted in more—not fewer—people in bondage. And so we see that sometimes the results of well-intentioned actions are not merely unexpected but tragic.

The cost of a pack of cigarettes in the United States has more than doubled over the last few years, because the federal and state governments have sharply increased cigarette taxes. These tax increases have reduced the supply of cigarettes and so pushed up prices. As we see in Chapter 9, "Smoking and Smuggling," this has led to a host of other developments. The number of smokers and the amount of smoking are both down, as would be predicted by the law of demand. Nevertheless, for people who continue to smoke in the face of higher taxes, things are worse: Not only is a larger share of their income going to the "evil weed," but they are also smoking stronger, more carcinogenic cigarettes. At the market level, higher cigarette taxes have also led to much more widespread smuggling of cigarettes as consumers seek to minimize the costs of the higher taxes.

Our final application of demand and supply analysis comes in Chapter 10, "Bankrupt Landlords, from Sea to Shining Sea." This chapter brings us back to the issue discussed in Chapter 5, the effects of government interference with free markets, in this case in the form of **rent controls**—legal ceilings on the rent that landlords may charge for apartments. Although the effects of rent controls are perhaps less tragic than some of the effects observed in Chapter 5, they are just as surprising and often as costly. We find, for example, that legal ceilings on rents have increased the extent of homelessness in the United States, have led to a rise in racial discrimination, and have caused the wholesale destruction of hundreds of thousands of dwelling units in our nation's major cities. We cannot escape one simple fact: Politicians may pass legislation, and bureaucrats may do their best to enforce it, but the laws of demand and supply ultimately rule the economy.

CHAPTER FIVE

Sex, Booze, and Drugs

Before 1914, cocaine was legal in this country; today it is not. Alcoholic beverages are legal in the United States today; from 1920 to 1933, they were not. Prostitution is legal in Nevada today; in the other forty-nine states, it is not.[1] All these goods—sex, booze, and drugs—have at least one thing in common: The consumption of each brings together a willing seller with a willing buyer, creating an act of mutually beneficial exchange (at least in the opinion of the parties involved). Partly because of this property, attempts to proscribe the consumption of these goods have met with less than spectacular success and have yielded some peculiar patterns of production, distribution, and usage. Let's see why.

When the government seeks to prevent voluntary exchange, it generally must decide whether to go after the seller or the buyer. In most cases—and certainly where sex, booze, and drugs are concerned—the government targets sellers because this is where the authorities get the most benefit from their enforcement dollars. A cocaine dealer, even a small retail pusher, often supplies dozens or even hundreds of users each day, as did speakeasies (illegal saloons) during Prohibition; a hooker typically services three to ten "tricks" per day. By incarcerating the supplier, the police can prevent several, or even several hundred, transactions from taking place, which is usually much more cost-effective than going after the buyers one by one. It is not that the police ignore the consumers of illegal goods; indeed, sting operations—in which the police pose as illicit sellers—often make the headlines. Nevertheless, most enforcement efforts focus on the supply side, and so shall we.

---

[1] These statements are not entirely correct. Even today, cocaine may be obtained legally by prescription from a physician. Prostitution in Nevada is legal only in those counties that have chosen to permit it. Finally, some counties in the United States remain "dry," prohibiting the sale of beer, wine, and distilled spirits.

Law enforcement activities directed against the suppliers of illegal goods increase the suppliers' operating costs. The risks of fines, jail sentences, and possibly even violence become part of the costs of doing business and must be taken into account by existing and potential suppliers. Some entrepreneurs will leave the business, turning their talents to other activities; others will resort to clandestine (and costly) means to hide their operations from the police; still others will restrict the circle of buyers with whom they are willing to deal to minimize the chances that a customer is a cop. Across the board, the costs of operation are higher, and at any given price, less of the product will be available. There is a reduction in supply, and the result is a higher price for the good.

This increase in price is, in a sense, exactly what the enforcement officials are after, for the consumers of sex, booze, and drugs behave according to the **law of demand:** The higher the price of a good, the lower the amount consumed. So the immediate impact of the enforcement efforts against sellers is to reduce the consumption of the illegal good by buyers. There are, however, some other effects.

First, because the good in question is illegal, people who have a **comparative advantage** in conducting illegal activities will be attracted to the business of supplying (and perhaps demanding) the good. Some may have an existing criminal record and are relatively unconcerned about adding to it. Others may have developed skills in evading detection and prosecution while engaged in other criminal activities. Some may simply look at the illegal activity as another means of thumbing their noses at society. The general point is that when an activity is made illegal, people who are good at being criminals are attracted to that activity.

Illegal contracts are usually not enforceable through legal channels (and even if they were, few suppliers of illegal goods would be foolish enough to complain to the police about not being paid for their products). So buyers and sellers of illegal goods must frequently resort to private methods of contract enforcement, which often entails violence.[2] Hence people who are relatively good at violence are attracted to illegal activities and have greater **incentives** to employ their talents. This is one

---

[2] Fundamentally, violence—such as involuntary incarceration—also plays a key role in the government's enforcement of legal contracts. We often do not think of it as violence, of course, because it is usually cushioned by constitutional safeguards and procedural rules.

reason why the murder rate in America rose to record levels during Prohibition and then dropped sharply when liquor was again made legal. It also helps explain why the number of drug-related murders soared during the 1980s and why drive-by shootings became commonplace in many drug-infested cities. The Thompson submachine gun of the 1930s and the MAC-10 machine gun of the 1980s were just low-cost means of contract enforcement.

The attempts of law enforcement officials to drive sellers of illegal goods out of business have another effect. Based on recent wholesale prices, $50,000 worth of pure heroin weighs about two ounces; $50,000 worth of marijuana weighs about twenty pounds. As any drug smuggler can tell you, hiding two ounces of contraband is a lot easier than hiding twenty pounds. Thus to avoid detection and prosecution, suppliers of the illegal good have an incentive to deal in the more valuable versions of their product, which for drugs and booze mean the more potent versions. Bootleggers during Prohibition concentrated on hard liquor rather than beer and wine; even today, moonshine typically has roughly twice the alcohol content of legal hard liquor such as bourbon, scotch, or vodka. After narcotics became illegal in this country in 1914, importers switched from the milder opium to its more valuable, more potent, and more addictive derivative, heroin.

The move to the more potent versions of illegal commodities is enhanced by enforcement activities directed against users. Not only do users, like suppliers, find it easier (cheaper) to hide the more potent versions, but there is also a change in relative prices due to user penalties. Typically, the law has lower penalties for using an illegal substance than for distributing it. Within each category (use or sale), however, there is commonly the same penalty regardless of value per unit. For example, during Prohibition, a bottle of wine and a bottle of more expensive, more potent hard liquor were equally illegal. Today, the possession of one gram of 90 percent pure cocaine brings the same penalty as the possession of one gram of 10 percent pure cocaine. Given the physical quantities, there is a fixed cost (the legal penalty) associated with being caught, regardless of value per unit (and thus potency) of the substance. Hence the structure of legal penalties raises the relative price of less potent versions, encouraging users to substitute more potent versions—heroin instead of opium, hashish instead of marijuana, hard liquor instead of beer.

Penalties against users also encourage a change in the nature of usage. Prior to 1914, cocaine was legal in this country and was used openly as a mild stimulant, much as people today use caffeine. (Cocaine was even an ingredient in the original formulation of Coca-Cola.) This type of usage—small, regular doses over long time intervals—becomes relatively more expensive when the substance is made illegal. Extensive usage (small doses spread over time) is more likely to be detected by the authorities than intensive usage (a large dose consumed at once), simply because possession time is longer and the drug must be accessed more frequently. Thus when a substance is made illegal, there is an incentive for consumers to switch toward usage that is more intensive. Rather than ingesting cocaine orally in the form of a highly diluted liquid solution, as was commonly done before 1914, people switched to snorting or injecting it. During Prohibition, people dispensed with cocktails before dinner each night; instead, on the less frequent occasions when they drank, they more often drank to get drunk. The same phenomenon is observed today. People under the age of twenty-one consume alcoholic beverages less frequently than people over the age of twenty-one. But when they do drink, they are more likely to drink to get drunk.

Not surprisingly, the suppliers of illegal commodities are reluctant to advertise their wares openly; the police are as capable of reading billboards and watching TV as potential customers are. Suppliers are also reluctant to establish easily recognized identities and regular places and hours of business because to do so raises the chance of being caught by the police. Information about the price and quality of products being sold goes underground, often with unfortunate effects for consumers.

With legal goods, consumers have several means of obtaining information. They can learn from friends, advertisements, and personal experience. When goods are legal, they can be trademarked for identification. The trademark cannot legally be copied, and the courts protect it. Given such easily identified brands, consumers can be made aware of the quality and price of each. If their experience does not meet expectations, they can assure themselves of no further contact with the unsatisfactory product by never buying that brand again.

When a general class of products becomes illegal, there are fewer ways to obtain information. Brand names are no longer protected by law, so falsification of well-known brands ensues. When products do not meet expectations, it is more difficult (costly) for consumers to punish suppliers. Frequently, the result is degradation of and uncertainty about product quality. The consequences for consumers of the illegal goods are often unpleasant and sometimes fatal.

Consider prostitution. In those counties in Nevada where prostitution is legal, the prostitutes are required to register with the local authorities, and they generally conduct their business in well-established bordellos. These establishments advertise openly and rely heavily on repeat business. Health officials test the prostitutes weekly for venereal disease and monthly for AIDS. Contrast this with other areas of the country, where prostitution is illegal. Suppliers are generally streetwalkers because a fixed, physical location is too easy for the police to detect and raid. Suppliers change locations frequently to reduce harassment by police. Repeat business is reported to be minimal; frequently, customers have never seen the prostitute before and never will again.

The difference in outcomes is striking. In Nevada, the spread of venereal disease by legal prostitutes is estimated to be almost nonexistent; to date, none of the registered prostitutes in Nevada has tested positive for AIDS. By contrast, in some major cities outside Nevada, the incidence of venereal disease among prostitutes is estimated to be near 100 percent. In Miami, one study found that 19 percent of all incarcerated prostitutes tested positive for AIDS; in Newark, New Jersey, 52 percent of the prostitutes tested were infected with the AIDS virus, and about half of the prostitutes in Washington, D.C., and New York City are also believed to be carrying the AIDS virus. Because of the lack of reliable information in markets for illegal goods, customers frequently do not know exactly what they are getting; as a result, they sometimes get more than they bargained for.

Consider alcohol and drugs. Today, alcoholic beverages are heavily advertised to establish their brand names and are carried by reputable dealers. Customers can readily punish suppliers for any deviation from the expected potency or quality by withdrawing their business, telling their friends, or even bringing a lawsuit. Similar circumstances prevailed before 1914 in this country for the hundreds of products containing opium or cocaine.

During Prohibition, consumers of alcohol often did not know exactly what they were buying or where to find the supplier the next day if they were dissatisfied. Fly-by-night operators sometimes adulterated liquor with far more lethal methyl alcohol. In tiny concentrations, this made watered-down booze taste like it had more kick, but in only slightly higher concentrations, the methyl alcohol blinded or even killed the unsuspecting consumer. Even in "reputable" speakeasies (those likely to be in business at the same location the next day), bottles bearing the labels of high-priced foreign whiskeys were refilled repeatedly with locally (and illegally) produced rotgut until their labels wore off.

In the 1970s, more than one purchaser of what was reputed to be high-potency Panama Red or Acapulco Gold marijuana ended up with low-potency pot heavily loaded with stems, seeds, and maybe even oregano. Buyers of cocaine must worry about not only how much the product has been cut along the distribution chain but also what has been used to cut it. In recent years, the purity of cocaine at the retail level has ranged between 10 percent and 95 percent; for heroin, the degree of purity has ranged from 5 percent to 50 percent. Cutting agents can turn out to be any of various sugars, local anesthetics, or amphetamines; on occasion, rat poison has been used.

We noted earlier that the legal penalties for the users of illegal goods encourage them to use more potent forms and to use them more intensively. These facts and the uncertain quality and potency of the illegal products yield a deadly combination. During Prohibition, the death rate from acute alcohol poisoning (due to overdose) was more than thirty times higher than today. During 1927 alone, twelve thousand people died from acute alcohol poisoning, and many thousands more were blinded or killed by contaminated booze. Today, about three thousand people a year die as a direct result of consuming either cocaine or heroin. Of that total, it is estimated, roughly 80 percent die from either an overdose caused by unexpectedly potent product or an adverse reaction to the material used to cut the drug. Clearly, *caveat emptor* ("let the buyer beware") is a warning to be taken seriously if one is consuming an illegal product.

We noted at the beginning of this chapter that one of the effects of making a good illegal is to raise its price. One might well ask, by how much? During the early 1990s, the federal government was spending about $2 billion a year in its efforts to stop the importation of cocaine from Colombia. One study concluded that these efforts had hiked the price of cocaine by 4 percent (yes, 4 percent) relative to what it would have been had the federal government done nothing to interdict cocaine imports. The study estimated that the cost of raising the price of cocaine an additional 2 percent would be $1 billion per year. More recently, Nobel Laureate Gary Becker and his colleagues have estimated that America's war on drugs costs at least $100 billion per year.

The government's efforts to halt imports of marijuana have had some success, presumably because that product is easier to detect than cocaine. Nevertheless, suppliers have responded by cultivating marijuana domestically instead of importing it or by bringing it in across the relatively open U.S.–Canadian border rather than from elsewhere. The net effect has been an estimated tenfold increase in potency due to the superior farming techniques available in this country and Canada, as well as the use of genetic bioengineering to improve strains.

A few years ago, most states and the federal government began restricting sales of cold medicines containing pseudoephedrine because that ingredient was widely used for making the illegal stimulant methamphetamine in home laboratories. The restrictions succeeded in sharply curtailing home production of "meth." They also led to a huge increase in imports of a far more potent version of meth from Mexico. Overall, it is estimated that neither consumption of nor addiction to methamphetamine was reduced by the restrictions. But overdoses from the drug rose sharply because of the greater purity of the imports.

Consider also the government's efforts to eliminate the consumption of alcohol during the 1920s and 1930s. They failed so badly that the Eighteenth Amendment, which put Prohibition in place, was the first (and so far the only) constitutional amendment ever to be repealed. As for prostitution, it is reputed to be "the oldest profession" and by all accounts continues to flourish today, even in Newark and Miami.

The government's inability to halt the consumption of sex, booze, or drugs does not mean that those efforts have failed. Indeed, the impact of these efforts is manifested in their consequences, ranging from tainted drugs and alcohol to disease-ridden prostitutes. The message instead is that when the government attempts to prevent mutually beneficial exchange, even its best efforts are unlikely to meet with spectacular success.

DISCUSSION QUESTIONS

1. The federal government currently taxes alcohol on the basis of the 100-proof gallon. (Alcohol that is 100 proof is 50 percent pure ethyl alcohol; most hard liquor sold is 80 proof, or 40 percent ethyl alcohol, whereas wine is usually about 24 proof, and most beer is 6 to 10 proof.) How would alcohol consumption patterns change if the gov-

ernment taxed alcohol strictly on the basis of volume rather than also taking its potency into account?

2. During Prohibition, some speakeasy operators paid bribes to ensure that the police did not raid them. Would you expect the quality of the liquor served in such speakeasies to be higher or lower than in those that did not pay bribes? Would you expect to find differences (for example, with regard to income levels) among the customers patronizing the two types of speakeasies?

3. The markets for prostitution in Nevada and New Jersey have two important differences: (1) Prostitutes in New Jersey face higher costs because of government efforts to prosecute them, and (2) customers in New Jersey face higher risks of contracting diseases from prostitutes because the illegal nature of the business makes reliable information about product quality much more costly to obtain. Given these facts, in which state would you expect the price of prostitution services to be higher? Which state would have the higher amount of services consumed (adjusted for population differences)? Explain your answer.

4. According to the surgeon general of the United States, nicotine is the most addictive drug known to humanity, and cigarette smoking kills perhaps 300,000 to 400,000 people a year in the United States. Why isn't tobacco illegal in America?

Expanding Waistlines

Americans are putting on the pounds. In the 1960s, the average American male weighed 168 pounds; today, he tips the scales at about 190. Over the same span, the average American woman put on a pound more than the men, rising to 165 pounds from her earlier 142 pounds. More significantly, the weight gain has been greater among people who were heavier to begin with. As a result, obesity in America has more than doubled: Nearly one-third of Americans now have a body mass index (BMI, a measure of weight relative to height) in excess of 30, the level at which doctors say a person passes from overweight to obese.[1] What explains these developments? Not surprisingly, economics has a lot to say on this question; in fact, some fairly simple changes in **demand** and **supply** explain why waistlines in America and elsewhere in the world have been expanding so quickly.

Actually, Americans put on weight throughout the twentieth century, largely as a result of two key factors. First, wages in sedentary occupations (those relying on brains rather than brawn) rose relative to those in active occupations. People responded by leaving jobs in manufacturing and agriculture and starting work in service and management jobs. This occupational switch reduced their calorie expenditures on the job and helped push up average weights. The second force at work was the decline in the relative price of food during the twentieth century; as predicted by the **law of demand,** this price decline induced people to eat more, pushing up their caloric intake and their body weights. Between about 1900 and 1960, the weight of

---

[1]In terms of the metric system, BMI $= K/M^2$, where K is weight in kilograms and M is height in meters. Using the English measurement system, BMI $= (703)(W/H^2)$, where W is weight in pounds and H is height in inches. BMIs in the range of 20–25 are considered healthy. Below 20 is thin, 25–30 is overweight, and 30 and above is obese—the range in which significant adverse health effects (ranging from diabetes to heart disease) begin to show up.

the average male rose 16 pounds, with similar but slightly smaller gains for the average female.

As it turns out, these weight gains during the first part of the twentieth century were probably a good thing from a health standpoint: Many Americans at the beginning of the century were actually malnourished, and the added poundage led to better health outcomes for them. The excess weight we added during the last fifty years or so is an entirely different matter, however. By the 1960s, average BMI in the United States was already at the high end of the healthy range of 20–25, so those extra pounds since then have pushed us further into the unhealthy categories of overweight and obesity.

How can we explain this recent surge in poundage? There are three key components. First, levels of physical activity have declined, although not nearly as much as many popular commentators would have us believe. The big move from active to sedentary employments took place before 1970, so it cannot explain the last forty years of weight gains. Still, caloric energy expenditures by both men and women in the United States have been falling. Americans are spending less time at work and on household chores and more time watching TV, looking at computer monitors, and talking on the phone. Overall, per capita caloric energy expenditures have dropped more than 25 percent since the 1960s. This is only a small part of the story, however; indeed, it can explain only a couple of the pounds Americans have added over the last forty years. The rest comes from higher caloric intake.

By far the most important reason for this higher caloric intake appears to be a change in the way food is prepared: Due to major changes in food processing technology, the "time cost" involved in preparing meals has fallen dramatically. Consequently, the **full cost** (money plus time cost) of food has dropped, leading to the consumption of significantly more calories. The result has been expanding waistlines.

In the 1960s, food was prepared in the home by family members and eaten there. Since then, there have been a series of technological innovations in food processing, including vacuum packing, flash freezing, improved preservatives and flavorings, and of course, the microwave. As a result, much food preparation now is done outside the home by manufacturers who specialize in that activity and then ship the packaged, prepared food to the consumer to be eaten at home or elsewhere. The result is that over the last forty years, the amount of time spent on food preparation and cleanup in the home has fallen by half. In addition, outside the home, convenient, tasty prepackaged foods are now a few steps away in a vending machine, rather than miles away in the nearest store. On both counts, the full cost of consuming food has declined, and people are consuming more calories. Moreover, they are doing it not by eating more calories at each meal but rather by eating more "meals" (actually snacks) during the day: Caloric intake during the traditional meals of breakfast, lunch, and dinner has remained nearly constant at about 1,800 per day for men and 1,400 per day for women. But both sexes have nearly doubled their intake of calories from snacks. Overall, caloric intake has risen almost 25 percent.

A few questions remain. First, are the additional calories that Americans are consuming each day—the equivalent of a Coke or a few cookies—really enough to account for the poundage we have been accumulating? The answer is yes. An extra 150 calories per day for men of average weight and activity levels will eventually lead to 11 pounds of excess waistline baggage. For women, the same 150 calories per day would eventually amount to an extra 13 pounds. (The weight gain from these extra calories eventually levels off because as people get heavier, they burn more calories just doing the things they usually do.)

The second question is, what started the revolution in food processing that made these extra calories cheaper? Although the answer to this is not completely settled, the most likely source may be found in the workforce decisions of women. Beginning around 1960, women began entering the workforce in unprecedented numbers; indeed, the **labor force participation rate** of women has doubled since then. Moreover, women have been moving into occupations and professions—such as medicine, law, and the upper ranks of business—in which annual earnings are much higher than in the traditional fields of female employment, such as teaching and nursing. On both counts, the **opportunity cost** of women's time has been rising, thus increasing the demand for laborsaving conveniences, such as prepared foods. The food industry has responded just as economics would predict.

A third question being asked by some people is this: Are Americans really better off due to the lower cost of food? Ordinarily, economists would argue that a technological improvement that lowers the costs of a good will definitely improve the lot of consumers. But in the present case, with more people becoming obese, the adverse health effects of the extra calories are becoming significant. The incidence of diabetes is rising, as is the number of people who are disabled due to obesity-related injuries or other health problems. Obesity cuts almost seven years off a person's life, about as much as smoking does, and obesity is now the largest single cause of rising Medicare expenditures—just at a time when the baby boom generation is becoming eligible for Medicare coverage.

As the poundage has piled up across the country, so have the sales of diet books, as well as the rate of expensive bariatric surgery (in which part of the stomach is stapled or tied shut to reduce caloric intake and absorption). All in all, some analysts have suggested, the lower cost of food may have made people *worse* off by inducing them to do something that they would rather not do—put on weight. This might be particularly the case for people who are said to have little self-control as to the amount they eat. While there may be something to this argument, we can consider a counterargument expressed in the following analogy: People who live in cold-weather climates, such as Montana, the Dakotas, and Minnesota, routinely complain about the weather in the winter. People in such climes also spend far more than the average person on clothes to offset the adverse effects of the cold weather. Surely we would not want to argue that such people are worse off for having chosen to live where they do rather than in warmer locales. Similarly, in the case of people who are said to lack control over the amount they eat, just who is it that should decide—and enforce—their caloric intake?

There is one final point to our story, one that illustrates amply the fact that even the best of intentions sometimes result in unintended consequences. Over the same period that Americans have been packing on the pounds, the taxes on cigarettes have risen sharply, even while the number of places where it is lawful to smoke has shrunk significantly. On both counts, the full cost of smoking (price per pack plus the hassle) has been rising, with the consequence that smoking has been on the decline in the United States. It is well known that people have a tendency to eat more when they stop smoking, and this very fact seems to be showing up in the national statistics on excess poundage. Where the full cost of smoking has risen the greatest, so has the incidence of obesity. In effect, people are being induced to substitute eating for smoking. This development reminds us that although people's behavior can easily be understood by examining the incentives they face, some of those incentives are difficult to forecast in advance.

DISCUSSION QUESTIONS

1. The technological changes in food preparation seem to have had a greater effect on the time costs of a meal than on the time costs of consuming extra calories during any given meal. What does economics predict about the resulting change in the number of meals consumed each day compared to the number of calories consumed per meal?

2. The changes in food preparation technologies of the past half-century resulted in the biggest reduction in time costs for married women. What does economics predict should have happened to the weight of married women relative to other people?

3. During the twentieth century, the cost of the automobile fell drastically, leading to a dramatic rise in the number of miles driven. But all of this driving also led to more automobile accidents, which now kill more than forty thousand people each year and maim hundreds of thousands more. Is it possible that the fall in the price of the automobile actually made Americans worse off? How much would your answer depend on whether those fatalities were among the people driving the cars as opposed to innocent bystanders, such as pedestrians and children? (*Hint:* Take a look at the chapters in Part Six, "Property Rights and the Environment.")

CHAPTER SEVEN

Is Water Different?

Mono Lake has gotten a reprieve. Over a fifty-year period, this California lake—our country's oldest lake and one of its most beautiful—shrank from more than 80 square miles in area to about 60. Why? Because in 1941, most of the eastern Sierra mountain water that once fed Mono Lake began disappearing down a 275-mile-long aqueduct south to Los Angeles, where it was used to wash cars, sprinkle lawns, and otherwise lubricate the lifestyle of Southern California. Environmentalists cried out that the diversion of water from Mono Lake must stop. Los Angelenos, who pay $350 per acre-foot for the water, claimed there were no viable alternative sources. Central California farmers, who pay but $12.50 per acre-foot for subsidized water from the western side of the Sierras, feared that diverting their own "liquid gold" to save Mono Lake would dry up their livelihood. Meanwhile, this migratory rest stop for hundreds of thousands of birds was disappearing.

Finally, prodded by the California Water Resources Control Board and aided by special funds voted by the state legislature, the city of Los Angeles agreed to drastically curtail its usage of Mono Lake water. Under the water-trading plan agreed to, Los Angeles will cut its usage of Mono Lake water by more than 80 percent until the lake's water level has risen 16 feet. Even after that elevation has been reached, the city will limit its use of Mono Lake water to less than half of its past use. To replace the water it is losing, Los Angeles will buy water from elsewhere, using state funds appropriated for this purpose.

The issues that have arisen over the future of Mono Lake are surfacing in hundreds of locations throughout the United States. Conservationists are increasingly concerned about the toxic contamination of our water supply and the depletion of our underground water sources. Extensive irrigation projects in the western states use more than 150 *billion* gallons of water a day—seven times as much water as all the nation's city water systems combined. The Ogallala aquifer (a 20-million-acre lake beneath the beef-and-breadbasket states of Colorado, Kansas, Nebraska, New Mexico, Oklahoma, and Texas) has been dropping by three feet per year because 150,000 wells are pumping water out faster than nature can replenish it.

Water problems are not confined to the United States. In China, water is being siphoned away from farmlands surrounding Beijing in order to meet rising urban and industrial demands, and some four hundred Chinese cities are now estimated to face water **shortages.** In the arid Middle East, water is a constant source of friction, and schemes to add to the region's supplies have included floating plastic bags of water southward across the Mediterranean and stirring the sea in the summer in the hopes of causing more rain to fall in the winter. In the island city-state of Singapore, half of the total land area of 247 square miles is set aside for collecting and storing water. Because there is no more room for additional reservoirs, Singapore has built desalination plants to convert seawater into drinking water. The result is more water, but the cost of freshwater produced in such a manner is seven to eight times higher than the current cost of treated water.

The common view of water is that it is an overused, precious resource and that we are running out of it. The economic analysis of the water "problem," however, is not quite so pessimistic. The physical amount of water in, on, and around the earth is fixed, but the amount of *usable* water is *not* fixed; that is, the **elasticity of supply** is positive. A higher price of water will call forth new sources of usable water: New wells will be dug, improved methods of reclaiming polluted water will be developed, and desalination of the world's oceans will increase. Thus an economic analysis of water is similar to an analysis of any other scarce resource, revealing that water is fundamentally no different from other scarce resources.

The water industry is one of the oldest and largest in the United States, and the philosophy surrounding it merits examination. Many commentators believe that water is unique and that it should not be treated as an **economic good,** that is, a **scarce good.** Engineering studies that concern themselves with demand for residential water typically use a so-called requirements approach. The forecaster simply predicts population changes and then multiplies those estimates by data showing the average amount of water currently used per person. The underlying assumption of such a forecast is that regardless of the price charged for water in the future, the same quantity will be demanded per person. Implicitly, then, both the short- and long-run **price elasticities of demand** are assumed to be zero.

But is this really the case? Perhaps not. To see why, let's look at a study of water prices in Boulder, Colorado, conducted by economist Steve Hanke. Boulder was selected by Hanke because a number of years ago, the water utility in that city installed water meters in every home and business that it supplied. Prior to that time, Boulder, like many other municipalities in the United States, had charged a flat monthly rate for water. Each household paid a specified amount per month no matter how much (or how little) water was used. In essence, the previous flat-fee system meant that a zero price was being charged at the margin (for any incremental use of water). The introduction of usage meters meant that a positive price for the marginal unit of water was now imposed.

Hanke looked at the quantity of water demanded both before and after the meters were installed in Boulder. He began by computing an index of water usage, relative to what he called the "ideal" use of water. (The term *ideal* implies nothing from an economic point of view. It merely indicates the minimum quantity of water required to maintain the aesthetic quality of each resident's lawn, taking into account such factors as average temperature and the effect of rainfall.) An index value of 100 meant that usage was exactly equal to the hypothetical ideal. A value of, say, 150 meant that residents were using 50 percent more than the ideal, whereas an index of 75 meant that usage was 25 percent less than Hanke's ideal figure of 100.

From the data in Table 7–1, which compares water usage in Boulder with and without metering, we find that individuals used much more water under the flat-rate system than they did under the metered-rate system. Column 1 shows the meter route numbers of the eight routes studied by Hanke. Column 2 shows the index of water usage for each of the routes during the unmetered period when a flat rate was charged for water usage. The data in column 3 show water usage on each route for the one-year period after the metering system was put into effect. Note that under the flat-rate system, every route used substantially more than the ideal amount of water, whereas under the metered system, six of the eight routes used less than the hypothetical ideal. Moreover, water usage dropped substantially on every route when metering was introduced, at which time each user was being charged for the actual amount of

TABLE 7–1   Water Usage in Boulder, Colorado, before and after the Introduction of Metering

(1) Meter Routes	(2) Index of Water Usage (Flat-Rate Period)	(3) Index of Water Usage (Metered-Rate Period)
1	128	78
2	175	72
3	156	72
4	177	63
5	175	97
6	175	102
7	176	105
8	157	86

Source: Adapted from Steve Hanke, "Demand for Water under Dynamic Conditions," *Water Resources Research,* vol. 6, no. 5, October 1970.

water used. Because less water is used in the presence of metering (which raises the price of incremental water), Hanke's data indicate that the quantity of water demanded is a function of the price charged for water. Hanke also found that for many years after the imposition of the metered-rate pricing system for water, the quantity of water demanded not only remained at a lower level than before metering but continued to fall slightly. That, of course, means that the long-run price elasticity of demand for water was greater than the short-run price elasticity of demand.

Would attaching a dollar sign to water help solve problems of recurring water shortages and endemic waste? Many economists feel it would. It is well known, for example, that much of the water supplied by federal irrigation projects is wasted by farmers and other users because they have no incentive to conserve water and curb overconsumption. The federal government, which has subsidized water projects since 1902, allots water to certain districts, communities, or farmers on the basis of previous usage "requirements." This means that if farmers in a certain irrigation district were to conserve on water usage by, say, upgrading their irrigation systems, their water allotment eventually would be reduced. As a result, a "use it or lose it" attitude has prevailed among users of federal water. Water supplied by federal water projects is also inexpensive for its users. The Congressional Budget Office has estimated that users pay only about 19 percent of the total cost of the water they get.

One would think that with growing worldwide concern over water conservation, the federal government would be trying to do its part to reduce waste. Let's first consider toilets—or water closets, as they are often called in the industry—a major source of residential water usage. In 1992, Congress mandated that all new water closets installed in the United States be "low-flow" models, which discharge only 1.6 gallons per flush, about half the rate per flush of regular toilets. The idea, it was claimed, was that low-flow toilets would reduce the amount of water that people "wasted" when they flushed. There were some problems with congressional reasoning on this issue. First, the basic low-flow toilet simply didn't work very well when attempting to dispose of some forms of waste, requiring that the user flush twice or even three times to accomplish the task. This, of course, eliminated all of the supposed water-conservation advantages of the low-flow model—and may also help explain why some people took to smuggling regular toilets in from Canada. Toilets have since been reengineered to make them work better with less water, sometimes assisted by compressed air. Such toilets cost up to ten times what regular water closets cost, however, and the air-assisted models have one additional problem—their operation briefly produces a noise level comparable to that of a loud vacuum cleaner. Just as important, Congress apparently failed to recognize that when water is flushed down the drain, it is not vaporized or sent into outer space. It is simply moved someplace else. The earth is a closed system, and flushing more water or more often simply moves water from one place to another more rapidly. Regular toilets may require that we devote more resources to treating wastewater, but they don't destroy the water. Indeed, many (although not all) cities actually return the treated water to the lake or river from which it was originally drawn, cleaner than it originally started.

The year after it gave us low-flow toilets, Congress authorized completion of the Central Utah Project (CUP). This project includes a series of dams, aqueducts, tunnels, and canals designed to collect water from the Colorado River drainage in Utah and transport it to the Great Basin. The cost of delivering this water to farmers for irrigation is estimated to be $400 per acre-foot. The water is used to produce additional crops yielding enough revenue to make the water worth $30 per acre-foot to the Utah farmers who receive it. But these farmers pay only $8 per acre-foot for the water—that is, only 2 *percent* of the cost of delivering the water to them!

Economists have suggested that raising the price of federal water would lead to more efficient and less wasteful water consumption. For example, a study by B. Delworth Gardner, an economist at Brigham Young University, concluded that a 10 percent rise in prices could reduce water use on some California farm crops by as much as 20 percent. Support for such a price increase is politically difficult, however, because federal law stipulates that ability to pay, as well as cost, must be considered when determining water prices.

An alternative solution involving the trading and sale of water rights held by existing federal water users has been proposed by some economists. Such a solution, it is felt, would benefit the economy overall because it could help curb water use, prevent water shortages, and lessen the pressure for costly new water projects. Trading and sales of water rights have already taken place in California, Oregon, and Utah. In addition, environmentalists were instrumental in helping arrange the water-trading plan for Mono Lake. Despite these modest successes, numerous federal and state laws have generally made such trading very difficult.

Until recent years, it had been thought that there was so much water we simply did not have to worry about it—there was always another river or another well to draw on if we ran short. Putting a price tag on water would require a substantial change in the way we have traditionally thought about water. Is this possible or even desirable? Well, events half a world away from Mono Lake may shed some light on this issue. In the Chinese capital of Beijing, an extended period of dry weather in a recent year caused the water levels in the city's reservoirs to drop sharply. The municipal State Council responded by raising the price of water for home use to $110 per acre-foot from its previous level of $80. For industrial and government users, the price hike was to $160 per acre-foot from the previous $125. Why were these actions taken? According to Liu Hangui, deputy director of the Beijing Water Conservancy Bureau, "The price adjustments were introduced to relieve the water shortage." Even communism, it would seem, is not enough to make water different.

DISCUSSION QUESTIONS

1. How much water does your neighbor "need"? Is your answer the same if you have to pay your neighbor's water bill?

2. Evaluate the following: "Although taxpayers foot the bill for federal water sold to farmers at subsidized prices, they also eat the crops grown with that water. Because the crops are cheaper due to the subsidized water, taxpayers get back exactly what they put in, so there is no waste from having subsidized water for farmers." Would you give the author of this quote an A or an F in economics?

3. During the drought that plagued California in the late 1980s and early 1990s, farmers in the state were able to purchase subsidized water to irrigate their crops, even though many homeowners had to pay large fines if they watered their lawns. Can you suggest an explanation for this difference in the treatment of two different groups of citizens in the state of California?

CHAPTER EIGHT

Slave Redemption
in Sudan

Sudan is Africa's largest nation. Located immediately south of Egypt, it encompasses nearly 1 million square miles and is home to 36 million people. It is also home to poverty, disease, civil war—and the emergence of modern-day slavery. The slave trade, in turn, has given rise to a humanitarian movement whose adherents seek to alleviate Sudan's misery by buying freedom for its slaves. Well-intentioned though they are, these humanitarian efforts may be making things worse.

Slavery is a centuries-old practice in Sudan, one that colonial British rulers finally managed to halt during World War I. The Sudanese gained independence in 1956, but despite ensuing periods of civil war, the slave trade initially remained a piece of history. This changed in 1989, when the National Islamic Front (NIF) took control of the government. The NIF quickly began arming the Muslim Baggara tribe in the northern part of the country to fight against the rebellious Christian tribes of the south. The Baggara had previously made a regular practice of enslaving members of the southern Dinka tribe, and once armed by the NIF, the Baggara resumed the slave raids the British had suppressed. This activity was further aided by the government, which supplied horses to the Baggara and permitted slave markets to open in the cities controlled by the NIF. Perhaps as many as twenty thousand Dinkas, mostly women and children, were enslaved and taken north, selling for as little as $15 each. The slaves were branded with the names of their owners and put to work as cooks, maids, field hands, and concubines.

Within a few years, word of the revived slave trade began filtering out of Sudan. In response, a variety of humanitarian groups from other nations began buying slaves in large batches and setting them free.

The process is called "slave redemption," and its purpose—ideally—is to reduce the number of people who are enslaved.

Raising money for slave redemption soon became big business, spreading rapidly among public schools and evangelical churches in the United States. A middle school in Oregon, for example, raised $2,500 to be used for slave redemption. Even more impressive was an elementary school class in Colorado: After the children's efforts caught the media's eye, the class raised more than $50,000 for slave redemption.

The largest of the humanitarian groups involved in slave redemption is Christian Solidarity International (CSI). This group says it has freed tens of thousands of slaves since 1995, most at prices of about $50 each. Other groups have purchased the freedom of several thousand additional slaves, sometimes at prices of up to $100 each.

Per capita income in Sudan is about $500 per year, which makes slave prices of $50 to $100 apiece quite attractive to the Baggara slave raiders. This is particularly true when the redeemers are buying in the south, where the targeted Dinkas live, and prices in the north, the traditional market for slaves, are as low as $15 apiece. In fact, says one individual who used to be active in slave redemption, "We've made slave redemption more profitable than narcotics." What are the consequences of such profitability?

There have been two sets of responses. First, on the **demand** side, the higher prices for slaves make it more costly for owners in the north to hold slaves. So rather than own slaves, some of them have offered their slaves to the redeemers. This, of course, is exactly the effect the slave redemption movement has desired. But there is also a **supply** response: When the market value of slaves rises due to an increase in demand (the demand of the slave redeemers), we expect an increase in the quantity supplied. That is, we expect the raiders who produce slaves by capturing them to engage in more of that activity. This is exactly what has happened in Sudan.

Slave redemption began in earnest in the mid-1990s, and according to local authorities, the number of slave raids grew sharply in response. Moreover, the size of a typical raiding party rose from roughly four hundred attackers to more than twenty-five hundred. What accounts for the increase? Slaves used to be traded in relatively small batches, but the redeemers prefer to buy in large lots—hundreds or more at a time. Collecting and assembling the number of slaves required to satisfy the redemption buyers thus requires considerably more manpower. Hence the slave trade has been transformed from a cottage industry into a large-scale business enterprise. Overall, it is estimated that the number of slaves captured in raids each year is greater now than at the inception of slave redemption.

Initially, it is likely that the impact of slave redemption was chiefly on the demand side; that is, the first slaves redeemed were almost surely "freed from slavery" in the sense that we would normally use that terminology. But once the stock of slave holdings in the north had adjusted downward in response to the newly elevated equilibrium price, there was only one place for the slave traders to get the slaves demanded by the redemption buyers. This was from the raiders who were now taking slaves for one purpose only—sale to the redeemers. Thus once the stock of slaves in the north had adjusted to its lower equilibrium level, *all* of the slaves subsequently "freed" by the redeemers were in fact individuals who never would have been enslaved had the redeemers not first made a market for them. In addition, because large numbers of new slaves now spend some time in captivity awaiting redemption, it is even possible that the total number of people in slavery at any point in time is actually *higher* because of the well-intentioned efforts of the slave redeemers.

As unpleasant as such reasoning is, it agrees with the opinions of people who observe the slave trade at first hand. As a local humanitarian worker says, "Giving money to the slave traders only encourages the trade. It is wrong and must stop. Where does the money go? It goes to the raiders to buy more guns, raid more villages. . . . It is a vicious circle." In a similar vein, the chief of one village that has been targeted by the slave raiders says, "Redemption is not the solution. It means you are encouraging the raiders."

In addition to encouraging the capture of new slaves, redemption also reduces any incentive for owners to set free their less productive slaves. Before slave redemption, about 10 percent of all slaves, chiefly older women and young children, were allowed to escape or even told to go home because the costs of feeding, clothing, and housing them exceeded their value to their owners. Now slaves who would have been freed on their own are instead held in captivity until a trader can be found to haul them south for sale to the redeemers.

The final effect of redemption has been to create a trade in fictitious slaves—individuals who are paid to pose as slaves for the purposes of redemption and who are then given a cut of the redemption price after they are "freed." Although redemption groups obviously try to avoid participating in such deals, observers familiar with the trade consider them a regular part of the redemption business.

Is there another way to combat slavery in Sudan? On the demand side, the U.S. government has long refused to negotiate with terrorists or pay ransom to kidnappers, because it believes that such tactics encourage terrorism and kidnapping. It recognizes that paying a ransom increases the profits of kidnapping, thus enticing more individuals into the trade.

On the supply side, the British were originally successful in ending the slave trade in Sudan and elsewhere in their empire by dispatching soldiers to kill or disarm slave raiders and by sending warships to close off maritime slave-trading routes. Sudan, of course, is an independent sovereign nation today; both the United Nations and the British electorate would likely oppose unilateral military action by the British government against Sudanese slave raiders. Yet even the people who used to be subject to British colonial rule have mixed feelings. When asked to compare the colonial British policies to the redeemers' policies of today, a schoolmaster in the affected area remarked, "If the colonial government were standing for election, I would vote for them." So too might the victims of the slave trade in Sudan.

DISCUSSION QUESTIONS

1. Is there anything in the historical British experience with the slave trade that suggests how the international community of today could reduce slavery in Sudan?

2. It appears that the actions of the slave redeemers have raised the **equilibrium price** of slaves. What does this imply about the number of slaves held by private owners in northern Sudan—as long as the **demand curve** for slaves is downward-sloping? What do the higher profitability and volume of slave trading today imply about the number of slaves held in inventory in the south for trading purposes, compared to the number that used to be held there?

3. How does the cost of "backhauling" a slave from the north down to the south, where the redeemers are purchasing, affect the extent to which the efforts of the redeemers cause slaves to be released from the existing stock in the north, compared to causing new slaves to be produced in the south?

4. Suppose the redeemers had succeeded in buying slaves without causing the equilibrium price of slaves to change at all. What would this imply about the elasticity of supply of new slaves? What would it imply about the number of slaves actually released from slavery in the north?

CHAPTER NINE

Smoking and Smuggling

Cigarette taxes have been in the news lately, and for good reason: Over the past few years, forty-two states and the federal government have hiked the taxes they levy on each pack of cigarettes. Higher federal and state taxes have helped push the average price of a pack of cigarettes in the United States to nearly $4.50.

A variety of motives are behind the increase in tax rates. In part, the higher taxes are an effort to reduce smoking, particularly among young people. Taxpayers often end up paying the tobacco-induced medical bills of smokers, through Medicare (for the elderly) and Medicaid (for the poor). Reducing the number of smokers, it is argued, will help cut these costs. In addition, given the current low state of public opinion about smoking, cigarette taxes are proving to be a politically palatable way of raising tax revenues. Sometimes (as in California) these receipts are used to fund antismoking advertising campaigns; other cigarette tax receipts are seen as a source of funds for publicly provided health care initiatives.

Cigarette prices have also been pushed up by a second force. Several years ago, the major tobacco companies settled a series of lawsuits filed by state governments. The companies agreed to pay $246 billion over twenty-five years into a fund to be distributed to the states. The purpose of the fund was said to be to help states promote antismoking campaigns. In fact, so far most of the states have spent most of the money on almost anything *but* antismoking campaigns. Roads have been paved, college scholarships funded, and budgetary shortfalls have been eliminated. Nevertheless, the settlement has had an antismoking impact along a different dimension. In the aftermath of the settlement, cigarette companies hiked their wholesale prices by up to $1.00 per pack. When added to state taxes that now range up to $2.57 (in the state of New Jersey), this helped push retail cigarette prices past $6.00 per pack in some places. Many smokers have responded by becoming ex-smokers.

There is little doubt that despite the addictive attributes of nicotine, higher cigarette prices make inroads on smoking—after all, the **demand curve** for cigarettes, like the demand curve for any other good, is downward-sloping. For each 10 percent that taxes push up the retail price, the number of packs sold drops by 4 to 8 percent. Interestingly, however, although smokers respond to higher taxes by smoking fewer cigarettes, they also tend to smoke cigarettes that are longer and have higher nicotine and tar content. This effect is so pronounced among people between the ages of eighteen and twenty-four that the average daily tar intake among the young people who continue to smoke is actually higher when the tax rate is higher. Because tar is believed to be the principal carcinogenic substance in cigarettes, higher taxes probably lead to *more* adverse health consequences among young smokers.

Smoking tends to be concentrated among lower-income individuals, which means that the burden of cigarette taxes also tends to be concentrated in this segment of the population. For example, one survey several years ago revealed that only 19 percent of people earning more than $50,000 per year smoked, whereas 32 percent of those earning less than $10,000 smoked. As a result, cigarette taxes consumed 0.4 percent of the income of smokers in the high-income group but 5.1 percent of the income of the low-income smokers. Indeed, it is estimated that more than half of the latest increases in federal cigarette taxes will be borne by people earning less than $25,000 per year.

Perhaps the most interesting consequence of changes in cigarette taxes, however, is the change in distribution channels that results. Cigarettes are both light and compact relative to their market value, and this becomes increasingly important when the taxes on them are raised. This makes cigarettes prime candidates for smuggling—and taxes are a prime stimulus to such smuggling. Worldwide, of the 1 trillion cigarettes exported from producing nations, it is estimated that roughly 300 billion were sold by smugglers, up from 100 billion in 1990. The chief reason for this smuggling is that cigarette taxes vary enormously around the world, creating price differences across nations of several dollars per pack.

For example, in Britain, where cigarettes cost about $9.00 per pack, it is estimated that half of all British smokers consume at least some smuggled cigarettes each year. About 25 percent of the cigarettes consumed in Spain are illegal, 20 percent of Italian cigarettes are black-market, and perhaps 40 percent of all cigarettes consumed in Hong Kong are contraband. In low-tax Luxembourg, it is estimated that only 15 percent of tobacco purchased is consumed in the country, with the rest being moved covertly to higher-tax locales elsewhere in Europe.

In 1991, the Canadian federal government raised cigarette taxes by 146 percent, yielding a price per pack of $3.50, compared to an average U.S. price of $1.00 at the time. Provincial governments soon followed suit with higher cigarette taxes of their own. By 1994, black-market cigarette consumption in Canada had jumped to 25 percent of total consumption, up from about 2 percent. How did this happen? When Canadian cigarettes are exported, they are exempt from Canadian cigarette taxes. Soon after the higher federal and provincial taxes went into effect, there was a huge rise in (tax-exempt) exports to the United States, where the cigarettes were promptly—and illegally—exported back to Canada. The federal and provincial governments were ultimately forced to slash their taxes down to about what they had been before the smuggling outbreak.

How big are the potential cigarette smuggling stakes in the United States? With an average $1.00-per-pack hike in combined state and federal taxes, the potential net revenue to smugglers would be on the order of $3 billion to $6 billion per year, even if only a quarter of all smokers turned to the black market. And where would these smuggled cigarettes come from? Almost anywhere. Mexico, a transshipment point for much of America's illegal drug imports, is one place. In the early 1990s, U.S. exports of cigarettes to Mexico went from 5 million packs a year to 150 million. Some of this was due to increased Mexican consumption, but a significant amount is believed to be due to reexports to California, which had tripled its cigarette taxes in 1989. In 2004, the federal government broke up a smuggling ring that had brought more than 100 million cigarettes into the United States from Mexico. Other likely sources of smuggled cigarettes are domestic U.S. military bases and Indian reservations, where cigarettes are generally tax-exempt. Both of these venues have been sources of bootleg cigarettes in the past, when combined federal and state taxes were far lower than they are now.

The potential problems facing states when they raise their cigarette taxes are magnified by the fact that other states represent potential sources of supply. Cigarette smuggling is sensitive to interstate tax differentials of only a few cents per pack, so state governments must consider the taxing behavior of other states or suffer the consequences. For example, the late 1940s saw an outbreak of smuggling when a significant number of states first began using cigarettes as a source of tax revenue. Another outbreak of smuggling occurred in the 1970s as states raised taxes to make up for other revenue losses caused by the recession of the early 1970s.

Michigan's experience reveals that the latest round of state cigarette tax increases is producing yet another epidemic of interstate smuggling. In 1994, Michigan hiked its tax to 75 cents per pack from 25 cents. Within just over a year, 20 percent of the cigarettes consumed in Michigan were smuggled in as smokers traveled to Ohio and Indiana to save more than one-third on the cost of a carton. With the tax in Michigan now at $2.00 per pack, compared to Indiana's 55.5 cents, Michigan smokers can save $15 per carton through a quick trip over the state line. There has also been a sharp rise in organized, large-scale heists of cigarettes, and even a major law enforcement push against cigarette bootlegging seems unable to quell the onslaught of illegal imports.

None of these developments would be surprising to the British, who two centuries ago relied on import tariffs to fund much of their government spending and suffered the consequences. Between 1698 and 1758, the standard tariff rate went from 10 percent to 25 percent. After further increases in tariffs during the American Revolution, smuggled goods accounted for a full 20 percent of all imports to Britain. Tea was particularly popular and thus heavily taxed. Indeed, the tax rate reached 119 percent, and by 1784, it was estimated that two-thirds of all tea consumed in Britain was contraband. Given the situation with cigarette taxes, cigarette smuggling seems headed the same way.

DISCUSSION QUESTIONS

1. Various state and federal laws specify that a pack of cigarettes must contain twenty cigarettes and that these cigarettes are limited in the total amount of tobacco they may contain. If such limits were not in place, when taxes per pack were raised, what would you expect to see happen to the number of cigarettes in a pack and the amount of tobacco in a cigarette?

2. In a world where transportation costs are positive, what effect would distance, from the point of production, be expected to have on the size of the tax that a state would find appropriate to levy on a pack of cigarettes?

3. In 1978, interstate trucking was deregulated in the United States, leading to greater competition in this industry and lower freight rates. In light of your answer to question 2, what effect would you expect trucking deregulation to have on the interstate pattern of cigarette taxes? In particular, what would happen to taxes in states distant from the major point of production in North Carolina relative to taxes in states closer to North Carolina?

4. Cigarettes that are smuggled from North Carolina to New York must pass through Virginia, Maryland, Delaware, and New Jersey along the way. Suppose that authorities in Delaware decide to raise taxes in the hope of discouraging smoking. What impact would this Delaware tax hike have on cigarette taxes in New York and New Jersey, compared to cigarette taxes in Maryland and Virginia?

CHAPTER TEN

Bankrupt Landlords, from Sea to Shining Sea

Take a tour of Santa Monica, a beachfront enclave of Los Angeles, and you will find a city of bizarre contrasts. Pick a street at random, and you may find run-down rental units sitting in disrepair next to homes costing $800,000. Try another street, and you may see abandoned apartment buildings adjacent to luxury-car dealerships and trendy shops that sell high-fashion clothing to Hollywood stars. Sound strange? Not in Santa Monica—known locally as the People's Republic of Santa Monica—where stringent rent-control laws once routinely forced property owners to leave their buildings empty and decaying rather than even bothering to sell them.

Three thousand miles to the east, rent-control laws in New York City—known locally as the Big Apple—have forced landlords to abandon housing units because the owners could no longer afford the resulting financial losses. Largely as a result of such abandonments, the city government of New York owns thousands of derelict housing units—empty, except for rats and small-time cocaine dealers. Meanwhile, because the controls also discourage new construction, the city faces a housing gap of two hundred thousand rental units—apartments that could easily be filled at current controlled rental rates if the units were in habitable condition.

From coast to coast, stories like these are commonplace in the two hundred or so American cities and towns that practice some form of **rent control**—a system in which the local government tells building owners how much they can charge for rent. Time and again, the stories are the same: poorly maintained rental units, abandoned apartment buildings, tenants trapped by housing gridlock in apartments no longer suitable for them, bureaucracies bloated with rent-control enforcers, and even homeless families that can find no one who will rent to them. Time and again, the reason for the stories is the same: legal limits on the rent that people may pay for a place to live.

Our story begins in 1943, when the federal government imposed rent control as a temporary wartime measure. Although the federal program ended after the war, New York City continued the controls on its own. Under New York's controls, a landlord generally could not raise rents on apartments as long as the tenants continued to renew their leases. Rent controls in Santa Monica are more recent. They were spurred by the inflation of the 1970s, which, combined with California's rapid population growth, pushed housing prices and rents to record levels. In 1979, the city of Santa Monica (where 80 percent of the residents were renters) ordered rents rolled back to the levels of the year before and stipulated that future rents could go up by only two-thirds as much as any increase in the overall price level. In both New York and Santa Monica, the objective of rent controls has been to keep rents below the levels that would be observed in freely competitive markets. Achieving this goal required that both cities impose extensive regulations to prevent landlord and tenant from evading the controls—regulations that are costly to enforce and that distort the normal operation of the market.

It is worth noting that the rent-control systems in New York and Santa Monica are slowly yielding to decontrol. For a number of years, some apartments in New York have been subject only to "rent stabilization" regulations, which are somewhat less stringent than absolute rent controls. In addition, New York apartments renting for over $2,000 per month are deregulated when a lease ends. In Santa Monica, the state of California mandated that, as of 1999, rent for newly vacant apartments could increase. Even so, in both cities, much of the rental market is dominated by rent controls. Accordingly, in this chapter we focus on the consequences of those controls.

In general, the unfettered movement of rental prices in a freely competitive housing market performs three vital functions: (1) It allocates existing scarce housing among competing claimants; (2) it promotes the efficient maintenance of existing housing and stimulates the production of new housing, where appropriate; and (3) it rations usage of housing by demanders, thereby preventing waste of scarce housing. Rent control prevents rental prices from effectively performing these functions. Let's see how.

Rent control discourages the construction of new rental units. Developers and mortgage lenders are reluctant to get involved in building new rental properties because controls artificially depress the most important long-run determinant of profitability—rents. Thus in one recent year, eleven thousand new housing units were built in Dallas, a city with a 16 percent rental vacancy rate but no rent-control statute. In that same year, only two thousand units were built in San Francisco, a city with a 1.6 percent vacancy rate but stringent rent-control laws. In New York City, the only rental units being built are either exempt from controls or are heavily subsidized by the government. Private construction of new apartments in Santa Monica also dried up under controls, even though new office space and commercial developments—both exempt from rent control—were built at a record pace.

Rent control leads to the deterioration of the existing supply of rental housing. When rental prices are held below free market levels, property owners cannot recover through higher rents the costs of maintenance, repairs, and capital improvements. Thus such activities are sharply curtailed. Eventually, taxes, utilities, and the expenses of the most rudimentary repairs—such as replacing broken windows— exceed the depressed rental receipts; as a result, the buildings are abandoned. In New York, some owners have resorted to arson, hoping to collect the insurance on their empty rent-controlled buildings before the city claims them for back taxes. Under rent controls in Santa Monica, the city insisted that owners wishing to convert empty apartment buildings to other uses had to build new rental units to replace the units they no longer rented. At a cost of up to $50,000 per apartment, it is little wonder that few owners were willing to bear the burden, choosing instead to leave the buildings empty and graffiti-scarred.

Rent control impedes the process of rationing scarce housing. One consequence of this is that tenant mobility is sharply restricted. Even when a family's demand for living space changes—due, for example, to a new baby or a teenager's departure for college—there can be substantial costs in giving up a rent-controlled unit. In New York City, landlords often charge "key money" (a large up-front cash payment) before a new tenant is allowed to move in. The high cost of moving means that large families often stay in cramped quarters while small families or even single persons reside in very large units. In New York, this phenomenon of nonmobility came to be known as *housing gridlock*. In Santa Monica, many homeowners rented out portions of their houses in response to soaring prices in the 1970s and then found themselves trapped by their tenants, whom they could not evict even if they wanted to sell their homes and move to a retirement community.

Not surprisingly, the distortions produced by rent control lead to efforts by both landlords and tenants to evade the rules. This in turn leads to the growth of cumbersome and expensive government bureaucracies whose job is to enforce the controls. In New York, where rents can be raised when tenancy changes hands, landlords have an incentive to make life unpleasant for tenants or to evict them on the slightest pretense. The city has responded by making evictions extremely costly for landlords. Even if a tenant blatantly and repeatedly violates the terms of a lease, the tenant cannot be evicted if the violations are corrected within a "reasonable" time period. If the violations are not corrected—despite several trips to court by the owners and their attorneys—eviction requires a tedious and expensive judicial proceeding. For their part, tenants routinely try to sublet all or part of their rent-controlled apartments at prices substantially above the rent they pay the owner. Because both the city and the landlords try to prohibit subletting, the parties often end up in the city's housing courts, an entire judicial system developed chiefly to deal with disputes over rent-controlled apartments.

Strict controls on monthly rents force landlords to use other means to discriminate among prospective tenants. Simply to ensure that the rent check comes every month, many landlords rent only to well-heeled professionals. As one commentator put it, "There is no disputing that Santa Monica became younger, whiter, and richer under rent control." The same pattern occurred under the rent-control laws of both Berkeley, California, and Cambridge, Massachusetts.

There is little doubt the bureaucracies that evolve to administer rent-control laws are cumbersome and expensive. Between 1988 and 1993, New York City spent $5.1 billion rehabilitating housing confiscated from private landlords. Even so, derelict buildings continued piling up at a record rate. The overflow and appeals from the city's housing courts clog the rest of New York's judicial system, impeding the prosecution of violent criminals and drug dealers. In Santa Monica, the Rent Control Board began with an annual budget of $745,000 and a staff of twenty people. By the early 1990s, the staff had tripled in size, and the budget was pushing $5 million. Who picked up the tab? The landlords did, of course, with an annual special assessment of $200 per unit levied on them. And even though the 1999 state-mandated changes in the law meant that apartment rents in Santa Monica can be increased when a new tenant moves in, the new rent is then controlled by the city for the duration of the tenancy. Indeed, the Rent Control Board conveniently maintains a Web site where one can go to learn the maximum allowable rent on any of the tens of thousands of rent-controlled residences in Santa Monica.

Ironically, the big losers from rent control—in addition to landlords—are often low-income individuals, especially single mothers. Indeed, many observers believe that one significant cause of homelessness in cities such as New York and Los Angeles is rent control. Poor individuals often cannot assure the discriminating landlord that their rent will be paid on time—or paid at all—each month. Because controlled rents are generally well below free market levels, there is little incentive for apartment owners to take a chance on low-income individuals as tenants. This is especially true if the prospective tenant's chief source of income is a welfare check. Indeed, a significant number of the tenants appearing in New York's housing courts have been low-income mothers who, due to emergency expenses or delayed welfare checks, have missed rent payments. Often their appeals end in evictions and new homes in temporary public shelters or on the streets. Prior to the state-mandated easing of controls, some apartment owners in Santa Monica who used to rent one- and two-room units to welfare recipients and other low-income individuals simply abandoned their buildings, leaving them vacant rather than trying to collect artificially depressed rents that failed to cover operating costs. The disgusted owner of one empty and decaying eighteen-unit building had a friend spray-paint his feelings on the wall: "I want to tear this mess down, but Big Brother won't let me." Perhaps because the owner had escaped from a concentration camp in search of freedom in the United States, the friend added a personalized touch: a drawing of a large hammer and sickle, symbol of the former Soviet Union.

It is worth noting that the ravages of rent controls are not confined to the United States. In Mumbai (Bombay), India, rents are still set at the levels that prevailed back in 1940. A two-bedroom apartment near the center of the city may have a controlled rent of as little as $8.50 per month. (Nearby, free market rents for an apartment of the same size can be as much as $3,000 per month.) Not surprisingly, landlords have let their rent-controlled buildings decay, and collapsing apartments have become a regular feature of life in this city of 12 million people. Over the past ten years, about ninety people have been killed in the collapse of more than fifty rent-controlled buildings. The city government estimates that perhaps one hundred more apartment buildings are on the verge of collapse.

Even Communist nations are not exempt from rent controls. In a heavily publicized news conference several years ago, the foreign minister of Vietnam, Nguyen Co Thach, declared that a "romantic conception of socialism" had destroyed his country's economy after the Vietnam War. Thach stated that rent control had artificially encouraged demand and discouraged supply and that all of the housing in Hanoi had fallen into disrepair as a result. Thach concluded by noting, "The Americans couldn't destroy Hanoi, but we have destroyed our city by very low rents. We realized it was stupid and that we must change policy."

Apparently, this same thinking was what induced the state of California to compel changes in Santa Monica's rent-control ordinance. The result of that policy change was an almost immediate jump in rents on newly vacant apartments, as well as a noticeable rise in the vacancy rate—exactly the results we would expect. Interestingly enough, however, prospective new tenants were less enthusiastic about the higher rents than many landlords had expected. The reason? Twenty years of rent controls had produced many years of reduced upkeep and thus apartments that were less than pristine. As one renter noted, "The trouble is, most of this area . . . [is] basically falling apart." And another complained, "I don't want to move into a place that's depressing, with old brown carpet that smells like chicken soup." Higher rents are gradually changing both the ambiance and the aroma of Santa Monica apartments—but only at the same rate that the market is allowed to perform its functions.

DISCUSSION QUESTIONS

1. Why do you think governments frequently attempt to control apartment rents but not house prices?

2. What determines the size of the key-money payments that landlords demand (and tenants offer) for the right to rent a controlled apartment?

3. Who, other than the owners of rental units, loses as a result of rent controls? Who gains from rent controls? What effect would the imposition of rent controls have on the market price of an existing single-family house? What effect would rent controls have on the value of vacant land?

4. Why do the owners of rental units reduce their maintenance expenditures on the units when rent controls are imposed? Does their decision have anything to do with whether they can afford those expenditures?

PART THREE

Labor Markets

Introduction

Almost everyone participates in the labor market, and most of us do so for most of our lives. In one sense, labor (or **human capital,** as it is sometimes called by economists) is no different from any other **economic good.** After all, labor is a **scarce good,** and thus the basic tools used by economists can be applied to understanding the markets for it. Nevertheless, special care is sometimes required to understand what appears to be going on in labor markets because not all aspects of these markets are what they seem to be.

As you will see in Chapter 11, "(Why) Are Women Paid Less?" since the middle of the twentieth century, there has been a revolution in the labor market as women have entered in unprecedented numbers. Yet even though women now regularly work in jobs formerly closed to them, the data still suggest that they are being paid less than men. Much of this seeming discrimination in pay is attributable to the occupational choices made by women: They work in less hazardous environments and take jobs that offer greater flexibility and fewer hours of work per week. Safe, flexible employment that demands fewer hours of work per week is desirable; once we correct for these job attributes, the real differences in pay between men and women are much smaller than they appear to be at first glance. Nevertheless, the question remains: Do women select such jobs because that is really their preferred choice, or are they forced into such work because discrimination by male business owners and managers gives women no real alternatives? This is an issue that only further study will resolve.

The issue of discrimination also arises when we examine what happens when the government interferes with the operation of labor markets. We examine this in Chapter 12, "The Effects of the Minimum Wage." As we shall see time and again in this book, the effects of government actions are not always what they seem, nor are they usually what their proponents claim for them. The chief losers from the **minimum wage**—disadvantaged minority teenagers—are often the very people who can least afford those losses, while those who claim to support the law on altruistic grounds are in fact likely to be the biggest winners. The message of this chapter may well be this simple piece of advice: When someone claims to be doing something *for* you, it is wise to ask what that person is doing *to* you.

The plight of the disadvantaged is the central focus of Chapter 13, "Immigration, Superstars, and Poverty in America." Over the past forty years, there is little doubt that people at the bottom of the income distribution in America have experienced a rising standard of living. Over the past fifteen to twenty years, however, this rise has slowed relative to the improving standard of living at the very top of the income distribution. Here we learn that several factors are likely at work, including the rising premium on education, technological changes that have helped top performers ("superstars") to earn even more, and high rates of immigration that have depressed wages near the bottom of the income distribution. Sadly, it also appears that some (though not all) government programs directed at improving life for the least fortunate have had just the reverse effect. Once again, we see that when it comes to important public issues, things are rarely what they seem.

As its title makes clear, Chapter 14, "A Farewell to Jobs," addresses the issues of employment in labor markets—in this case, the claim that American firms are exporting jobs, to the detriment of American workers. In recent years, many American corporations have begun **outsourcing** service work (such as technical and customer support) to workers located in foreign lands, especially India. Despite claims regarding the novelty (and supposed harm to the economy) of this activity, outsourcing is no different from any other form of trade. When Americans purchase, say, technical support from a company in a foreign land, that service is provided by residents of India rather than by residents of the United States; to this extent, employment in technical support is lower in America than it otherwise would be. But foreigners only *sell* us goods in the expectation that they will be able to *buy* something from us in return. Ultimately, then, **imports** (purchases) of services or goods from abroad must result in more **exports** of goods or services to foreign lands—and this implies more employment in those export industries. Like all voluntary trade, international trade creates wealth for the trading partners. The residents of each land are making the most of their **comparative advantage** in producing different goods and services, and government restrictions on such activities serve only to make us worse off.

(Why) Are Women Paid Less?

Since the middle of the twentieth century, there has been a revolution in the job market. Women have entered the paid workforce in unprecedented numbers. In 1950, for example, only about one-third of working-age women were in the paid workforce; today, fully 60 percent are. And because the male **labor force participation rate** has fallen from 89 percent to 76 percent over this period, women now account for almost half of the paid workforce in America. There has also been an overwhelming change in the nature of paid work done by women. Fifty years ago, careers for women outside of nursing or teaching were unusual. Today, women comprise nearly half of the newly minted attorneys and physicians starting work each year. Over the same fifty-year period, there has been a transformation of wages, too. In 1950, median earnings of women were only two-thirds as high as those paid men. Today, women earn 80 percent of what men are paid.

Reread that last sentence. On average, for every dollar a man earns, a woman gets paid 80 cents. Can this possibly be true? Consider this fact: Nearly 70 percent of employers' costs are accounted for by labor. An employer who hired exclusively women at 80 cents on the dollar could cut labor costs by 20 percent relative to an employer who hired only men. This would yield added profits of about 14 percent of sales—which would *triple* the **profit** earned by the typical firm. If women are paid 20 percent less than men, how could any employer possibly afford to hire anyone *but* women?

At this point you may be saying to yourself, "Surely, there are differences between men and women other than their sex that can help account for this "gender gap" in earnings." And you would be correct. Earnings are determined by experience, education, marital status, and age, for example. But even when economists control for all of these individual characteristics, using nationwide data, such as from the U.S. Census Bureau or the Bureau of Labor Statistics, unexplained differences between the pay of men and women persist. Men with the same measured individual characteristics are paid at least 10 percent more than women, and some studies find a difference twice that size.

The widespread opinion of many observers is that the unexplained gap between the pay of men and women is chiefly the result of discrimination against women. The reasoning is simple. Most business owners and senior managers are men, and given a choice between hiring a man or a woman, the "old-boy network" operates in favor of the man. According to this view, women can get the job only if they agree to accept lower wages.

Consider this fact, however: For more than forty years, it has been illegal to discriminate in the workforce on the basis of race or sex. Two major federal agencies, the Equal Employment Opportunity Commission and the Office of Federal Contract Compliance, are wholly or largely devoted to ensuring that this antidiscrimination mandate is enforced. As interpreted by the courts, the law now says that if the statistical *appearance* of lower wages for women (or minorities) is present in a workplace, the employer is *presumed* to be guilty of discrimination and must prove otherwise. No one thinks that federal agencies do a perfect job at enforcing the law here or elsewhere, but it is hard to believe that a persistent 20 percent pay difference could escape the notice of even the most nearsighted federal bureaucrat.

A hint of what might be going on begins to emerge when economists study the payroll records of individual firms—using actual employee information that is specific and detailed regarding location of the firm, type of work, employee responsibilities, and other factors. These analyses reveal that the so-called wage gap between men and women is much smaller—typically no more than 5 percent—and often there is no gap at all. The sharp contrast between firm-level data and economywide data suggests that something may be at work here besides (or in addition to) outright sex discrimination.

That something is actually three things. First, women's pay is extremely sensitive to whether or not they have children. In Britain, for example, where this issue has been studied intensively, the average pay earned by a woman begins to fall shortly before the birth of her first child and continues to drop until the child becomes a teenager. Although earnings begin to revive once the first child passes the age of twenty or so, they never fully recover. The earnings drop associated with motherhood is close to one-third, and only one-third of that drop is regained after the nest is empty. American data suggest that the same pattern is present on this side of the Atlantic.

The parenthood pay declines suffered by women stem from a variety of sources: Some are put on the "mommy track," with reduced responsibilities and hours of work; others move to different employers around the time their first child is born, taking jobs that offer more flexibility of work schedules but offer correspondingly lower pay as well. Overall, a woman with average skills who has a child at age twenty-four can expect to receive nearly $1 million less compensation over her career, compared to one who remains childless. It is worth emphasizing that no similar effect is observed with men. In fact, there is some evidence that men with children are actually paid *more* than men without children. These findings strongly suggest a fact that will come as no surprise to most people: Despite the widespread entry of women into the labor force, they retain the primary responsibility for child care at home, and their careers suffer as a result.

The second factor at work in explaining male-female wage differences is occupational selection. Compared to women, men tend to be concentrated in paid employment that is dangerous or unpleasant. Commercial fishing, construction, law enforcement, firefighting, truck driving, and mining, to name but a few, are occupations that are much more dangerous than average and are dominated by men. As a result, men represent 92 percent of all occupational deaths. Hazardous jobs offer what is known as a **compensating differential,** extra pay for assuming the differential risk of death or injury on the job. In equilibrium, these extra wages do no more than offset the extra hazards. So even though measured earnings *look* high relative to the educational and other requirements of the jobs, appearances are deceiving. After adjusting for risk, the value of that pay is really no greater than for less hazardous employment—but the appearance of higher pay contributes to the measured gender gap.

The third key factor influencing pay is hours of work. Men are more than twice as likely as women to work in excess of fifty hours a week in paid employment. Overall, the average paid workweek for men is about 15 percent longer than it is for women. Men are also more likely than women to be in full-time, rather than part-time, paid employment, and the wage differences here can be huge. Working an average of forty-four hours per week versus thirty-four hours per week, for example, yields more than twice the pay, regardless of sex. This substantial gender gap in hours of paid work is due in part to the "mommy track" phenomenon, but the question that remains is, does this constitute discrimination on the part of employers, or is it the result of choices by women?

Although we cannot answer that question definitively, there is reason to believe that some differences in occupational choice (and thus in pay) are due to discrimination. For example, the highest-paying blue-collar jobs are typically union jobs, and industrial and crafts unions have had a long history of opposition to women as members. Or consider medicine. Women are becoming much more numerous in specialties such as dermatology and radiology, where schedules tend to be more flexible, hours of work can be limited, and part-time practice is feasible. But many physicians would argue that the noticeable underrepresentation of women in the high-paying surgical specialties is partly the result of discrimination against women, rather than reflecting the occupational choices preferred by women. If this argument is correct, then even if women in a given specialty are paid the same as men in that specialty, the exclusion of women from high-paying slots will lower their average wages and make them worse off.

The extent of sex discrimination in the workplace is unlikely to be definitively settled anytime soon. Measured earnings differences, even those that account for experience, education, and other factors, clearly overstate the true pay gap between equally qualified men and women. Just as surely, however, given the heavier parenting demands typically made on women, even when they receive equal pay, it is not for equal work.

DISCUSSION QUESTIONS

1. Suppose an employer offers a base wage of $20 per hour for the first forty hours of work each week and overtime pay of $30 per hour for any hours beyond forty per week; the employer allows workers to choose their own hours of work. Suppose employee A chooses to work thirty-six hours per week and employee B chooses to work forty-two hours per week. Compute the average weekly earnings for

employees A and B, and compute the "earnings gap" (in percentage terms) between them. In your view, does this observed earnings gap constitute discrimination? Justify your conclusion.

2. A recent British study found that married men earned more than unmarried men—but only if their wives did *not* have full-time paid employment. Suggest an explanation for this finding. (*Hint:* In which case is a man more likely to share in the household responsibilities, including child care?)

3. Women who own their own businesses earn net profits that are only half as large as the net profits earned by men who own their own businesses. First, consider why women would be willing to accept lower profits. Could this reflect poorer options for women as employees? Alternatively, could it reflect other attributes of self-employment that women might find more advantageous than do men? Then think about why women do earn lower profits. Is this evidence of discrimination? If so, by whom? If not, what else might account for the lower profits?

4. Why do you think we have laws that prohibit discrimination in pay based on sex or race but permit employers to discriminate in pay based on education or experience?

CHAPTER TWELVE

The Effects of the Minimum Wage

Ask workers if they would like a raise, and the answer is likely to be a resounding yes. But ask them if they would like to be fired or have their hours of work reduced, and they would probably tell you no. The effects of the minimum wage are centered on exactly these points.

Proponents of the **minimum wage**—the lowest hourly wage firms may legally pay their workers—argue that low-income workers are underpaid and therefore unable to support themselves or their families. The minimum wage, they say, raises earnings at the bottom of the wage distribution, with little disruption to workers or businesses. Opponents claim that most low-wage workers are low-skilled youths without families to support. The minimum wage, they say, merely enriches a few teenagers at the far greater expense of many others, who can't get jobs. Most important, opponents argue, many individuals at the bottom of the economic ladder lack the skills needed for employers to hire them at the federal minimum. Willing to work but unable to find jobs, these people never learn the basic job skills needed to move up the economic ladder to higher-paying jobs. The issues are clear—but what are the facts?

The federal minimum wage was instituted in 1938 as a provision of the Fair Labor Standards Act. It was originally set at 25 cents per hour, about 40 percent of the average manufacturing wage at the time. Over the next forty years, the legal minimum was raised periodically, roughly in accord with the movement of market wages throughout the economy. Typically, its level has averaged between 40 and 50 percent of average manufacturing wages. In response to the high inflation of the late 1970s, the minimum wage was hiked seven times between 1974 and 1981, reaching $3.35 per hour—about 42 percent of manufacturing wages. President Ronald Reagan vowed to keep a lid on the minimum wage, and by the time he left office, the minimum's unchanged level left it at 31 percent of average wages. Legislation passed in 1989 raised the minimum to $3.80 in 1990 and $4.25 in 1991. Five years later, Congress raised it in two steps to $5.15 per hour. By the time you read this, it is likely that the minimum wage will have been increased again.

About half a million workers earn the minimum wage; another 1.5 million or so take home even less because the law doesn't cover them. Supporters of the minimum wage claim that it prevents exploitation of employees and helps people earn enough to support their families and themselves. Even so, at $5.15 per hour, a full-time worker earns only about half of what the government considers enough to keep a family of four out of poverty. In fact, to get a family of four with one wage earner up to the poverty line, the minimum wage would have to be nearly $10.00 per hour.

Yet opponents of the minimum wage argue that such calculations are irrelevant. For example, two-thirds of the workers earning the minimum wage are single, and they earn enough to put them above the poverty cutoff. Moreover, about half of these single workers are teenagers, most of whom have no financial obligations, except perhaps clothing and automobile-related expenditures. Thus opponents argue that the minimum wage chiefly benefits upper-middle-class teens who are least in need of assistance at the same time that it costs the jobs of thousands of disadvantaged minority youths.

The debate over the minimum wage intensified a few years ago when research suggested that a change in the New Jersey minimum wage had no adverse short-run impact on employment. Further research by other scholars focusing on Canada reveals more clearly what happens when the minimum wage is hiked. In Canada, there are important differences in minimum wages both over time and across different provinces. These differences enabled researchers to distinguish between the short-run and long-run effects of changes in minimum wages. The short-run effects are indeed negligible, as implied by the New Jersey study. But the Canadian research shows that in the long run, the adverse effects of a higher minimum wage are quite substantial. In the short run, it is true that firms do not cut their workforce by much, if at all, in response to a higher minimum. But over time, the higher costs due to a higher minimum wage force smaller firms out of business, and it is here that the drop in employment shows up clearly.

The Canadian results are consistent with the overwhelming bulk of the U.S. evidence on this issue, which points to a negative impact of the minimum wage on employment. After all, the number of workers demanded, like the quantity demanded for all goods, responds to price: The higher the price, the lower the number desired. There remains, however, debate over how many jobs are lost due to the minimum wage. For example, when the minimum wage was raised from $3.35 to $4.25, credible estimates of the number of potential job losses ranged from 50,000 all the way up to 400,000. When the minimum was hiked to $5.15, researchers suggested that at least 200,000 jobs were at stake. More recently, some economists estimate that a hike in the federal minimum wage to $7.25 would ultimately cause between 800,000 and 1.6 million people to lose their jobs. With a workforce of over 150 million persons, numbers like these may not sound very large. But most of the people who don't have jobs as a result of the minimum wage are teenagers; they comprise only about 5 percent of the workforce but bear almost all of the burden of forgone employment alternatives.

Significantly, the youths most likely to lose work due to the minimum wage are disadvantaged teenagers, chiefly minorities. On average, these teens enter the workforce with the fewest job skills and the greatest need for on-the-job training. Until and unless these disadvantaged teenagers can acquire these skills, they are the most likely to be unemployed as a result of the minimum wage—and thus least likely to have the opportunity to move up the economic ladder. With a teen unemployment rate more than triple the overall rate and unemployment among black youngsters hovering around 30 percent, critics argue that the minimum wage is a major impediment to long-term labor market success for minority youth.

Indeed, the minimum wage has an aspect that its supporters are not inclined to discuss: It can make employers more likely to discriminate on the basis of sex or race. When wages are set by market forces, employers who would discriminate face a reduced, and thus more expensive, pool of workers. But when the government mandates an above-market wage, a surplus of low-skilled workers results, and it becomes easier and cheaper to discriminate. As former U.S. Treasury

Secretary Lawrence Summers noted, the minimum wage "removes the economic penalty to the employer. He can choose the one who's white with blond hair."

Critics of the minimum wage also argue that it makes firms less willing to train workers lacking basic skills. Instead, companies may choose to hire only experienced workers whose abilities justify the higher wage. Firms are also likely to become less generous with fringe benefits in an effort to hold down labor costs. The prospect of more discrimination, less job training for low-skilled workers, and fewer fringe benefits for entry-level workers leaves many observers uncomfortable. As the economist Jacob Mincer of Columbia University noted, the minimum wage means "a loss of opportunity" for the hard-core unemployed.

Despite these adverse effects of the minimum wage, many state and local governments believe that people with jobs should be paid a wage on which they can "afford to live." In the decade after the hike in the federal minimum to $5.15, nearly 20 states and perhaps 150 localities decided that even $5.15 wasn't high enough to achieve this goal, and so these governments mandated that state or local minimum wages (sometimes called "living wages") be even higher—at levels ranging from $5.70 throughout Wisconsin to $9.50 an hour in Santa Fe, New Mexico (an amount that is scheduled to go to $10.50 an hour by the time you read this). In some cases, as in Baltimore, Maryland, the local minimum wage applies only to workers at firms that do business with the relevant government entity. But in the case of the Santa Fe minimum wage and all state-determined minimums, the law applies to all but a few firms that are declared exempt because of their very small size or their industry (such as agriculture).

When Congress and the president agreed to raise the minimum wage in 1996, it was only after a heated battle lasting months. Given the stakes involved—an improved standard of living for some, a loss of job opportunities for others—it is not surprising that discussions of the minimum wage soon turn to controversy. As one former high-level U.S. Department of Labor official said, "When it comes to the minimum wage, there are no easy positions to take. Either you are in favor of more jobs, less discrimination, and more on-the-job training, or you support better wages for workers. Whatever stance you choose, you are bound to get clobbered by the opposition." When Congress and the president face this issue, one or both usually feel the same way.

DISCUSSION QUESTIONS

1. Are teenagers better off when a higher minimum wage enables some to earn higher wages but causes others to lose their jobs?

2. Are there methods other than a higher minimum wage that could raise the incomes of low-wage workers without reducing employment among minority youngsters?

3. Why do you think organized labor groups, such as unions, are supporters of a higher minimum wage, even though their members all earn much more than the minimum wage?

4. Is it possible that a higher minimum wage could ever *raise* employment?

CHAPTER THIRTEEN

Immigration, Superstars, and Poverty in America

In 1965, the poorest 20 percent of households in the United States received about 4 percent of total income. Today, after more than forty years of government efforts to relieve poverty, the bottom 20 percent still receive about 4 percent of total income. More than 35 million Americans lived in poverty in the mid-1960s; more than 35 million U.S. citizens *still* live in poverty, despite the expenditure of hundreds of billions of dollars in aid for the poor. In the richest country in the world, poverty is remarkably resilient.

If we are to understand why, we must begin by getting the facts straight. First, even though the absolute number of Americans living in poverty has not diminished over the past four decades, population growth has brought a modest reduction in the *proportion* of impoverished Americans. As conventionally measured, more than 17 percent of Americans lived in poverty in 1965; today, a bit over 12 percent of the population is below the poverty line.

Second, traditional methods of measuring poverty may be misleading because they focus solely on the *cash income* of individuals. In effect, government statisticians compute a "minimum adequate budget" for families of various sizes—the "poverty line"—and then determine how many people have a cash income below this line. Yet major components of the federal government's antipoverty efforts come in the form of **in-kind transfers** (transfers of goods and services rather than cash) such as Medicare, Medicaid, subsidized housing, food stamps, and school lunches. When the dollar value of these in-kind transfers is included in measures of *total* income, the standard of living of persons at lower income levels has improved substantially over the years.

There is disagreement over how much of these in-kind transfers should be included in measures of the total income of recipients.[1] Nevertheless, most observers agree that these transfers, plus the earned income tax credit (which gives special tax rebates to low-income individuals), are major sources of income for people at the bottom of the income distribution. Adjusting for these transfers and taxes, it seems likely that over the past forty years, the proportion of Americans living below the poverty line has been cut roughly in half. Just as important, the standard of living for the poorest 20 percent of the population has doubled since the mid-1960s. In short, the number of poor individuals in this country has declined significantly, and those who remain poor are generally better off than the poor of forty years ago.

Whatever measure of income we use, it is crucial to remember that most Americans exhibit a great deal of **income mobility**—they have a tendency to move around in the income distribution over time. The most important source of income mobility is the "life-cycle" pattern of earnings: New entrants to the workforce tend to have lower incomes at first, but most workers can enjoy rising incomes as they gain experience on the job. Typically, annual earnings reach a maximum at about age fifty-five. Because peak earnings occur well beyond the **median age** of the population (now about thirty-seven), a "snapshot" of the current distribution of earnings will find most individuals on the way up toward a higher position in the income distribution. People who have low earnings now are likely, on average, to have higher earnings in the future.

Another major source of income mobility stems from the operation of Lady Luck. At any point in time, the income of high-income people is likely to be abnormally high (relative to what they can expect on average) due to recent good luck—they may have just won the lottery or received a long-awaited bonus. Conversely, the income of people who currently have low incomes is likely to be abnormally low due to recent bad luck, for example, because they are laid up after an automobile

---

[1]There are two reasons for this disagreement. First, a given dollar amount of in-kind transfers is generally less valuable than the same dollar amount of cash income because cash offers the recipient a greater amount of choice in his or her consumption pattern. Second, medical care is an important in-kind transfer to the poor. Inclusion of all Medicaid expenditures for the poor would imply that the sicker the poor got, the richer they would be. Presumably, a correct measure would include only those medical expenses that the poor would have to incur if they were *not* poor and thus had to pay for the medical care (or medical insurance) out of their own pockets.

accident or have become temporarily unemployed. Over time, the effects of Lady Luck tend to average out across the population. Accordingly, people with high incomes today will tend to have lower incomes in the future, while people with low incomes today will tend to have higher future incomes; this means that many people living below the poverty line are there temporarily rather than permanently.

The impact of the forces that produce income mobility are strikingly revealed in studies examining the incomes of individuals over time. During the 1970s and 1980s, for example, among the people who were in the top 20 percent of income earners at the beginning of the decade, less than *half* were in the top 20 percent by the end of the decade. Similarly, among the people who were in the bottom 20 percent income bracket at the beginning of the decade, almost half had moved out of that bracket by the end of the decade. Nevertheless, over the past fifteen to twenty years many observers have found two developments troubling. First, the degree of income mobility in the United States has declined: The chances of moving up or down the income distribution, although still high, are less than they were in 1990. Second, although incomes of the poor are rising, incomes of the rich are rising even faster. Thus the distribution of income in the United States is becoming less equal.

One measure of this growing inequality is seen in the rising proportion of the population that is *far* above the poverty line. In 1969, for example, only about 4 percent of all people in America had incomes seven times greater than the poverty level. Today, about 19 percent of Americans have incomes that high (above $135,000 for a family of four). Much of this jump in incomes at the top of the income distribution has come at the very top. Twenty-five years ago, for example, people in the top 10 percent of earners in America pulled in about 31 percent of total income; today, they garner 37 percent. And most of this jump is in even more rarified company. The top 1 percent of earners used to account for 9 percent of total income; today, they take in 16 percent. The overall picture is thus one in which incomes are rising throughout the income distribution but rising the fastest at the very top. This pattern, which first became apparent during the 1990s, is one that economists are seeking to explain. Much work remains to be done, but a few answers are beginning to emerge.

First, there is no doubt that education is important: People with a college degree earn two-thirds more than those with a high school diploma. And people who are high school dropouts can expect to be mired near the bottom of the income distribution for most of their lives. Individuals near the top of the educational pyramid seem to have fared the best of all: Those with business, law, medical, or other postgraduate degrees have experienced earnings gains outpacing all other education groups. Skill commands a premium in the market, and that premium seems to be growing.

This phenomenon is heightened by the so-called superstar effect. Technological changes have vastly expanded the size of the economic market that top performers can serve. Because of cell phones, videoconferencing, and e-mail, for example, top business managers can effectively direct far larger enterprises than used to be the case. Sports and entertainment stars can now use cable TV and the Internet to reach audiences of tens (or hundreds) of millions, far more than the tens of thousands who can attend a live performance. And these additional customers are each willing to pay for these services, so the incomes of those at the very top have multiplied correspondingly.

So much for why income at the top has grown so fast. Why has income growth at the bottom been sluggish? One reason has surely been the huge influx of immigrants to the United States in the past fifteen years. New immigrants typically earn far less than long-term residents. When large numbers of them are added to the mix of people whose incomes are being measured, *average* income can fall, even when the incomes of all individuals are rising. But new immigrants have also added to competitive pressures in labor markets for less skilled individuals. On balance, it appears that immigration has probably lowered the wages of high school dropouts in America by 4 to 8 percent. And although this seems small, remember that it is occurring among people whose incomes are already low.

Public policy has also taken its toll on the incomes of people at the bottom. The war on drugs, for example, has saddled literally millions of individuals with criminal records, and the impact has been disproportionately greatest on African Americans, whose incomes were lower to begin with. For example, since 1990, more than 2 million African American males have served time in jail on serious (felony) drug charges. Once they return to the workforce, they find that their felony records exclude them from most jobs—and not just jobs in the middle or at the top. Often convicted felons cannot find positions that pay more than $8 per hour. The result is that the incomes of such individuals are sharply diminished, which means more poverty.

The expansion of Social Security Disability Insurance (SSDI) has also likely contributed to income stagnation at the bottom. Originally established in 1956 as a program to help individuals under age sixty-five who are truly disabled, SSDI has become the federal government's fastest-growing transfer program. It now accounts for about $50 billion in federal spending per year. It allows even those who are not truly disabled to receive payments from the government when they do not work. Since 1990, the number of people receiving disability payments from the Social Security Administration has more than doubled to over 5.5 million. This is not surprising when you consider that the real value of the monthly benefits a person can collect has gone up 50 percent in the last thirty years, and eligibility requirements have been eased. The federal government spends more on disability payments than it does for food stamps or for unemployment benefits.

What does this mean? Simply that people who might have worked through chronic pain and temporary injuries—particularly those without extensive training and education—now choose to receive a government disability benefit instead. The average Social Security disability payment is over $800 a month, tax-free. For many at the lower echelon of the job ladder, $800 a month tax-free seems pretty good. For the truly disabled, SSDI and related federal disability programs have definitely made life better. But experts believe that many disability recipients are now being drawn out of higher-paying jobs by the tax-free status of disability pay, combined with the fact that it enables them to spend more time with family and friends. This development also means that measures of income inequality have risen because even though disability recipients are clearly better off as a result of the program, their incomes as measured by government statisticians are markedly lower.

There is one bright spot on the poverty policy front, however. It is the "welfare reform" program undertaken in 1996. Previously, low-income families had been eligible to receive—for an unlimited duration—federal payments called Aid to Families with Dependent Children. The program was changed in 1996 to become Temporary Assistance to Needy Families. Limits were placed on the length of time individuals could receive payments, and all recipients were given additional **incentives** and assistance to enhance their job skills and enter or reenter the labor force.

The full impact of this policy change is still being studied, but it now appears that it has modestly raised incomes among individuals at the bottom of the income distribution.

Although the resilience of poverty in America is discouraging to the poor and to analysts who study their plight, it is useful to consider these issues in an international context. In other industrialized nations, such as in Japan and Europe, people at the bottom of the income distribution sometimes (but not always) fare better than the poor in America. Although the poor typically receive a somewhat larger *share* of national income than in America, the national income in which they are sharing is lower. Thus compared to America, the poorest 10 percent of the population has a higher average income in Japan and Germany but a lower average income in the United Kingdom and Italy.

In developing nations—which is to say, for the vast majority of people around the world—poverty has a completely different meaning than it does in America. In Africa and much of Asia, for example, it is commonplace for people at the bottom of the income distribution to be living on the equivalent of $400 per *year* or less—in contrast to the $10,000 to $15,000 per year they would earn in America. As we noted in Chapter 4, "The Mystery of Wealth," this staggering difference in living standards is due to the vast differences in legal and economic **institutions** that are observed around the world. In America, as in many other industrialized nations, these institutions both give people the incentives to put their talents to work and protect them from having their assets expropriated by the government. Thus the best antipoverty program anyone has ever seen is the creation of an institutional environment in which human beings are able to make maximum use of the talents with which they are endowed.

DISCUSSION QUESTIONS

1. Why do most modern societies try to reduce poverty? Why don't they do so by simply passing a law that requires that everybody have the same income?

2. How do the "rules of the game" help determine who will be poor and who will not? (*Hint*: How did the Civil Rights Act of 1964, which forbade discrimination on the basis of race, likely affect the

incomes of African Americans compared to the incomes of white Americans?) Explain your answer.

3. Which of the following possible in-kind transfers do you think raises the true income of recipients the most: free golf lessons, free transportation on public buses, or free food? Why?

4. Consider three alternative ways of helping poor people get better housing: government-subsidized housing that costs $3,000 per year, a housing **voucher** worth $3,000 per year toward rent on an apartment or a house, or $3,000 per year in cash. Which would you prefer if you were poor? On what grounds might you make your decision?

CHAPTER FOURTEEN

A Farewell to Jobs

Let's take a trip back to the late 1980s. The foremost problem on some economists' minds is the merciless competition that American firms face from Asian manufacturers. "Japan, Inc." and its neighbors, for example, have started turning out computer memory chips at ever lower prices. The result is sharply declining profits for U.S. chipmakers and—according to chipmakers and their political supporters—a dire threat to U.S. jobs. The issue of looming job losses in this and other industries dominates the political scene. Chip industry leaders try to persuade members of Congress that the United States will lose its technological edge unless the federal government steps in to protect U.S. chipmakers. Experts are even prophesying that without government protection and help, U.S. microelectronics will be "reduced to permanent, decisive inferiority within ten years."

Now flash forward to the mid-2000s, when the most frequently recurring issue in domestic-policy debates has been much the same. To be sure, the details—which country is "stealing" jobs from which industry—have changed, but not by much. Indeed, as early as the presidential election of 2004, so-called foreign **outsourcing** of **white-collar jobs** had become as un-American as desecrating our flag. A well-known TV business analyst on CNN, Lou Dobbs, even began a listing of all of the "unpatriotic" U.S.-based companies that were "sending this country's jobs overseas." The House of Representatives tried to pass measures to prevent any type of outsourcing for the Department of State and the Department of Defense. Representative Don Manzullo (R.-Ill.) said, "You just can't continue to outsource overseas time after time after time, dilute the strategic military base, and then expect this Congress to sit back and see the jobs lost and do nothing." (This was from a member of the same House of Representatives that, twenty years earlier tried to outlaw competition from foreign automakers because the U.S. auto industry supposedly faced "imminent collapse.")

According to Craig Barrett, CEO of Intel (the world's largest chipmaker), American workers today face the prospect of "300 million well-educated people in India, China, and Russia who can do effectively any job that can be done in the United States." In a similar vein, Forrester Research has predicted that 3.3 million service jobs will "move offshore" by 2015. Five hundred thousand of those jobs will supposedly be in computer software and services. The 2004 Democratic presidential nominee, John Kerry, had a name for the leaders of companies that "export" such jobs: "Benedict Arnold CEOs." And when the chair of the Council of Economic Advisers publicly stated that foreign outsourcing of service jobs wasn't such a bad idea, numerous politicians lambasted him, arguing that foreign outsourcing of domestic service jobs was the biggest plague ever to hit the U.S. economy.

To understand the hot-button issue of outsourcing service employment to workers located abroad, you have to go back to our chapter-opening scenario. What actually happened after the "Asian invasion" of computer chips and other high-tech items in the late 1980s? The result was not the demise of Silicon Valley. Rather, American high-tech companies responded to the challenge by identifying the things at which they were best and leaving the rest to their foreign competitors. They became innovative. They led the way in personal computing and the development of the Internet. They became the engine of job creation throughout the 1990s. Indeed, we can look back through American business history and find numerous other periods in which foreign competition has threatened a particular sector of the economy. In spite of that competition—and regardless of the outcome for the sector involved—the American economy has continued to prosper.

This was not the first time the resilience of the labor market surprised people. Back in the 1960s, for example, numerous experts predicted that the rise of the computer and robots for use in businesses was going to lead to mass joblessness and poverty. Instead, computers and automation have produced staggering productivity increases throughout nearly every industry. They have helped make possible the 72 million jobs created over the past forty years and the doubling of **real per capita income** over that span. This is hardly the outcome predicted by experts in the 1960s, but then, predicting the future of the labor market has never been easy. Consider the track record of the Bureau of Labor Statistics (BLS), recognized as America's foremost source of information and expertise on the labor market. Twenty years ago, the BLS predicted that the number of gas station attendants and travel agents in America would rise sharply; in fact, employment in both occupations has fallen. And of the twenty occupations that the BLS predicted would suffer the greatest job losses over those twenty years, fully half of them have *grown*, often robustly.

What we have witnessed is a continual testing of a concept that is central to all of economics: **comparative advantage.** The nineteenth-century economist David Ricardo got it right two centuries ago, and no one has disproved him since—although U.S. corporate executives facing stiff foreign competition try to do so all the time. In a nutshell, the principle of comparative advantage says that if an individual, firm, or nation is singularly good at doing one thing (has low **costs** of doing it), it must, *by definition,* be less good at doing other things (face higher costs of doing them). Comparative advantage implies that there is a niche for everyone and that those niches can best be filled (and our wealth increased the most) if we permit unfettered freedom of trade, both domestically and internationally, and allow all participants to focus on what they do best.

Consider the current situation: Like their counterparts in the United States, engineers and technicians in India have the capacity to provide both computer programming and innovative new technologies. Indian programmers and high-tech engineers earn one-quarter of what their counterparts earn in the United States. Consequently, India is able to do both jobs at a lower dollar cost than the United States: India has an **absolute advantage** in both. In other words, it can produce a unit of programming for fewer dollars than the United States, and it can also produce a unit of technology innovation for fewer dollars. Does that mean that the United States will lose not only programming jobs but innovative technology jobs, too? Does that mean that our standard of living will fall if the United States and India engage in international trade?

David Ricardo would have answered no to both questions—as we do today. While India may have an absolute advantage in both activities, that fact is *irrelevant* in determining what India or the United States will produce. India has a comparative advantage in doing programming in part because such activity requires little **physical capital.** The flip side is that the United States has a comparative advantage in technology innovation partly because it is relatively easy to obtain capital in this country to undertake such long-run projects. The result is that Indian programmers will do more and more of what U.S. programmers have been doing in the past. In contrast, American firms will shift to more and more innovation. The United States will specialize in technology innovation; India will specialize in programming. The business managers in each country will opt to specialize in activities in which they have a comparative advantage. As in the past, the U.S. economy will continue to concentrate on what are called the "most best" activities.

The principle here is no different from what we regularly observe among world-class athletes. Typically, they have the physical and mental skills that would enable them to beat virtually anyone else in any of several sporting activities. They have an absolute advantage in athletics. Yet they invariably end up specializing in *one* sport, the one in which they have a comparative advantage. They do this because they are so good in that sport *relative* to other sports that their earnings would be lower if they "wasted" their time in those other sports. Exactly the same thing is happening with the Indian engineers and technicians, just as it happens in all other endeavors.

Let's return to the general issue of outsourcing services to foreign workers. Computer programming is just one area in which such outsourcing is occurring. This outsourcing also extends, somewhat amazingly, to U.S. income tax return preparation. The fact is that accounting firms small and large use workers in India to prepare returns for U.S. clients. At least a quarter of a million returns each year are being prepared by Indians in Bangalore and Mumbai. Moreover, U.S. hospitals are sending (via the Internet, of course) computer-image X-rays to India for physicians and medical technicians there to prepare before the images are resent to the United States for a final diagnosis.

Sending overseas white-collar jobs that are labor-intensive—answering simple complaints, taking orders over the phone, explaining basic computer setup, and reading simple medical-test results—is no different from what we did when we bought lower-priced computer chips from Japan and other Asian countries in the 1980s. Nor is it fundamentally different from what we did when we started importing more labor-intensive textiles in the 1980s and 1990s. Because of foreign competition, specific industries throughout time have been forced to be more innovative and cost-conscious, but overall, the number of jobs in the United States has consistently grown, decade after decade. Indeed, at least for the high-tech industrial sector, the aftermath of the "Asian invasion" of the 1980s was a **productivity** boom.

The fact is that there is little evidence that well-paying jobs are being "sent overseas." The average unemployment rate for college-educated workers in the postrecession year 2003 was only 3 percent. The average for 1992, the last postrecession year, was higher—3.2 percent. And since 2003, employment growth among college-educated workers has been six times greater than for less educated workers.

Jobs disappear in this economy and everywhere else—normally, because of **technological change.** (Actually, jobs disappear in the U.S. economy at the rate of 1 million per *week* as workers quit or are fired; but in a typical year, slightly *more* than a million jobs per week are created as workers accept new employment.) It is also true that manufacturing employment in America continues to shrink. But the decline in manufacturing jobs is not unique to the United States. Indeed, despite talk of "losing" manufacturing jobs to China and elsewhere, the number of manufacturing jobs in foreign countries such as China is shrinking *faster* than it is in the United States!

Wealth-enhancing technological change is relieving human beings of the necessity of performing mind-numbing, repetitive, dangerous factory jobs. It is making us more productive, and we are collectively better off as a result, even though some individuals may be worse off. But the only way to protect *everyone* from the effects of technological change is to prevent all technological change. Not only would this impoverish us if we tried it, but we would fail in our attempts because other nations would gleefully step into the technology-leading shoes we had vacated.

Indeed, the reason that U.S. companies can outsource service jobs to India, China, and elsewhere is *because* of technological change—dramatic improvements in telecommunications and computing. One thing you can be absolutely certain of is this: The political brouhaha over "exporting" jobs will eventually die out, but technological change will never stop. We don't know what the next great innovation cycle will be or which sectors will be affected. When they are affected, though, some politicians will jump on the bandwagon and declare that a new threat to the American economy has emerged. You'll then hear much pontification about how foreigners are destroying the U.S. economy. But remember this: For the past 250 years, technological change is what has enabled us to become richer as a nation; indeed, in the United States, every generation over this span has been roughly 50 percent richer than the one that preceded it. It is true that along the way, some people in the whale blubber–rendering and buggy-whip industries have had to move on to other employments. But as long as humans can think, technology will change, and jobs along with them. Our only option is to decide whether we want to get rich by embracing these changes or get poor by rejecting them.

DISCUSSION QUESTIONS

1. What is the difference between buying automobiles, clothes, and DVD players from abroad and buying low-cost labor services, such as call-center services, from abroad?

2. Given the possibility of continued outsourcing of programming services abroad, what do you think will happen to the demand for degrees in computer sciences in the United States over time?

3. In what way can immigration be thought of as "insourcing" jobs, that is, bringing the people into America to do the jobs here? Suppose we had decided a century ago (as many politicians advocated at the time) to stop this "insourcing" threat to Americans by eliminating all immigration. Would our nation be better or worse off? Would you even be an American?

PART FOUR

Market Structures

Introduction

The competitive model employed in our discussion of **demand** and **supply** assumes that firms on both sides of the market satisfy the conditions of **pure competition.** For sellers of goods, this means the **demand curve** they face is **perfectly elastic:** Suppliers must take the market price as given because any attempt by them to raise their price above the market price will result in the loss of *all* of their sales. Similarly, purchasers in the competitive model face a **supply curve** that is also perfectly elastic. The market price is given, and any attempt by them to purchase at less than that price will be unsuccessful—no one will sell to them.

The conditions of pure competition imply that buyers and sellers have no effect individually on market prices. Even a casual glance at the world suggests that the conditions of pure competition are not always met. Sometimes, as is the case for major corporations, the firms are large enough relative to the market that significant changes in their purchase or sale decisions will have an effect on prices. In other cases, buyers or sellers are "unique," in that no other buyer or seller offers exactly what they do. (Classic examples include the superstars of sports and entertainment, who will sell less of their services if they raise their prices but will still sell some.) Sometimes firms that would otherwise be pure competitors join to form a **cartel,** acting as a single decision-making unit whose collective output decisions affect the market price.

When a seller's decisions affect the price of a good, economists usually call the firm a **monopoly.** Literally, this means "single seller," but what is actually meant is that the firm faces a downward-sloping demand curve for its output, so that its decisions affect the price at which its output is sold. When a buyer's decisions affect the market price, we term the firm a **monopsony,** or "single buyer." This means that the firm faces a positively sloped supply curve, so that its purchasing decisions affect the price at which it buys goods. (Some economists use the term **price searcher** to mean any firm, buyer or seller, whose decisions affect market prices, and who must therefore search for—or decide on—the price that maximizes the firm's profits. Following this terminology, a pure competitor would be called a **price taker,** for such a firm takes the market price as given.)

The starting point for our examination of market structures is Chapter 15, "Monopsony and Competition in Health Care." Americans spend a lot on health care. In fact, one dollar out of every six we spend goes to health care—to pay for physicians, hospitals, pharmaceuticals, and medical devices. This is not merely the highest spending rate in the world. It is roughly *double* the rate observed in the typical industrialized country. Why do we spend so much, and what do we get in return? The answers lie in the fact that in America, in sharp contrast to most industrialized nations, there is wide-open competition in the demand for health care. Most wealthy countries around the world have so-called single-payer national health-insurance systems: The national government collects taxes and uses the proceeds to pay for health care for everyone. The good news of such a system is that everyone is covered. But the bad news is that a single government agency in each country acts as a monopsony buyer of health-care services on behalf of everyone. Individuals are either prevented from buying health care on their own or limited by government rules as to what they may buy. Like other monopsonies, these national health-insurance systems force down the prices of the goods they buy, such as drugs, medical devices, and physicians' and nurses' services. This in turns reduces the quantities of those goods and services that suppliers will provide, particularly in the long run. Because both prices and quantities are driven down by the monopsony national health-care systems, total spending on health care is reduced. That's the good news. The bad news (at least if you are a consumer of health-care services) is that less health care is provided.

As we note in Chapter 16, "Big Oil, Big Oil Prices?" oil is something else that has been expensive in America recently, and plenty of people think that big oil companies are the culprits. Make no mistake, the big oil companies are definitely price searchers: They can raise their price above their **marginal cost** and still sell plenty of oil. But their absolute size (measured in billions of dollars of sales or hundreds of billions in assets) is no sure guide to *how much* they are able to raise their prices. In the case of petroleum products, such as gasoline, that ability seems to be limited to something like pennies per gallon, rather than the far larger sums often attributed to big oil. Those pennies per gallon that oil companies squeeze out of us are enough to make for big **profits,** but they aren't enough to explain the oil (and gasoline) price surges of the 1970s or the 2000s. To do that, we need to move on to our next chapter.

As you will see in Chapter 17, "Contracts, Combinations, and Conspiracies," the rigors (and low profits) of competition are such that firms often try to devise ways to avoid competing. One of the most popular is the cartel, which is simply a collective agreement by many or all firms in an industry to reduce total output so that the price of the product—and thus the profits of the cartel's members—can be raised. Cartels generally are illegal in the United States, but the National Collegiate Athletic Association (NCAA) is a cartel that is both legal and flourishing. Cartels are more commonly observed in international markets. Here we examine three international cartels, in the markets for oil, diamonds, and caviar. In each case, we find that although the **incentives** to form cartels are great, even greater are the incentives to cheat on the cartels almost as soon as they are formed. The overriding message of this chapter is that despite their enormous profit potential, competitive pressures make cartels inherently unstable and thus generally short-lived.

Whatever the degree of competition, firms are always seeking ways to raise profits. Often this means developing new products and striving to offer superior service. But sometimes, as you will see in Chapter 18, "Coffee, Tea, or Tuition-Free?" it simply means adjusting prices on existing products. The practice of charging prices that differ among customers in ways not due to differences in the marginal costs of supplying them is called **price discrimination.** Although technically illegal in the United States, it is routinely observed in markets ranging from airline travel to college financial aid. In the case of air travel, you are almost certainly the beneficiary of price discrimination, paying a lower price than you would if price discrimination were completely eliminated. But don't feel too smug: By the time you start traveling for business rather than pleasure, you are likely to be on the wrong end of the price discrimination, paying plenty so that the college kid in the seat next to you can enjoy spring break in a sunny clime.

Speaking of college, you may have noticed that it has gotten pretty expensive, a topic we investigate in Chapter 19, "College Costs (. . . and Costs and Costs)." The market structure in which colleges operate is called **monopolistic competition:** Sellers (in this case, colleges) are offering similar products for sale but using advertising to differentiate their products from those offered by other sellers. Chapter 18 made clear that colleges have enough market power to price-discriminate among students. Nevertheless, there is enough competition among colleges that the structure of this market does not seem capable of explaining the high *average* price of a college education these days. To do that, we must look at a host of other factors that have come into play in this market in recent years, most notably, a rising demand for college education.

As Chapter 20, "Keeping the Competition Out," demonstrates, enlisting the government to hamstring or exclude competitors is probably the most reliable means of ensuring that you are protected from the rigors of competition. Perhaps for this reason, the array of markets in which the government stifles competition is nothing short of remarkable. Here we examine just a handful, ranging from taxicabs to hair braiding, but the list could have gone on and on. In each case, the method is the same: Usually under the guise of "consumer protection," the government prevents entry by some firms into a market, thereby reducing supply in that market. The effect is much the same as that produced by a fully enforced cartel. Firms thus protected by the government enjoy both a higher price for their product and a larger **market share.** The consumers, supposedly "protected" by their government, are usually the big losers due to higher product prices and reduced selection among suppliers.

CHAPTER FIFTEEN

Monopsony and Competition in Health Care

Americans spend a lot on health care. In fact, one dollar out of every six we spend goes to health care—to pay for physicians, hospitals, pharmaceuticals, and medical devices. This is not merely the highest spending rate in the world. It is roughly *double* the rate observed in the typical industrialized country. Why do we spend so much, and what do we get in return? Some surprising features of competition in health-care markets help answer both questions.

First things first: One reason we spend a lot on health care is because it is a **luxury good:** that is, the **income elasticity of demand** for health care is greater than 1. So when the income of the typical consumer rises by, say, 10 percent, that consumer will want to buy *more* than 10 percent more health care. One consequence is that the *share* of income the consumer spends on health care will grow as the consumer gets richer. Indeed, this pattern of spending is observed around the world in countries large and small, rich and poor. When incomes rise, people spend larger shares of their incomes on health care.

But even this pattern is not enough to explain the high spending in the United States. Based on our **per capita income** and the observed patterns of spending in other nations, we would be expected to spend about 12 percent of our income on health care. In fact, we spend about 16 percent of it there. So even accounting for the fact that Americans are rich and rich people buy more health care, we still spend heavily on it.

For many years, economists thought technology explained our high spending. America is a world leader in applying technological advances in health care. Many of these advances are developed in America, and whether they originate here or not, we generally adopt them far faster than other nations and use them more intensively. Whether it is magnetic resonance imaging (MRI) or computed tomography (CT) scans for diagnosing injuries or illness, stents for keeping clogged arteries open, or less invasive surgical techniques for replacing knees and hips, Americans want the best. And because the best is also typically the most expensive, we end up spending a lot on the "latest and greatest."

Even so, until recently, it has been difficult to understand exactly why so much innovation in health-care technology happens in the United States and why that technology spreads so quickly and so widely here. But the solution to this mystery is beginning to emerge. In America, in sharp contrast to most industrialized nations, there is wide-open competition in the demand for health care. Most wealthy countries around the world have so-called single-payer national health-insurance systems: The national government collects taxes and uses the proceeds to pay for health care for everyone.

The good news of such a system is that everyone is covered. But the bad news is that a single government agency in each country acts as a **monopsony** buyer of health-care services on behalf of everyone. Individuals are either prevented from buying health care on their own or limited by government rules as to what they may buy. Like other monopsonies, these national health-insurance systems force down the prices of the goods they buy, such as drugs, medical devices, and physicians' and nurses' services. This in turns reduces the quantities of those goods and services that suppliers will provide—particularly in the long run. Because both prices and quantities are driven down by the monopsony national health-care systems, total spending on health care is reduced. That's the good news. The bad news (at least if you are a consumer of health-care services) is that less health care is provided.

Although national health systems date back to before 1920 in Europe, Americans have resisted the idea, preferring to rely instead on a mixture of self-payment and health insurance. Modern health insurance in the United States emerged in the decade before World War II with the creation of Blue Cross (for hospital services) and Blue Shield (for physicians' services). But private health insurance really began to take off as a result of a few pivotal events. During World War II, for example, wage and price controls prevented employers from using wages to compete for labor. But the 1942 Stabilization Act allowed firms to adopt employee insurance plans. Such plans spread rapidly, in part due to a 1943 federal ruling that employer payments for employee medical and hospitalization insurance were not taxable as employee income. Then in

1954, changes to the tax laws widened the applicability and ensured the long-term security of this tax-exempt status of employee health insurance. As a result, between 1940 and 1960, the number of people in America with health insurance soared from about 12 million to over 130 million, with about 330 million different policies in force by 1960. And under virtually all of these policies, individuals had great latitude in choosing their health-care providers, who in turn had virtually complete discretion in deciding what health-care services would be provided. And the insurance companies picked up the tab.

In 1965, the U.S. government made its first important foray into this market with the creation of the Medicare program, health insurance for people aged sixty-five and above, and Medicaid, which is health insurance for low-income individuals. Initially, premiums for Medicare were heavily subsidized by the federal government, but the program otherwise operated much like private health insurance: It paid for whatever services physicians and hospitals provided, at whatever "usual and customary" fees they charged. A 1983 change in Medicare began limiting reimbursements according to diagnosis-based fee schedules, but physicians and hospitals still retained great autonomy in deciding on the services they provided patients and thus the level of spending on those patients. Medicaid is now structured similarly, but because it is jointly administered with the federal government by each individual state, there is considerable diversity in its operations across the country.

For our purposes, the key difference between the American system and the single-payer system found in most other developed nations lies in the degree of **competition** in each. As noted earlier, the single-payer monopsony system limits competition for health-care services. This helps keep health-care prices down, but it also reduces the level of health-care services provided to individuals. Under the competitive system found in the United States, people with health insurance have much greater freedom of choice in selecting the health-care providers they use and the health-care services they receive. The higher demand for health care here pushes up health-care prices. This in turn gives potential suppliers of those services the **incentives** to develop new ways to meet those demands. Moreover, because hospitals and other health-care providers know that insured individuals are willing to consume the "latest and greatest" in health-care innovations, these suppliers are willing to invest in them. Thus, for example, hospitals build new cardiac-care centers knowing that insured patients won't flinch at price tags of $40,000 and up for the procedures they offer. As one expert put it, "If you produce expensive new things for medical care, people will buy them."

The accompaniment to high spending on health care in the United States is a high-tech, service-intensive health-care system. Physicians spend far more time with their patients in America than they do in single-payer systems such as in the United Kingdom and Canada because there are more physicians per capita here and because they are explicitly rewarded for providing medical services rather than for simply seeing patients. There are also far more highly trained specialists in the United States because the greater demand for their services increases the economic **rate of return** to specialized training. America also has many more MRI machines, CT scanners, and positron emission tomography (PET) scanners than are seen in the typical single-payer monopsony system. This diagnostic equipment is critical to the early and accurate diagnosis of many injuries and illnesses. The combination of more oncologists (cancer specialists) and the widespread use of sophisticated diagnostic equipment is then reflected in the quality of the services delivered. For example, breast cancer and prostate cancer are two of the most frequently diagnosed cancers; the survival rates for these diseases are much higher in the United States than in other industrialized nations. Similarly, the most effective—and most expensive—new drugs on the market are far more likely to be prescribed in America than they are elsewhere. Perhaps for these reason, tens of thousands of Canadians come south to America each year to get the health-care services they cannot obtain at any price in the monopsony system they face at home.

All of this state-of-the-art health care comes at a cost, of course. In addition to the 16 percent of GDP we spend on it, some of the cost comes in the form of health care that *doesn't* get consumed. Because the insurance-fueled demand for health care in America pushes up prices, the 15 percent of all Americans who have no health insurance can face staggering bills if they suffer a major illness or accident.[1] It is clear that

---

[1]Some people argue that the lack of health insurance in America plays a key role in elevating our infant mortality rate. But data from the U.S. Census Bureau and the Centers for Disease Control and Prevention suggest that lack of health insurance is unlikely to explain our high infant mortality. It is among Hispanics that the lack of health insurance is by far most prevalent, yet their infant mortality rate is essentially the same as among white non-Hispanics. Blacks have health insurance rates nearly as high as among whites, yet their infant mortality rates are three times higher. Other important factors are clearly at work here, although physicians have not yet determined what they are.

because of the high cost of health care in America, many uninsured persons delay treatment for their medical problems and thus prolong or worsen their suffering while others simply do without health care altogether. Although federal law requires hospitals to treat people who are in need of care, it cannot prevent people from declining such care because they fear the financial consequences. This is a cost of the American system that discomfits many observers.

Interestingly enough, even though the Medicare system is essentially a single-payer monopsony system, the elderly in America do not suffer the long service delays and low quality that plague the elderly in other industrialized nations. Instead, they are free to choose whatever health-care providers they wish to patronize, and the quality of the care they get is every bit as good as that provided to people who have private insurance. This seeming anomaly is due precisely to the very existence of that huge private insurance market in the United States. The elderly have a clear benchmark against which they can evaluate the services they consume and the out-of-pocket expenses they incur. Any attempt by the government to treat them more poorly than the private sector would be immediately apparent—and immediately protested. Hence the federal government has never been able to squeeze down prices or restrict services the way that monopsony health-care systems have in other nations. This is indeed an illustration of one of the advantages of a market in which competition is allowed to thrive: Consumers can benefit even from the actions of competitors they never patronize.

DISCUSSION QUESTIONS

1. How does the **elasticity of supply** influence how a higher **demand** for Medicare gets translated into more medical care rather than into a higher price for medical care? Explain your answer using specific values for the elasticity of supply to illustrate your general reasoning.

2. How does the fact that Canadians (and other foreign nationals) come to America for health care tend to influence the measured share of our GDP that is devoted to health care in America? (*Hint*: Does their spending show up in the numerator used to calculate that share? Does their income show up in the denominator?)

3. People between the ages of eighteen and thirty-five are substantially overrepresented among those without health insurance. Suggest some reasons why this is the case. Does this situation make you more or less concerned about the incidence of uninsured persons than you would be if people aged forty-five to sixty-four were overrepresented among the uninsured?

4. How is the structure of Medicare influenced by the fact that senior citizens (people aged sixty-five and above) are much more likely to vote than members of any other age group?

CHAPTER SIXTEEN

Big Oil, Big Oil Prices?

The milk crates began disappearing at an unprecedented rate in 2005. Berkley Farms in Northern California started "losing" about fourteen hundred crates a day, 30 percent more than the company had been losing in a previous average year. Velda Farms in Winter Haven, Florida, reported a similar increase in missing milk crates. About the same time, police investigators in Southern California noticed an increase in the number of large SUVs that were being abandoned in the Los Angeles River bed and set on fire.

What do these seemingly unrelated events—missing milk crates and burning SUVs—have in common? The answer is the high price of oil and petroleum-based products. Consider first the sudden outbreak of flaming SUVs. When the price of premium-grade gas rose to $3.50 a gallon in California in 2005, the resale value of used SUVs plummeted. Many owners of those cars found themselves "upside down," meaning they owed more on their car loans than the cars were worth. So arson seemed like a good solution to this financial problem. Pay someone to steal the car and set it on fire. Then collect from the auto insurance company and start over again, presumably with a smaller car.

As for the missing milk crates, well, the thieves who stole them knew exactly where they were. As oil prices climbed, the prices for petroleum-based resin climbed too. Milk crates are made of such resin. At the same time that Californians were paying record **nominal prices** for gas, petroleum-based resin prices were hitting nominal-price peaks also. Resin can be recycled. At higher resin prices, there were greater **incentives** for thieves to steal milk crates to sell them to recyclers. And so they did.

Although the days of $3.50-per-gallon gas may be a vague memory by the time you read this, the public and political outcry over high gasoline prices will return with a vengeance the next time prices jump. As the title of this chapter suggests, there is a common view that big oil—multibillion-dollar oil companies—is behind big oil prices, which translate into higher prices for gas at the pump. Let us first look at the notion of what "big" means.

To be sure, today's oil companies are huge. They have to be, because exploring for oil is a costly and risky venture. But certainly, you may think, an oil company worth many billions of dollars must have plenty of **monopoly power** in the marketplace. After all, in 2006, the market valuation of ExxonMobil hit $400 billion. Shell and BP were both worth over $200 billion at that time, while Chevron was valued at "only" $125 billion.

As it turns out, however, the absolute size of a corporation is rarely a good indicator that it is a monopoly. For a company to be effective in raising prices much above the competitive level, it has to have a large *share* of the total market. To put things in perspective, the three largest privately owned oil companies in the world are ExxonMobil, Shell, and BP. *Added together,* they are smaller than the Saudi Arabian Oil Company. And none of the three private firms is as big as any of the national oil companies of Mexico, Venezuela, or China.

Make no mistake, the big oil companies in America can and do influence the price you pay at the pump. One example of this is found in **zone pricing,** in which oil companies vary their prices depending on local market conditions. For example, they might charge a nickel or a dime a gallon more at stations near an upscale university, where the SUV-driving students won't bother to drive an extra mile to save a buck on a tankful of gas. A nickel here and a dime there pretty soon adds up to real money when you are selling *billions* of gallons a year. But it doesn't add up to the price swings in petroleum products that America witnessed in the mid-2000s.

In fact, those price swings are worth a look. All of the headlines about the price of a barrel of oil reaching historic highs in the mid-2000s—over $70 per barrel—meant very little because prices were always presented *uncorrected for inflation.* In modern times, if we correct the price of oil for inflation, it reached its peak in January 1981, when it was almost $90 per barrel in 2007 dollars.

Consider, by contrast, the price of oil and gasoline in the 1800s. In 1859, when Colonel Edwin Drake struck oil in Pennsylvania, you could buy a barrel of oil for $4. Of course, if you adjust that $4 for changes in the price level and in the standard of living between then and now, it would be the equivalent of $1,200 per barrel today. As you might imagine, there was a surge in oil drilling and discoveries after word of Drake's discovery spread, which pushed prices ever downward. By 1896, when Henry Ford's first quadricycle went on sale, the price of gasoline at the pump was, in terms comparable to today's income, about $10 a gallon. (This may help explain why Ford designed his vehicle to run on ethanol.) In the years since, the prices of crude oil and its derivatives have gone up and down (actually, mostly down) in response to global **demand** and **supply,** just as the prices of all other resources, products, and services vary in response to demand and supply over time.

About thirty years ago, the Organization of Petroleum Exporting Countries (OPEC) curtailed oil production sharply; this pushed the price of oil up by a factor of 5 (from $18 per barrel in 2007 prices to about $90 per barrel). In response, oil users in developed countries, especially the United States, became more energy-efficient, just as we would expect under the **law of demand.** Today, we use only 50 percent as much energy for every dollar of production as we did in 1973. Moreover, since 1980, the share of consumer spending that goes for energy has been slashed by over a third. So when the **real price** of oil doubled between 2003 and 2006, it was a lot less painful than it had been in the 1970s.

Nevertheless, many people have been claiming that the latest spike in oil prices is different. We have had energy crises in the past, but nothing like what awaits us, they say. All you have to do is look at the titles of some recent books on the energy problem: *The Empty Tank, Out of Gas,* and *The Coming Economic Collapse: How You Can Thrive When Oil Costs $200 a Barrel.* As it turns out, experts from the federal government have been telling Americans that we are running out of oil for quite a long time. In 1914, for example, the Interior Department announced that there was only a ten-year supply of oil left. That same department told us in 1939 that there was a thirteen-year supply. Then in 1951, we were told that oil wells would run dry in the mid-1960s. President Jimmy Carter in the 1970s said that we would use up all **proven reserves** of oil in the world by the end of the 1980s.

Something is wrong here. The economy of every developed country in the world depends critically on oil to keep it going. If the world is running out of oil, we would expect the real price of oil to rise over time under these circumstances. But it hasn't—because global oil reserves are increasing, not decreasing. In 1970, Saudi Arabia had about 90 billion barrels of proven reserves. Since then, Saudi Arabia has pumped and sold over 100 billion barrels of oil. The wells should have run dry in the desert there, but they did not. In fact, Saudi Arabia now says that there are still 270 billion barrels left under the ground. And the proven oil reserves in Canada, which were tiny in 1970, are now bigger than Saudi Arabia's. The explanation is that every time there is a sustained jump in oil prices, exploration for more oil increases. So far, this has paid off with improved technology for finding and extracting oil and with more oil reserves. For example, oil companies now routinely extract oil from the bottom of the ocean at the same real cost they spent four decades ago drilling just a hundred feet down into the earth in Texas. Over the long haul, the result of this process is that real prices have trended downward.

Hysteria over the possibility of running out has occurred with other resources, too. At the end of the nineteenth century, there were numerous articles about industry grinding to a halt because we were running out of coal. Yet today there is a five hundred years' supply. What is happening with oil, coal, and many other resources is that the lure of profits induces companies to invest in better technology to create and sell more of these commodities.[1]

This process of exploration and discovery takes place over many years, even decades—it is a long-run process. In the short run, which can last several years, the **elasticity of supply** of oil and many other natural resources is relatively low: A large percentage increase in price will call forth only a small percentage increase in quantity supplied in the short run. Hence it is possible for economic or political developments to cause large changes in market prices. In the mid-2000s, hurricanes temporarily slashed supply from U.S. sources, and political upheaval in the Middle East and Africa cut supplies there too. Moreover, demand was elevated by the Chinese government, which was trying to acquire large amounts of oil to ensure that its rapidly growing economy would remain well lubricated. Reduced supplies combined with the added demand from China produced the price spike.

Interestingly enough, in the case of oil, outrage can arise when prices *fall*. In the weeks leading up to the congressional elections of 2006, the price of gasoline fell 20 percent. Many people complained

---

[1]This assumes that the **property rights** to these resources are well defined, enforceable, and transferable. As we discuss in Chapter 27, "Bye-Bye Bison," if such conditions are not met, this process of conserving existing resources and expanding new sources of them cannot be expected to occur.

that the drop was the result of a conspiracy between big oil and the government to alter the outcome of the elections. What people over-looked was that gas prices *typically* fall between Labor Day and the first week of November because the end of the summer vacation season reduces the demand for gasoline well before the onset of winter increases the demand for heating fuel.

Make no mistake, big oil companies take big risks and make big **profits.** And they are extremely good at squeezing that last nickel or dime a gallon out of us—money we might get to keep if this market were more competitive. But even though a nickel here and a nickel there soon adds up to big profits, it does not add up to price swings of $1 per gallon of gas or $40 per barrel of oil. To understand that, you have to go back to the old familiar forces of demand and supply.

DISCUSSION QUESTIONS

1. In the 1970s, during different periods, Americans had to line up and wait to get gas. Today, even when there are periodic disruptions in the oil market, we rarely, if ever, have to wait a long time to fill up. Why? (*Hint:* During the 1970s, the federal government imposed wage and price controls.)

2. If the size of proven oil reserves keeps going up, what can you say about the term *proven* as it is used by geologists? How would an economist define "proven reserves"?

3. The price at the pump for gasoline, whether it is $2 or $3, is certainly higher than it was, say, fifteen years ago. Nonetheless, Americans have not switched in great numbers to small, lightweight cars that consume less gas. Indeed, we remain a nation of large cars. Americans do love big cars, but what might be some other reasons for not downsizing?

4. When big oil companies make big profits, where do those profits go? (*Hint:* Over 50 percent of adult Americans own shares in American corporations, either directly or indirectly.)

Contracts, Combinations, and Conspiracies

The Sherman Act of 1890 outlaws any "contract, combination, . . . or conspiracy, in restraint of trade or commerce" in the United States. Translated from the legalese, this means that firms in America cannot lawfully join with competitors to form a **cartel** to raise prices above the competitive level.[1] Because successful cartels have the potential for great profits, there are strong **incentives** to form them. Usually, however, if the government discourages them, or even if it does not actively encourage them, cartels are difficult to keep together. This is because a cartel must meet four requirements if it is to be successful:

1. *Share.* It must control a large share of actual and potential output, so that other producers of the good it sells will not be able to depress prices by expanding output significantly.
2. *Substitutes.* Consumers must regard alternatives to the cartel's product as being relatively poor substitutes, and these substitutes must be few in number and relatively inelastic in supply; such factors all reduce the **elasticity of demand** facing the cartel, helping it to raise prices.
3. *Stability.* There must be very few outside factors that tend to disturb cost or demand conditions in the industry, so that the cartel is not continually having to make new price and output decisions in response to changing conditions.

---

[1]Despite this, many American agricultural producers are legally permitted to collectively agree to raise their prices on products ranging from almonds to oranges. They do so under the umbrella of "marketing orders," which effectively are cartels approved and enforced by the U.S. Department of Agriculture.

4. *Solidarity.* It must be relatively easy for the cartel to maintain solidarity by identifying and punishing members who cheat on the cartel agreement with price cuts.

All successful cartels have been able to meet these requirements to some extent. Conversely, it has been a breakdown in one or more of these factors that has been the downfall of each of them that has failed. In general, successful cartels are international in character. They are either effectively beyond (or exempt from) national laws forbidding them or encouraged by or made up of governments themselves.

One of the most famous and most successful cartels has been the Organization of Petroleum Exporting Countries (OPEC). Formed in 1960, its members have included many major oil-producing countries, such as Algeria, Indonesia, Iran, Iraq, Kuwait, Libya, Nigeria, Saudi Arabia, and Venezuela. OPEC had little impact on the price of oil until the outbreak of the Middle East war in 1973 provided the impetus for cohesive action. Saudi Arabia, Kuwait, and several other Arab nations sharply reduced their production of oil; because the **demand curve** for oil is downward-sloping, this reduction in supply pushed oil prices—and thus the **profits** of OPEC members—up sharply. On January 1, 1973, one could buy Saudi Arabian crude oil for about $9.75 per barrel (in 2007 dollars). Within one year, the price of crude had risen to $31.25 per barrel; by the next year, $40.00; and by the end of the decade, to $80.00 per barrel with no end in sight.

Several forces combined to send oil prices in the opposite direction by the mid-1980s. At least partly in response to the high prices charged by OPEC, worldwide output of oil from other sources began to grow, led by rising production on Alaska's North Slope and by aggressive marketing of the oil flowing out of the Norwegian and British fields located in the North Sea. Eventually, this additional production significantly reduced the **market share** controlled by OPEC members and thus helped reduce their stranglehold on price.

The most important problem for OPEC, however, as for so many cartels, has been cheating on the cartel agreement by its members. Whenever there are numerous firms or countries in a cartel arrangement, there will always be some that are unhappy with the situation, perhaps because they think they are not getting enough of the profits. They cheat by charging a slightly lower price than the one stipulated by the cartel, a move that will result in a very large increase in the cheater's revenues (and thus profits). The potential for cheating is a constant threat to a cartel's existence, and when enough of a cartel's members try to cheat, the cartel breaks up.

In the case of OPEC, war between the member nations of Iran and Iraq during the 1980s precipitated a major outbreak of cheating as those two nations expanded production beyond their **quotas,** using the extra sales to finance heavy military expenditures. Expressed in 2007 dollars, the price of crude oil plunged to less than $20 per barrel in 1986, when cheating on output quotas spread throughout the cartel. Saudi Arabia, the world's largest producer of crude, finally restored order when it threatened to double its output if other OPEC members did not adhere to their quotas. Crude oil prices hovered around $25 to $30 per barrel from then until early 2004, when they started a sharp climb due to rising world demand. After peaking at over $70 per barrel, prices subsequently dropped by 20 percent.

The difficulties faced by cartels are also illustrated in the diamond market, where DeBeers, the famous diamond company, once controlled as much as 80 percent of the world supply but now can claim only a 50 percent market share. DeBeers itself produces about 30 percent of the world's diamond output and controls the marketing of another 20 percent through a cartel called the Diamond Trading Company (DTC). Under the direction of DeBeers, the DTC has long restricted the sale of rough-cut diamonds to keep their prices at levels that maximize the profits of its members. After many years of profitable success, however, the diamond cartel has hit rough times. Cartel profits spurred searches for new sources of supply, and major discoveries have been made in Australia and Canada. Moreover, Russia, which accounts for about one-fourth of world output, has defected from the DTC cartel to market its diamonds through the Lev Leviev Group, the top DTC competitor. The combined effect of increased supplies and cartel defections has been to push the inflation-adjusted price of top-quality diamonds down to less than half the levels they achieved twenty-five to thirty years ago.

The Russians have had troubles with their own historically successful cartel, the one that controls—or controlled—the supply of fine caviar. The principal source of some of the world's best caviar is the Volga River delta, where Kazakhstan and Russia (both former members of the Soviet Union) share a border at the northern end of the Caspian Sea. Both the temperature and the salinity of the water in the delta make it the ideal spawning ground for sturgeon, the long-nosed prehistoric fish whose eggs have for centuries been prized as the world's finest caviar. Originally, the Russian royal families ran the show, eating what they wanted of the harvest and then controlling the remaining supplies to their advantage.

When the Russian Revolution disposed of the Romanov dynasty in 1917, the new Communist regime quickly saw the potential profits to be had from cornering the market on caviar. Hence, for the next seventy-five years or so, a Soviet state-dominated cartel controlled the nation's caviar business from top to bottom. Although the Soviet sturgeon were considerate enough to produce an annual catch of some 2,000 tons of caviar, the Communist cartel allowed only 150 tons out of the country. As a result, a state-supplied kilogram (2.2 pounds) of top-grade black caviar costing $5 or less on the Moscow black market commanded $1,000 or more in New York.

The demise of the Soviet Union spawned trouble, however, for **competition** reared its ugly head. As it turns out, the largest sturgeon fisheries fell under the jurisdictions of two different autonomous republics—Russia and Kazakhstan—each of which wanted to own and operate its own lucrative caviar business. Moreover, a variety of individuals, including enterprising Caspian Sea fishermen from these republics, staked private claims and in some cases set up their own **export** channels (behavior officially termed "black market piracy"). The effect of this capitalist behavior was a 20 percent drop in the official caviar export price during the first year of autonomy, plus an escalation of competition since then.

Caviar consumers were pleased at this turn of events, but old-line suppliers were not quite so happy. "We don't need this kind of competition," complained one. "All of these small rivals mean that prices will fall and the market will be ripped apart. This is a delicacy—we need to keep it elite." Recent years have seen a sharp upswing in world caviar prices, although not because Russia and Kazakhstan have managed to get competition under control. Instead, it turns out that pollution from leftover Soviet industry in the area has sharply reduced the region's sturgeon population. The resulting decline in the amount of harvestable caviar drove costs and prices up and profits even lower. Adding insult to injury, firms in America (whose costs are not affected by the Soviet pollution) have entered the caviar market in response to the higher prices, intensifying the price-cost squeeze that the former Soviet republics are suffering. And so just as Soviet citizens found that communism wasn't all that it was cracked up to be, it appears some of them are now learning that capitalism may be more than they bargained for—but perhaps no less than Karl Marx warned them about.

Oddly enough, despite the Sherman Act and other tough antitrust laws, one of the longest-running cartels can be found right here in the

United States. The National Collegiate Athletic Association (NCAA), which operates under a special exemption from the antitrust laws, sets the rules not only for how intercollegiate sports competition takes place but also for how athletes are recruited and paid. And under NCAA rules, college athletes are not paid much. Indeed, as a practical matter, compensation for collegiate athletes is limited to the cost of room, board, books, and tuition at their university or college, an amount that typically ranges from $20,000 to $40,000 per year. Now this might sound like pretty good pay to you, and indeed, for a field hockey player or college wrestler, it probably is. But for the so-called revenue sports of college athletics, most notably football and basketball, such sums amount to a pittance compared to what these athletes would bring on the open market. (This, of course, is exactly the point: Universities are joined together in the NCAA in part simply to keep down the costs of college athletics.) In the case of football, this issue has been studied quite intensively, so we actually have a good idea of what top college players are worth. Over a four-year college career, a player who ends up getting drafted by a professional team is underpaid by about $2 million. And while lesser players are underpaid by lesser amounts, numbers like these make it clear that despite encouraging open competition on college playing fields, when it comes to competition in the marketplace, the NCAA is guilty of unsportsmanlike conduct.

DISCUSSION QUESTIONS

1. Why are all cartels inherently unstable?

2. Would it be easier to form a cartel in a market with many producers or one with few producers?

3. What happens to the producers of caviar made from other types of fish eggs (such as salmon, whitefish, and trout) when the price of the finest sturgeon caviar changes? Would these firms ever have an incentive to help the governments of Russia and Kazakhstan reestablish the caviar cartel?

4. If the members of your class were to attempt to form a study-reduction cartel in which everyone agreed to study less, which individuals would have the most to gain from the cartel? Which ones would have the greatest incentive to cheat on the cartel?

CHAPTER EIGHTEEN

Coffee, Tea, or Tuition-Free?

A few years ago, the Internet retailing giant Amazon.com received some unwanted publicity when it was revealed that the company was charging different prices for movies sold to different customers. Amazon insisted that the price differences were random and amounted to an effort to simply test the market. But some customers complained that Amazon was using the practice to tailor prices to customer characteristics, charging more to people who were likely to be willing to pay more. The flap over Amazon's "market test" soon died out, but as time passes, Internet firms and other companies are finding it almost irresistible to regularly charge different prices to different customers. The reason is simple: By tracking people's buying habits, firms can get a pretty good idea of how to engage in **price discrimination** among their customers and thus increase their **profits.**

Now, price discrimination not only sounds like something that should be illegal, it *is* illegal, at least under some circumstances. Despite that, it is routinely practiced by businesses of all descriptions—and perhaps even by the college you attend. Interestingly, although price discrimination definitely benefits the firms (or colleges) that engage in it, you may benefit, too. Let's see how.

First things first: Price discrimination is defined as the existence of price differences across customers for the same good that are not due to differences in the **marginal costs** of supplying the customers. Thus price discrimination can occur when marginal costs are the same across customers but prices are different or when prices are the same despite differences in marginal costs. An example of the former occurs when pharmacies or movie theaters charge lower prices to "senior citizens" than to other customers. An example of the latter can be found at "all-you-can-eat" buffets, where the price is the same for all diners, even though some eat much more food than others.

Three conditions must exist for a firm to engage in price discrimination. First, the firm must be, at least to some extent, a **price searcher**—it must be able to raise price above marginal cost without losing all of its sales to rivals. Second, there must be identifiable differences across customers in their willingness (or ability) to pay different prices for the same good. Third, the firm must be able to prevent customers who pay lower prices from reselling the good to customers who otherwise would be charged higher prices—or else customers eligible for the lowest price will buy on behalf of all customers.

The objective of price discrimination is, of course, higher profits for the firm that engages in it. To see how this might work, consider a firm selling to two identifiable groups of customers, say, retirees and working people. Also suppose that the retirees have lower income and so perhaps have a higher **price elasticity of demand** for the good—that is, they tend to be more sensitive to changes in price. In this case, it may be possible for the firm to reallocate sales among customer groups, lowering prices slightly to retirees and raising them somewhat to working people, thereby getting more revenue at the same costs, and so earning higher profits. Of course, to be able to accomplish this, the firm must be able to distinguish between the two groups. (This ability is often approximated by offering the lower prices only to persons who can prove they are older and thus more likely to be retired.) Moreover, the firm must be able to prevent resale from low-price buyers to other customers; in the case of prescription medicines, pharmacies are aided by federal and state laws that forbid such resale, while in the case of movie theaters, the person getting the lower price generally must attend the movie personally to get the lower price. (This helps explain why movie rental companies like Blockbuster are less likely than movie theaters to offer senior-citizen discounts: It would be too easy for seniors to rent movies on behalf of younger people who wish to avoid the higher prices applicable to them.)

If you have ever traveled on an airplane, you are likely to have been a beneficiary of price discrimination (although your parents—or their employers—may have been victims of such discrimination if they fly on short-notice business trips). Prior to 1978, the fares charged by airlines in the United States were regulated by the federal government, so all airlines offered the same government-approved fares; discounts were rare beyond late-night ("red-eye") or weekend flights.[1] Once deregulation occurred, airlines quickly discovered there were large differences in the price elasticity of demand across customers. Business travelers typically had a lower price elasticity of demand and hence were willing to pay higher fares than leisure travelers. Fares charged business travelers are now higher than they used to be, even though leisure fares are significantly lower than they were in the days of government regulation.

The precision and effectiveness with which the airlines engage in price discrimination have been rising steadily over time, thanks to a process known as "yield management." Combining sophisticated statistical techniques and massive historical databases, together with computerized up-to-the-minute bookings, the airlines can predict with almost pinpoint accuracy how many business customers will want seats on a given flight—and how much they'll be willing to pay. As a result, says one industry insider, "high fares get higher and low fares get lower."

The process begins months before a flight ever departs, as the airline divides the seats on a plane into as many as seven or more different fare classes, or categories. Initial fares on a flight are established for each of the categories, and the yield-management computers begin the process of monitoring the reservations, comparing them to historical patterns. If advance bookings are slow, the airline will move seats to low-fare categories. But if business travelers buy higher-priced, unrestricted tickets sooner than expected, the yield-management computer removes seats from discount categories and holds them for last-minute business passengers that are predicted to show up.

A host of techniques are used to optimize the blend between filling the seats on a plane and getting the highest possible fare for each seat. In the weeks leading up to a flight, the level of fares assigned to each category may be adjusted up or down based on the latest moves by competitors, and as the flight date approaches, lower-priced categories are likely to be closed out altogether. Moreover, some people seeking

---

[1]Those fares were also considerably higher on average than they are today because the federal government agency responsible for regulating the airlines also prevented them from competing on the basis of price.

reservations may be told a given flight is "sold out" even though passengers using that flight as a connector to another of the airline's routes may find ample seating—for a price, of course. The result of all this fine-tuning is that passengers on the same flight from, say, Chicago to Phoenix, may pay round-trip fares that vary by a factor of 5—ranging, say, from $280 for the lowest-priced seats to $1,400 for the top fares.

Interestingly, the same yield-management techniques refined by the airlines are now being used by universities when they decide on financial-aid packages offered to students. After all, given the nominal tuition at a university, a more generous financial-aid offer can be thought of as a lower price, and students, like everyone else, behave according to the **law of demand.** Universities have found, for example, that they can offer less generous aid packages to students who apply for early admission because such students are more eager to attend; as one financial-aid consultant notes, "Those who have the most interest in the school are going to be less price sensitive." In a similar vein, some colleges have found that people who come for campus interviews are more interested in attending; the response has been to offer slightly less generous aid packages to such students, even though the colleges routinely recommend that students come for interviews.

In addition to these regular features of price discrimination in financial-aid offers, universities also monitor their enrollment figures each year, just as the airlines watch bookings by fare category. If a school is getting, say, too many premed students and not enough in the humanities, financial-aid offers will be adjusted accordingly, with bigger than usual aid offers being made to the students the school is trying to attract. Schools that are noted for excellence in one area but are trying to maintain a balanced mix of majors have become particularly adept at the financial-aid game. As the enrollment vice president for Carnegie Mellon University notes, without sophisticated adjustments to the blend of aid packages offered, "I'd have an institution full of engineers and computer scientists and I wouldn't have anybody in arts and design." Carnegie Mellon also recognizes the importance of competition in determining the prices it charges: After admitted students are notified of their aid offers in the spring, they are invited to fax the school any better offers they receive from other colleges. Using money from a special fund set aside for the purpose, the university generally meets competing offers received by desirable students.

Price discrimination has also shown up in the news lately on the international front. Most major pharmaceutical companies price-discriminate based on the nationality of the people buying their drugs. Partly because incomes in other nations are lower than in the United States, people in other nations have higher elasticities of demand than American citizens. Consequently, pharmaceutical companies sell prescription drugs elsewhere at lower prices than they do in the United States. But one of these other nations is Canada, and American senior citizens have found that by getting on a bus (or even just visiting the Web site of a Canadian pharmacy), they can save a bundle on their prescriptions.[2] Although this practice is technically illegal, neither the United States, nor Canada has stopped it. In fact, by the time you read this, Congress may have legalized the importation of prescription drugs from other nations.

Price discrimination certainly profits the firms that practice it, but there is an entirely different question—one that cannot be answered by economics—as to whether it is fair. Most college students who can stay over a Saturday night or make reservations a month in advance probably don't mind the lower fares made possible by price discrimination. But business travelers are far from pleased with the high fares they must pay to get where they want, when they want, usually on short notice. "They've got you, and they know it," says one executive. The flip side, of course, is that without the extra revenue generated by price discrimination, some companies or colleges would be hard-pressed to survive. Indeed, when asked about the equity of fine-tuning aid packages to willingness to attend rather than ability to pay, one financial-aid official noted he had little choice in the matter: "I could make it very fair—and be out of business."

DISCUSSION QUESTIONS

1. First-class passengers generally pay higher fares than coach passengers, even when they take advantage of advance-purchase discounts. Is this price discrimination? (*Hint:* Seats in first class are generally

---

[2]Another reason for lower prices in Canada is that it has a nationalized health-care system, meaning that the government buys drugs on behalf of all Canadians. This practice makes the Canadian government a **monopsonist** (literally, "single buyer"), with the power to force drug prices down below what they otherwise would be.

leather rather than fabric and are about 50 percent wider than coach seats. Also, there are more flight attendants per passenger in the first-class section.)

2. Is it price discrimination when a professional football team charges, say, $150 per ticket for 50-yard-line tickets in the lower deck and $30 per ticket for upper-deck tickets overlooking the end zone?

3. What factors other than income are likely to affect willingness to pay? How will differences in these factors among its customers affect the likelihood that a firm will engage in price discrimination?

CHAPTER NINETEEN

College Costs (. . . and Costs and Costs)

There is an old saying that "you get what you pay for." The implication of this aphorism is that if you want higher quality, you must pay a higher price. If that were true in higher education, college students today should be receiving triple the education quality they received three decades ago. For that is how much college costs have risen (after correcting for inflation). Few of you reading this book will have had any firsthand knowledge of the quality of higher education that long ago. Your authors do, however. We can tell you (although unscientifically) that the quality of a college education on average today is not three times better than it was thirty years ago. So what is happening here?

First, it must be noted that the rapid pace of technological change and the explosion of new sources of information have both put a premium on individuals with top skills. And this gets translated in part into a demand for people who are better educated. Thus, according to the College Board and other sources, the economic returns to college education have risen. Thirty years ago, male college graduates earned 19 percent more than men with a high school diploma. Female college graduates earned 35 percent more. Today, male college graduates earn 63 percent more and female college graduates 70 percent more. Moreover, the unemployment rate for college graduates is half the unemployment rate for the general population. Consequently, a college education is worth more now than before in the market, so people are willing to pay more for it.

Still, the rise in the annual cost of college has been staggering, and it has been accompanied by an increase in the number of years it takes to finish a degree. Thirty years ago, at both public and private colleges, it took just a little over four years for the typical student to graduate. These days, the average student in a private college takes 5.3 years to graduate. The average public university student takes 6.2 years to complete his or her studies. Someone going to a private university who does not receive any form of financial aid ends up paying about $200,000 for that degree. Hence many people are now arguing that college costs can't be fully justified by the economic returns.

There are literally thousands of colleges and universities in the United States. The existence of so many competitors would seem to qualify the industry structure in higher education as perhaps not perfect competition but at least **monopolistic competition.** In a monopolistically competitive industry, producers and sellers are offering similar products for sale, albeit ones with slight variations in features or quality. And in such an industry, there are not tens of thousands of producers, as there might be in a perfectly competitive one, but there are a large number. Monopolistic competition is characterized by advertising and **product differentiation**—and so is higher education. In a monopolistically competitive industry, though, prices and quality are, at least in the long run, related—higher prices can only be obtained by providing higher quality. Why? Because of intense competition among firms, which means that in the long run, businesses in monopolistically competitive industries cannot make **economic profits.** We should also add that because consumers patronizing the typical firm in such an industry are each paying the full cost of whatever they purchase, they are careful to keep tabs on those costs and to switch their patronage when they can cut their costs by doing so. This obviously adds to the competition among firms and helps keep prices in line with product quality.

How well does the model of monopolistic competition seem to apply to higher education? There is one way in which it clearly does not: Virtually all colleges and universities are not for profit. You can buy and sell the shares of Apple, Microsoft, and Google, and as a shareholder, you can extract the profits out of the companies via the dividends they pay. You can do neither for Harvard, Yale, MIT, or any of the state-financed higher education institutions. In the for-profit world, businesses that are well run and have consequently higher profits see their share values go up. Managers and employees in the best-run businesses are often rewarded with higher paychecks. Nothing of this nature resembles the "marketplace" for higher education. There is no "bottom line." It is difficult to measure workers' (staff, faculty, and administrators') **productivity.** Consequently, there are reduced **incentives** for those who run universities to use their **resources** more efficiently. This means that costs are higher for any given level and quality of output. (This is not to say that people who work in higher education are less capable than anyone else; rather, the incentive structure is different.)

But colleges have been not-for-profit for a long time, so we really need to look elsewhere to see what has changed recently that might affect their costs or the prices they charge relative to those costs. Let's look first at the "superstar" phenomenon discussed in Chapter 13. Because of changing technology, the economic returns to those in the very highest echelons of performance have risen relative to the returns for the typical performer. Among colleges, this has intensified competition for superstar faculty and for (potential) superstar students—especially students who might eventually become very rich and subsequently donate large sums of money to their alma mater.

This competition gets translated into higher average costs. For example, salaries of the very best faculty and administrators are far above the average. In this circumstance, even if the salary of a typical professor doesn't budge, average salaries will rise, and this must be paid for somehow. Similarly, to help attract superstar faculty, the university must offer them the best labs and computer facilities. Again, this raises costs and must be paid for by someone, probably you.

The scramble for superstars has also been translated into a new pricing policy by universities, which have learned by watching major companies (such as airlines) about charging what the market will bear. As we note in Chapter 18, because of cheaper and more powerful computing capacity, private firms have been able to set up algorithms that estimate the maximum amount they can charge customers, depending on the time of day, the time of year, and so forth. When a different price is charged to different people for the same good or service, we call this **price discrimination**—and it is something that institutions of higher learning are getting increasingly good at doing. Via an elaborate analysis of information on family incomes, colleges give discounts in the form of scholarships and other ways to potential and actual students that have a higher **price elasticity of demand.** Because competition is greatest for the best students, the big discounts are being used to attract those—the ones with high SAT scores who will improve the college's position in the *U.S. News & World Report* rankings of the country's best colleges. At the same time prices are cut for top students (via lucrative scholarships), prices are hiked for most other students, the merely very good or average ones, via higher tuition. And because the "list prices" for tuition that get reported in the press don't reflect the discounts given to top students, costs appear to be higher than they actually are.

This quest for the best students also gets translated into **nonprice competition** among universities. Students are interested in academic quality, to be sure. But even the brightest won't turn up their noses at luxurious dormitories, elegant dining facilities, spa-quality recreational centers, and winning athletic programs. All of these are expensive to provide, and so measured costs go up even further. Now, once we adjust for the quality of the offerings, it is possible that the **quality-constant price** is not in fact changing due to these improvements. But the news media don't report prices adjusted for quality, and so the headlines tell us only that prices are up.

Over the past decade, one additional factor has entered into the college cost equation. Numerous states have instituted lotteries that earmark all or part of their net proceeds for education. In at least fifteen states, an important part of the lottery funding is channeled through students in the form of scholarships. These scholarships are typically based on high school performance and are then continued (or not) based on the student's ensuing college performance. Such scholarships increase the demand to go to college, which in turn puts upward pressure on tuition.

Many students (up to two-thirds at some universities) who use the scholarships to start college don't make grades good enough to keep the scholarships after their first or second year. Meanwhile, they have finished part of their education and also have come to "know the ropes" at their college and accumulated a host of friends. This reduces their **elasticity of demand** at that school. As a result, many students who lose their scholarships stay on in school, even some who would not initially have started the process without the scholarship. When their financial-aid money gets recycled to bring in new students, the upward press on tuition continues, because existing students are staying around, too. So the next time you see a billboard advertising the "millions" that your state's lottery has channeled into education, keep in mind that unless you are a superstar, not much of it may have gone toward *your* education.

DISCUSSION QUESTIONS

1. Describe the similarities between the health-care sector and its problems and the higher education sector and its problems. Why do these two sectors in our economy have similar problems?

2. According to one study, the salaries of full professors at this nation's most prestigious universities have risen over 50 percent (corrected for inflation) in the past twenty-five years. What causes universities to offer such high salaries? What benefits do prestigious universities receive from "superstar" faculty members?

3. According to researcher Richard Vedder, only 21 cents of every added dollar that universities have spent over the past twenty-five years has gone to student instruction. Where did the other 79 cents go? If you are an undergraduate today, what tangible benefits of these increased university resources can you see around you?

4. Why do universities discount their fees to attract superstar athletes?

CHAPTER TWENTY

Keeping the Competition Out

Most competitors hate **competition.** And who can blame them? After all, if a firm can keep the competition out, **profits** are sure to rise. How high they will rise obviously varies by industry, but the lowly taxicab market gives some indication of what is at stake.

In New York City, the number of taxicabs is limited by law—limited, in fact, to one cab for every six hundred people, in a town where many people don't own cars. To legally operate a taxi in New York, one must own a taxi medallion, a city-issued metal shield affixed to the cab's hood. Although the number of taxi medallions in New York is fixed by law, you are free to buy one from a current owner, assuming that you can come up with the prevailing market price, which exceeds $400,000. That price, we should note, does not include the taxi itself—although it does entitle you to the right to work a seventy-hour week, subject to robbery, rude customers, and the erratic driving habits of other cabbies. And lest you think New York taxi drivers are crazy to pay such sums, keep this in mind: Because the city keeps the competition out, the taxi business is so lucrative that the medallions can be used as collateral to borrow money at favorable interest rates, and any cabbie who wants to leave the business can immediately find a buyer for his medallion, usually at a price that will bring even more profit. In fact, the long-run **rate of return** on New York taxi medallions compares favorably with the long-run rate of return on stocks listed on the New York Stock Exchange.

Keeping the competition out works this way: Reducing the number of firms in an industry decreases the supply of the good, thus driving up its price. Firms that remain thus enjoy both a higher price for their product and a larger market share. Consumers lose, however, suffering not only from higher prices but also from fewer alternative sources of supply from which to choose. Another group of losers are the firms who are excluded. They are forced to go into lower-paying pursuits for which they are not as well suited. The higher profits enjoyed by the firms that are protected from competition thus come at the expense of consumers and excluded competitors; the net result is also an overall loss to society as a whole, because the limit on competition reduces the total extent of mutually beneficial exchange.

Note that we said that the number of taxi medallions in New York is limited by the government. This is typical. Even though many government agencies (for example, the Federal Trade Commission and the Department of Justice at the federal level) are supposed to promote competition, getting the government involved is usually the most effective way to *stifle* competition. Consider telephones. It used to be that both long-distance and local telephone markets were regulated by the federal government. In 1984, the long-distance market was deregulated, and AT&T had to begin competing with MCI and Sprint for customers. The result was a 40 percent drop in inflation-adjusted long-distance rates. Local telephone service continued to be regulated by the Federal Communications Commission (FCC), however, and over the same period of time, local phone rates *rose* 40 percent in real terms— chiefly because the FCC has kept competition out of the local phone service market.

The government of Mexico has been even more successful in protecting phone giant Telmex from competition. Formerly a state-owned company, Telmex was privatized in 1990, with the understanding that the government would gradually but steadily end the firm's **monopoly.** The thought was nice, but the monopoly remains. Telmex has effectively been permitted to prevent potential entrants to the Mexican phone market from connecting through its dominant switching equipment. The result has been sky-high connection charges and virtually no new connections. Hence there are now only ten telephones per hundred inhabitants of Mexico. In Poland, the fellow member of the Organization for Economic Cooperation and Development with the next fewest number of lines, there are twenty telephones per hundred inhabitants. In addition to poor service, the lack of competition also shows up in prices, which sharply hamper Mexican businesses. For example, residential long-distance calls within Mexico cost 50 percent more than such calls in the United States, and international business calls made from Mexico cost nearly four times as much as such calls placed from its neighbor to the north.

Many of the decision makers who work for the government agencies that limit competition are lawyers, so it is not surprising that competition among lawyers is limited. For example, in every state but one (California), the number of law schools is capped by state law, thereby restricting entry into the profession and driving up earnings. Real estate agents are also well represented among the members of state legislatures, and so it may come as no surprise that they, too, have been successful in keeping the competition out. In addition to having to pass examinations to be licensed, real estate agents are prohibited—at their own request—from engaging in all sorts of competitive behavior. In a dozen states, agents are prohibited from discounting their prices even if they perform less than the usual amount of services for their customers. In eight states, real estate agents are not permitted to perform fewer services than the local realty association specifies, even if the customer does not want those services. These crimps on competition make life both comfortable and profitable for real estate agents, but it's not such a good deal for home buyers and sellers. In the United States, the average real estate agent's commission is 5.1 percent of the sale price of the home; the average commission in other countries is 3.6 percent. Thus by keeping the competition out, real estate agents in America are able to charge about one-third more for their services than people providing the same services in other nations.

Sometimes the government gets involved in some unlikely markets in its efforts to prevent the ravages of competition from taking their toll. Consider hair braiding. Some African Americans like to have their hair straightened in beauty shops, a procedure that requires a touch-up every four weeks, for an average monthly cost (excluding cutting and styling) of about $100. An alternative is to get one's hair braided at a braiding salon. There are now about ten thousand of these salons across the country. Braids need maintenance only once every ten weeks, cutting the cost to $50 per month. The same low cost and convenience that make braiding salons attractive to consumers also make them threatening to the conventional beauty shops that straighten hair, especially in fashion-conscious California. Claiming that they are seeking to protect consumers, agents of the California Barbering and Cosmetology Board regularly raid the salons of unlicensed hair braiders. Not surprisingly, the hair braiders think the state is actually trying to protect state-licensed cosmetologists at beauty shops, who must spend $6,000 for sixteen hundred hours of training to get their licenses. Indeed, one of the braiders, Ali Rasheed, argues that the marketplace is better than state licensing boards at protecting consumers. "It's simple," he says. "If I mess up your hair, you don't come back. You spread the word. And very quickly I'd be out of business." Perhaps so, but it looks like the state of California doesn't want to give consumers that option.

Back in New York, there is an example of the fact that the government likes to protect itself from competition, too. New York City is well known for its massive public transit system, comprising both subways and bus lines. What is not so well known is that mass transit in New York City started off as private enterprise. The first horsecars and elevated trains in the city were developed by private companies. Moreover, even though New York's first subway was partly financed by a loan from the city, it was otherwise a private operation, operated profitably at a fare of a nickel (the equivalent of less than a dollar today).

New York's politicians refused to allow fares to rise during the inflation of World War I, yielding financial losses for the private transit companies. Promising to show the private sector how to run a transit system efficiently while simultaneously offering to protect the public from the "dictatorship" of the transit firms, the city took over the subway, merged it with the bus line, and promptly started raising fares. Despite fare increases double the inflation rate, however, costs have risen even faster, so that today, even though the basic fare is $2, the city *loses* $2 a passenger because fares don't cover costs.

Enter the jitneys, privately owned vans that operate along regular routes, like buses, but charge as little as $1 a passenger and make detours for pickups and dropoffs on request. Actually, we should have said "attempted entry" by the jitneys, because the New York City Council—at the insistence of the public transit system—has denied operating permits to almost all jitney operators who have applied. The council says it is only seeking to prevent the vans from causing accidents and traffic problems, but even fully insured drivers who have met federal requirements for operating interstate van services are routinely denied permits. Thus most of the hundreds of jitneys operating in New York City are doing so illegally. Even the few jitneys that have managed to get licensed are forbidden from operating along public bus routes—in the name of public safety, of course.

Transportation economists such as Daniel Klein of Santa Clara University have argued that public transit systems could once more be profitable—instead of losing an average of 50 cents on the dollar—if the jitneys were given a chance. "Government has demonstrated that it has no more business producing transit than producing cornflakes. It should concentrate instead on establishing new rules to foster competition," says Klein. Unfortunately for the jitneys and their customers, however, that competition would come at the expense of New York's public transit system. Thus for the foreseeable future, it seems the jitneys will have to compete only by breaking the laws, because, like most competitors, the New York City mass transit system just hates competition.

DISCUSSION QUESTIONS

1. Consider two different ways of beating your competition. One way is to offer your customers lower prices and better service. The other is to get a law passed that raises your competitors' costs—for example, by imposing special operating requirements on them. Can you see any difference between these two methods, assuming that both succeed in keeping your competition out?

2. Although governments at all levels sometimes act to prevent some individuals from competing with others, the federal government is probably the most active in this role, state governments are less active, and local governments are the least active. Can you explain this pattern?

3. Is there any difference between prohibiting entry by a group of firms and levying a special tax on those firms?

Political Economy

Introduction

The chief focus of economics has always been on explaining the behavior of the private sector. Yet dating back at least to the publication of Adam Smith's *Wealth of Nations* in 1776, economists have never missed an opportunity to apply their theories to additional realms of behavior. For the past forty years or so, much of this effort has been devoted to developing theories that explain the actions of governments, as well as the consequences of those actions. This undertaking is often referred to as the study of **political economy,** for it often involves a mixture of politics and economics. As the selections in Part Five hint, economists do not yet have a unified theory of government. Nevertheless, they are making progress and are sometimes able to offer surprising insights.

It is fair (and no exaggeration) to say that farmers understand and have exploited the nuances of political economy as well as anyone in this nation, a point we elaborate on in Chapter 21, "Raising Less Corn and More Hell." More than seventy years ago, American farmers convinced the federal government to guarantee that farmers receive prices for their crops well above the **equilibrium prices** and that taxpayers and consumers of food should bear the costs of making these high prices "stick." Ever since, consumers have faced higher prices for many crops because of various **target prices** and **price-support programs,** and taxpayers have faced higher tax bills as well. Indeed, the average American household pays almost $500 a year in higher food prices and higher taxes due to federal programs benefiting "farmers"—even though most of this money actually ends up in the pockets of shareholders in giant agribusiness corporations. Moreover, as the experience of New Zealand reveals, government farm programs are *not* necessary to protect the vitality or **productivity** of the farm sector. Twenty-five years ago, New Zealand brought a halt to all of its efforts to protect farmers from competition. The result was innovation, cost cutting, and aggressive international marketing by New Zealand farmers, who are now stronger and more productive than ever before.

One of the first things that economists had to learn about government decision making is that the costs of government policies are always higher than promised and the benefits are always lower. This simple proposition forms the centerpiece of Chapter 22, "Killer Cars and the Rise of the SUV," which explores the implications of federal rules that specify the minimum fuel efficiency permitted for new cars sold in the United States. Sometimes the effects of the federal regulations are surprisingly pervasive—as when they induce one-third of American drivers to switch from cars to trucks in response to federal fuel economy rules. Sometimes the effects are at least moderately expensive—as when they induce companies to spend millions of dollars redesigning vehicles, not to make them more fuel-efficient but solely to satisfy the peculiar accounting conventions of the regulations. And sadly, sometimes the effects of the regulations are tragic. Reliable estimates suggest that the federal fuel economy standards have forced automakers to downsize their cars to such an extent that they have become less crashworthy. It is estimated that three thousand Americans lose their lives in traffic accidents every year as a result of these particular regulations.

Crime rates that won't go down, coupled with criminals who seem impervious to law enforcement, have led many people to ask a simple disturbing question: Is there any effective way to fight crime? Although economic theory says the answer to this question is yes, many empirical estimates obtained by economists have said, well, "Maybe." Yet as you will see in Chapter 23, "Crime and Punishment," new evidence is shedding light on the answer to this question. Indeed, it is increasingly clear that the two central tools of traditional law enforcement—police to apprehend the criminals and prisons to punish them—may be every bit as effective as their proponents claim in discouraging criminal activity. Two lessons that emerge from this chapter are that politicians are likely to continue pouring more money into law enforcement and that those resources are going to have a growing impact in reducing crime in America.

For thirty years, the nation struggled with the baby boom generation as it graduated from bassinets to BMWs. For the next thirty years, we will have to grapple with the problems that arise as the boomers progress from corporate boardrooms to nursing homes. As we note in Chapter 24, "The Graying of America," the United States is aging at the fastest rate in its history. As the nation ages, two major problems in political economy are emerging. First, we must face the issue of paying the Social Security and Medicare bills of the rapidly growing elderly portion of the population. Second, as increasing numbers of people retire, there will be fewer workers capable of bearing the growing tax burden. America must learn new ways of harnessing the productive capabilities of the elderly and accept that, as much as we may wish otherwise, the elderly may simply have to fend for themselves.

Our final foray into political economy takes place on the road—sitting somewhere in a traffic jam. Travel on most roads in the United States (and elsewhere in the world) is "free," in the sense that one does not have to pay a direct monetary price to commute to work or take a Sunday drive. Yet as you will see in Chapter 25, "Heavenly Highway," roads are in fact **scarce goods,** meaning that their use must ultimately be rationed somehow. In most places in the world, during parts of most days, the scarce space on roads is rationed by the valuable time of drivers, in the form of traffic congestion. Not only do traffic jams yield economic losses that are avoidable, but advancing technology is making it ever cheaper to avoid those losses. Many governments are reluctant to take advantage of that technology. In examining the reasons for that reluctance, we also come to a better understanding of why, despite the great advantage of having prices ration scarce goods, we often choose instead to rely on nonprice rationing. Nevertheless, we also see that successes on both sides of the Atlantic in **congestion pricing** reveal that, as with other goods, putting a price on highway travel can make us much better off.

CHAPTER TWENTY-ONE

Raising Less Corn and More Hell

When politician Mary Lease stumped the Kansas countryside in 1890, she urged the farmers to raise "less corn and more hell," and that is just what they have been doing ever since.

The two decades before World War I witnessed unparalleled agricultural prosperity in the United States. This "golden age of American farming" continued through the war as food prices soared. The end of the war, combined with a sharp depression in 1920, brought the golden age to a painful halt. Even the long economic recovery from 1921 to 1929—the Roaring Twenties—did little to help American farmers. European countries were redirecting their resources into agricultural production, and new American **tariffs** on foreign goods severely disrupted international trade. Because food **exports** had been an important source of farmers' incomes, the decline in world trade reduced the **demand** for American agricultural products and cut deeply into food prices and farm income.

The sharply falling food prices of the 1920s led farmers to view their problem as one of overproduction. Numerous cooperative efforts were made, therefore, to restrict production, but virtually all of these efforts failed. Most crops were produced under highly competitive conditions, with large numbers of buyers and sellers dealing in products that were largely undifferentiated: One farmer's corn, for example, was the same as any other farmer's corn. Thus producers were unable to enforce collective output restrictions and price hikes on a voluntary basis. But what farmers failed to do by voluntary means in the 1920s, they accomplished via government directives in the 1930s. An effective farm **price-support program** was instituted in 1933, marking the beginning of a policy of farm subsidies in the United States that continues today.

We can best understand the results of price supports and other government farm programs by first examining the market for agricultural commodities in the absence of government intervention. In that competitive market, a large number of farmers supply any given commodity, such as corn. The sum of the quantities that individual farmers supply at various prices generates the **market supply** of a commodity. Each farmer supplies only a small part of the market total. No one farmer, therefore, can influence the price of the product. If one farmer were to raise the price, buyers could easily purchase from someone else at the **market-clearing, or equilibrium, price.** And no farmers would sell below the market-clearing price. Thus every unit of output sold by farmers goes for the same price. The price received for the last (or *marginal*) unit sold is exactly the same as that received for all the rest. The farmer will produce corn up to the point that if one more unit were produced, its production cost would be greater than the price received. Notice that at higher prices, farmers can incur higher costs for additional units produced and still make a profit. Because all farmers face the same basic production decision, all farmers together will produce more at higher prices. Indeed, no farmer will stop producing until he or she stops making a profit on additional units. That is, each farmer will end up selling corn at the market-clearing price, which will equal the costs of production plus a normal profit.[1]

Now, how has the usual price-support program worked? The government has decided what constitutes a "fair price." Initially, this decision was linked to the prices farmers received during "good" years—such as during agriculture's golden age. Eventually, the government-established price was simply the result of intense negotiations between members of Congress from farm states and those from nonfarm states. The key point, however, is that except for the years of World War II, the "fair" price decreed by the government has generally been well above the equilibrium price that would have prevailed in the absence of price supports. This has encouraged farmers to produce more, which ordinarily would simply push prices back down.

How has the government made its price "stick"? There have been two methods. For the first several decades of farm programs, it agreed to buy the crops, such as corn, at a price, called the **support price,** that was high enough to keep farmers happy but not so high as to enrage too many

---

[1]For society as a whole, this is actually a cost of production, because it is required to keep the farmer growing corn instead of changing to an alternative occupation.

taxpayers. As a practical matter, these purchases have been disguised as "loans" from a government agency—loans that never need be repaid. The government then either stored the crops it purchased, sold them on the world market (as opposed to the domestic market) at prices well below the U.S. support price, or simply gave them away to foreign nations under the Food for Peace program. In each instance, the result was substantial costs for taxpayers and substantial gains for farmers. Under the price-support system, the American taxpayers routinely spent more than $10 billion *each year* for the benefit of corn farmers alone. Smaller but still substantial subsidies were garnered by the producers of wheat, peanuts, soybeans, sorghum, rice, and cotton, to name but a few.

In an effort to keep the size of the surpluses down, the government has often restricted the number of acres that farmers may cultivate. Under these various **acreage-restriction programs,** farmers wishing to participate in certain government subsidy programs were required to keep a certain amount of land out of production. About 80 million acres, an area the size of New Mexico, have at one time or another been covered by the agreements. Enticed by high support prices, farmers have always been ingenious in finding ways to evade acreage restrictions. For example, soybeans and sorghum are both excellent substitutes for corn as a source of livestock feed. So farmers agreed to cut their corn acreage and then planted soybeans or sorghum on the same land. This action aggravated the corn surplus and forced the government to extend acreage restrictions and price supports to soybeans and sorghum. Similarly, faced with limitations on the amount of land they could cultivate, farmers responded by cultivating the smaller remaining land far more intensively. They used more fertilizers and pesticides, introduced more sophisticated methods of planting and irrigation, and applied technological advances in farm machinery at every opportunity. As a result, agricultural output per man-hour is now *twelve times* what it was sixty years ago.

There were a couple of problems with the price-support system. First, because it kept crop prices high, it kept consumers' food bills high as well. People were spending an extra $5 to $10 billion on food each year. Another problem with the price-support system was the fact that the surplus crops piled up year after year in government warehouses. Not only was storing the surpluses expensive, but it also eventually became politically embarrassing. For example, at one point, the federal government had enough wheat in its storage bins to make seven loaves of bread for every man, woman, and child *in the world.*

To help get rid of accumulated surpluses, in the early 1980s the government tried a new payment-in-kind (PIK) program. Instead of writing checks to farmers, the PIK scheme authorized the U.S. Department of Agriculture to give farmers surplus commodities that were left in storage due to price supports. Farmers could use the commodities as livestock feed or simply sell them at the going market price. The PIK program got rid of leftover surpluses and encouraged exports initially, but only at great cost—roughly $30 billion a year. Moreover, the law locked many farmers into growing the same crop year after year, regardless of market conditions. If farmers didn't plant a specified percentage of their "crop base" each year, their subsidy payments were subsequently reduced. The result was huge crop costs for the government in the lucrative (for farmers) corn and wheat programs.

The federal government also switched to a system in which it set a **target price** that was guaranteed to farmers but let the price paid by consumers adjust to whatever lower level it took to get consumers to buy all of the crops. Then the government simply sent a check to farmers for the difference between the target price and the market price. This brought consumers' food bills down and eliminated government storage of surplus crops, but it also meant that the cost to taxpayers—up to $25 billion per year—was painfully clear in the huge checks being written to farmers.

The original price-support program hid its subsidies by making it appear as though the crop surpluses were the result of American farmers' simply being "too productive" for their own good. With the direct cash payments made under the target-price system, however, it became apparent that the government was taking money out of taxpayers' pockets with one hand and giving it to farmers with the other. Moreover, the target-price system, like our other agricultural programs, geared the size of the subsidies to the amount of output produced by the recipients. Thus small farmers received trivial amounts, while giant farms—agribusinesses—collected enormous subsidies. The owners of many huge cotton farms and rice farms, for example, received payments totaling more than $1 million apiece.

This fact illustrates who actually benefits from federal farm programs. Although these programs have traditionally been promoted as a way to guarantee decent earnings for low-income farmers, most of the benefits have in fact gone to the owners of very large farms, and the larger the farm, the bigger the benefit. In addition, *all* of the benefits from price supports ultimately accrue to *landowners* on whose land price-supported crops are grown.

In the mid-1990s, the Republican-controlled Congress made what turned out to be a futile attempt to reduce agricultural subsidies. On April 5, 1996, a *New York Times* headline read, "Clinton Signs Farm Bill Ending Subsidies," reflecting the fact that Congress had enacted and Clinton signed the seven-year Freedom to Farm Act. The 1996 reforms were supposed to increase farmer flexibility and remove market distortions by moving away from price-support payments for wheat, corn, and cotton. In their place, farmers would receive "transition payments." The taxpayer was supposed to save billions of dollars.

It was not to be. Beginning in 1998, Congress passed large farm "supplemental bills" each year, each costing billions of dollars per year—in money that goes directly from your paycheck to the bank accounts of the largest agribusiness corporations in America. Then, in 2002, Congress passed the most expensive farm bill in the history of the United States, with an advertised price tag of over $191 billion for a ten-year period. (The actual price tag is turning out to be even higher.) President Bush said, when he signed the bill, "This nation has got to eat." He further said, "Our farmers and ranchers are the most efficient producers in the world. . . . We are really good at it."

We are also really good at subsidizing farmers, and most of them are not poor. In one recent year, when farm profits were $72 billion, the federal government handed out $25 billion in subsidies to farmers, almost 50 percent more than it spent on welfare payments for poor families. Millionaires such as Ted Turner and David Rockefeller receive hundreds of thousands of dollars a year in taxpayer-financed agricultural subsidies. When you add to the $191 billion of direct subsidies to the almost $300 billion of higher food prices that will result over the ten years of the program, you will see that the average American household will pay almost $4,400 in higher food prices and higher taxes. As always, two-thirds of all farm subsidies will go to the top 10 percent of farms, most which earn over $250,000 annually. Thus, large agribusinesses continue to be the chief beneficiaries of our generous agricultural policy.

Farmers can now receive payments for growing crops they used to grow but don't grow anymore. In fact, if they sell their land to someone else, the right to receive these payments goes with the land. So in many cases, even if the land is subsequently carved up into lots on which people build homes, the happy homeowners are eligible for such "direct payments," made because years ago the land was used to grow, say, rice. The price tag in one recent year: $1.3 billion. Farmers also receive payments to compensate them for losses they don't actually incur. To see how this works, let's suppose the government's target price for corn is $2.00 per bushel and that a farmer manages to sell his crop for $2.30 per bushel during a period of the year when prices were a bit higher than usual. If at any time during the year the price per bushel fell below $2.00, say, to $1.80, the farmer can claim a "deficiency payment" from the government. In this case, he would be eligible for 20 cents per bushel (= $2.00 − $1.80) for every bushel produced, even though he actually sold his corn at $2.30.

Perhaps we should not complain too much about farm programs in the United States, for at least we don't have Japanese farm programs. In Japan, a combination of subsidies for domestic farmers and tariffs on imported food have pushed farm incomes to a level roughly *double* the average income in the country as a whole. They also have driven up the price of an ordinary melon to $100 (yes, one hundred dollars). Even the Europeans seem to find lavishing largesse on farmers irresistible. In recent years, Americans have been shelling out about $40 billion a year for farm subsidies. The European Union (EU) has been spending more than $130 billion a year on farm subsidies. To be sure, the EU is about 50 percent more populous than the United States, but even adjusting for this, the huge spending there means that the average EU citizen is spending twice as much subsidizing farmers as we spend here.

Politicians from the farming states argue that we cannot abandon our farmers because the United States would end up with too many bankrupt farms and not enough food. But there is evidence from at least one country that such a scenario is simply not correct. In 1984, New Zealand's Labor government ended all farm subsidies of every kind, going completely "cold turkey" without any sort of transition to the new era of free markets for food. Agricultural subsidies in New Zealand had accounted for more than 30 percent of the value of agricultural production, even higher than what has been observed in the United States. The elimination of subsidies in New Zealand occurred rapidly, and there were no extended phaseouts for any crops. Despite this, there was no outbreak of farm bankruptcies. Indeed, only 1 percent of farms have gone out of business in New Zealand since 1984. Instead, the farmers responded by improving their techniques, cutting costs, and aggressively marketing their products in export markets.

The results have been dramatic. The value of farm output in New Zealand has increased by more than 40 percent (in constant-dollar terms) since the subsidy phaseout. The share of New Zealand's total annual output attributed to farming has increased from 14 percent to 17 percent. Land productivity has increased on an annual basis a little over 6 percent. Indeed, according to the Federated Farmers of New Zealand, the country's experience thoroughly debunked the myth that the farming sector cannot prosper without government subsidies.

Are any members of the U.S. Congress listening?

DISCUSSION QUESTIONS

1. American corn farmers receive billions of dollars in taxpayer subsidies each year. These subsidies allow them to sell their grain at prices below what it costs to produce it, particularly for export markets. How do U.S. corn subsidies hurt Mexican farmers?

2. If it is so obvious that farm subsidies hurt consumers, why do such subsidies continue to be voted in by Congress? (*Hint:* Revisit the discussion of **rational ignorance** in Chapter 2, "Ethanol Madness.")

3. What groups would be the major beneficiaries of the elimination of farm subsidies in the United States?

CHAPTER TWENTY-TWO

Killer Cars and the Rise of the SUV

Things are not always what they seem.
—Phaedrus, circa 8 C.E.

If there were a Murphy's Law of economic policymaking, it would be this: *The costs are always higher than promised, and the benefits are always lower.* The federal law that regulates automobile fuel economy provides just one example of this fundamental principle and along the way demonstrates that what Phaedrus had to say two thousand years ago is true today.

Our story begins in the 1970s, when the United States was in the middle of a so-called energy crisis. The Organization of Petroleum Exporting Countries (OPEC), a **cartel** of major oil-producing countries, had succeeded in raising the prices of petroleum products (including gasoline) to record-high levels. Consumers reacted by conserving on their use of gasoline and other petroleum products, and Congress responded by enacting legislation mandating energy conservation as the law of the land. One of these laws, known as the corporate average fuel economy (CAFE) standard, requires that each auto manufacturer's passenger cars sold in this country meet a federally mandated fuel economy standard. The new car fleets for the year 2007, for example, had to average 27.5 miles per gallon (mpg) of gasoline. If an automaker sells a gas-guzzler that gets only 15 mpg, somewhere along the line it must also sell enough gas-sipping subcompacts so that the average fuel economy of the entire fleet of cars sold by the company works out to 27.5 mpg. If an automaker's average fuel economy is worse than 27.5 mpg, the corporation is fined $5 per car for each 0.1 mpg it falls short. For example, if General Motors were to fail to meet the CAFE standard by only 1 mpg, it could be subject to penalties of about $200 million per year.

The CAFE standard was first introduced at a time when the price of gasoline, measured in today's dollars, was over $3 per gallon. During the mid-1980s, price cutting by members of the OPEC cartel, combined with a rise in oil production elsewhere, sent gasoline prices into free fall. With gasoline now less expensive (in inflation-adjusted dollars) than it was in the 1970s, the legally mandated CAFE standard of 27.5 mpg almost certainly results in cars that don't consume *enough* gasoline. This seems like a strange conclusion, so we want to be sure we understand why it is correct.

There is no doubt that conserving gasoline is a good thing, for gasoline is a **scarce good.** If we are able to accomplish the same objectives (such as making a trip to the grocery store) and use less gasoline in doing so, the money that would have been spent on gas can now be spent on other goods. Yet conserving gasoline is itself a costly activity. In the extreme case, we could engage in 100 percent conservation of gasoline, but doing so would mean giving up automobiles altogether! Somewhat more realistically, reducing the amount of gasoline that cars burn requires that they be lighter, have smaller engines, and be smaller and sometimes less crash-resistant. To meet the CAFE standards, for example, automobile manufacturers had to switch to production techniques that are more costly, use materials (such as aluminum and high-tech plastics) that are more easily damaged in accidents and more costly to repair, and design engines that are less responsive and more difficult and expensive to repair. Although these are all things that probably would make sense if the price of gas were $4 per gallon, many economists believe that with gas at $2 or even $3 per gallon, the principal effect of the CAFE standard is to raise consumers' total transportation costs: The costs of conserving on gasoline exceed the savings from consuming less of it.

But the costs of the CAFE standard are measured not just in terms of the dollars and cents of reduced economic efficiency. They are also measured in terms of people whose lives are lost as the result of the law—thousands of lives every year.

The seemingly obvious way to respond to a law that requires enhanced fuel efficiency is to redesign engines so that they burn less fuel. Indeed, the automakers have done exactly this. But another highly effective means of reducing the fuel appetite of automobiles is to downsize them by making them smaller and lighter. A major study by Robert Crandall of the Brookings Institution and John Graham of Harvard University found that the CAFE standard forced automakers to produce cars that are about 500 pounds lighter than they would have been without the law. A 500-pound weight reduction implies a 14 percent increase in the fatality risk for the occupants of a car involved in an accident. That translates into approximately three thousand additional deaths per year, plus another fifteen thousand or so serious nonfatal injuries each year.

Apparently, consumers have not been happy with the lighter and less powerful cars or with their higher attendant risk of death. So they found a way out. Light trucks, which include vans, pickups, and sport utility vehicles (SUVs), have been subject to a less demanding fuel economy standard. In contrast to the standard for cars, established in 1978 at 18.0 mpg and now at 27.5 mpg, the CAFE standard for light trucks, initially set in 1980 at 17.5 mpg, is 22.5 mpg for the 2008 model year. Hence the CAFE standards were initially less stringent for light trucks than for cars, and they have been raised less sharply (up 29 percent for light trucks, versus 53 percent for cars).

Frustrated—and safety-conscious—consumers have thus been able to substitute light trucks for passenger cars and thereby escape some of the consequences that Congress would otherwise have inflicted on them. Indeed, according to research by the economist Paul E. Godek, CAFE has induced millions of consumers to move away from small cars and into larger, higher-powered SUVs and other light trucks. Between 1975 and 1995, the light-truck share of passenger vehicles rose to 41.5 percent from 20.9 percent. Godek estimates that without CAFE, the light-truck share would have been only 29.2 percent. Hence about three-fifths of the rise in the light-truck **market share** has been induced by the CAFE standards. By the year 2005, the market share for SUVs and other light trucks had reached fully 50 percent of the passenger vehicles sold each year, a remarkable transformation in the market in just twenty-five years.

The original goal of CAFE was (in part) to induce substitution from large cars to small ones. But the rise of the SUV has to some extent frustrated this intent. Two consequences have resulted. First, light trucks are less fuel-efficient than passenger cars, so fuel economy has risen less than if light-truck substitution had not been possible. A rough estimate is that overall fuel economy has been reduced by about 1 mpg.

More important are the consequences in the area of passenger vehicle safety. Despite their name, light trucks are heavier than cars. Because there are more light trucks on the road with CAFE-lightened cars, drivers of those cars are now at increased risk of death in crashes involving light trucks. This effect has made national headlines from time to time as people have worried about the adverse effects for the occupants of small cars that tangle with large SUVs.

Beginning a few years ago, it also became apparent that because of their high center of gravity, SUVs and other light trucks are much more likely than passenger vehicles to roll over in an accident. The results can be deadly, particularly for occupants who are not wearing a seat belt. Nevertheless, the higher mass of light trucks that protects their occupants from cars also protects them from heavy trucks, trees, wildlife, and other threats. On balance, and particularly with recent improvements in the stability of SUVs, the ability to substitute light trucks for the cars made lighter by CAFE has probably saved the lives of some of the people who made this switch. But for the occupants of smaller cars and for pedestrians and motorcyclists, the switch has been deadly. Indeed, it is estimated that for every life a light truck saves among its occupants in a crash, it likely kills at least four other people using these other modes of transportation. The overall result is more deaths on the highways.

One mystery in the CAFE story remains, and that is why the law was originally enacted. If the real objective of CAFE was fuel economy (and thus, in part, environmental protection), this could have been accomplished much more cheaply with a direct tax on gasoline. According to Godek, the structure of the law suggests a different congressional motive. CAFE treats domestic and imported cars separately. Manufacturers must meet the standard for both fleets, so they can't simply import fuel-efficient cars to bring up the average mileage of their domestic cars. Instead, they must make more small cars here in America. Thus CAFE has protected the jobs of domestic autoworkers—giving us one more example of a law supposedly enacted to achieve a high-minded goal that instead serves chiefly to insulate a U.S. industry from the rigors of **competition.**

So the next time a minivan takes your parking place or an oversized four-wheeler tailgates you, remember this: Their owners are just trying to prevent Congress from killing them to save jobs in Detroit.

DISCUSSION QUESTIONS

1. Why do you think Congress passed the CAFE standard?

2. Does your answer to question 1 imply either that consumers do not know what is in their own best interest or that firms will not voluntarily provide the goods (including fuel economy) consumers want to purchase?

3. Suppose that Congress really knows what the best average fuel economy for automobiles is. How do you think "best" is (or should be) defined? Do the costs and benefits of achieving a particular level of fuel economy play a role in determining that definition?

4. If Congress wanted to increase the average fuel economy of cars, could it accomplish this by imposing a tax on gasoline? What are the advantages and disadvantages of using taxes rather than standards to achieve an improvement in fuel economy?

CHAPTER TWENTY-THREE

Crime and Punishment

The city of Detroit, Michigan, has twice as many police per capita as Omaha, Nebraska, but the violent crime rate in Detroit is four times as high as in Omaha. Does this mean that police are the source of violent crime? If that sounds like an odd question, consider this: Between 1970 and 1995, the number of Americans in prison tripled as a share of the population, while the violent crime rate doubled and the property crime rate rose 30 percent. Does sending people to prison actually encourage crime?

Few people would answer either question in the affirmative, yet there is still widespread concern that crime pays and that there is little that policymakers can do about it. In a nation in which about 20 percent of all households can expect to be victimized by a serious crime in any given year, it is little wonder that people are asking some tough questions about law enforcement. Do harsher penalties discourage people from committing crimes? Will longer prison sentences reduce the crime rate? Are more police the answer? Crime costs its victims more than $200 billion every year in America, even as we are spending roughly $100 billion per year in public monies to prevent it, so answers to questions such as these are clearly important.

There is one thing we can be sure of at the start: Uniformly heavy punishments for all crimes will lead to a larger number of *major* crimes. Let's look at the reasoning. All decisions are made at the margin. If theft and murder will be punished by the same fate, there is no marginal deterrence to murder. If a theft of $5 is met with a punishment of ten years in jail and a theft of $50,000 incurs the same sentence, why not go all the way and steal $50,000? There is no marginal deterrence against committing the bigger theft.

To establish deterrents that are correct at the margin, we must observe empirically how criminals respond to changes in punishments. This leads us to the question of how people decide whether to commit a crime. Here we might look to Adam Smith, the founder of modern economics, who observed:

> The affluence of the rich excites the indignation of the poor, who are often both driven by want, and prompted by envy, to invade his possessions. It is only under the shelter of the civil magistrate that the owner of that valuable property, which is acquired by the labour of many years, or perhaps by many successive generations, can sleep a single night in security. He is at all times surrounded by unknown enemies, whom, though he never provokes, he can never appease, and from whose injustice he can be protected only by the powerful arm of the civil magistrate continually held up to chastise it. The acquisition of valuable and extensive property, therefore, necessarily requires the establishment of civil government.[1]

Thus, Smith concluded, theft will be committed in any society in which one person has substantially more property than another. If Smith is correct, we can surmise that the individuals who engage in theft are seeking income. We can also suppose that before acting, a criminal might look at the anticipated costs and returns of criminal activity. These could then be compared with the net returns from legitimate activities. Hence individuals engaging in crimes may be thought of as doing so on the basis of an assessment in which the benefits to them are perceived to outweigh their costs. The benefits of the crime of theft are clear: loot. The costs to the criminal would include, but not be limited to, apprehension by the police, conviction, and jail. The criminal's calculations are thus analogous to those made by an athlete when weighing the cost of possible serious injury against the benefits to be gained from participating in a sport.

If we view the supply of offenses in this manner, we can devise ways in which society can lower the net expected benefit for committing any illegal activity. That is, we can figure out how to reduce crime most effectively. Indeed, economists have applied this sort of reasoning to study empirically the impact of punishment on criminal activity. The two areas on which they have focused are (1) the impact of increasing the probability that criminals will be detected and apprehended by, for example, putting more police on the street, and (2) the role of punishment by, for example, imprisonment.

---

[1] Adam Smith, *An Inquiry into the Nature and Causes of the Wealth of Nations*, 1776, bk. 5, ch. 1.

Surprisingly, at least to an economist, the early empirical answers to these questions came back rather mixed. The impact of imprisonment on crime rates appeared quite small, often little different from zero. Moreover, most of the early studies that attempted to estimate the impact of police on the crime rate found either no relationship or found that having more police on the force appeared to *increase* the crime rate!

The problem researchers have encountered in estimating the impact of police or prison terms on criminal activity is simple in principle but difficult to correct: Because people who live in areas with higher crime rates will want to take measures to protect themselves, they are likely to have larger police forces and to punish criminals more severely. Thus even if more police and more severe penalties actually do reduce crime, this true effect may be masked or even seem to be reversed in the data because high-crime areas will tend to have more police and higher prison populations.

Economic research has begun to unravel these influences, however, offering us the clearest picture yet of the likely effects of police and imprisonment on the crime rate. The key is to find factors that strongly influence the number of police in a community or the size of a state's prison population but do not otherwise affect the crime rate. For example, it turns out that election cycles tend to have a strong independent effect on the size of police forces. Because crime is such a hot political issue, both mayors and governors have strong **incentives** (and the ability) to push for more police funding in election years. So even though police forces in major cities tend to remain constant in nonelection years, they grow significantly in election years. These increases in policing, in turn, have clearly detectable effects in reducing crime.

The strongest deterrent effect of police appears to be on violent crimes such as murder, rape, and assault. In fact, the **elasticity** of violent crime with respect to police is about −1.0. Accordingly, a 10 percent increase in a city's police force can be expected to produce about a 10 percent decrease in the violent crime rate in that city. With regard to property crimes, such as burglary, larceny, and auto theft, the impact of having more police is smaller but still significant. In this case, the estimated elasticity is about −0.3, meaning a 10 percent increase in the police force will yield about a 3 percent reduction in property crimes. The implications for a city like Detroit are quite striking. Increasing the police force by 10 percent would mean adding about 440 officers. These estimates imply that as a result, the city could expect to suffer about 2,100 fewer violent crimes each year and about 2,700 fewer property crimes.

Researchers have also been able to isolate the role of imprisonment on deterring crime. Once again, the effects are strongest for violent crime. A 10 percent decrease in a state's prison population can be expected to increase the violent-crime rate in that state by about 4 percent. In the case of property crime, a 10 percent decrease in prison population will yield about a 3 percent rise in burglaries, larcenies, and auto thefts in the state. Perhaps not surprisingly, many states have been constructing new prisons.

Separate research has found that juvenile criminals respond to incentives, just as their adult counterparts do. From the mid-1970s to the mid-1990s, juvenile crime soared relative to adult crime, which has led many commentators to worry about a generation of juveniles who are seemingly undaunted by the threat of imprisonment. In fact, it appears that soaring juvenile crime was largely the result of changes in the incentives juveniles faced: Over this same period of time, violent-crime imprisonment rates for juveniles fell 80 percent relative to those for adults. Hence the chances of violent young criminals being jailed dropped to only about half those of violent adult criminals. Moreover, the change in penalties that occurs as youths become subject to adult laws (usually at age eighteen) has a strong effect on their behavior. In states tough on youth but easy on adults, violent-crime rates rise 23 percent at age eighteen, but in states that are easy on juveniles and tough on adults, such crime drops 4 percent at age eighteen. Incentives, it seems, still matter.

Are the growing expenditures on crime prevention worthwhile? According to what we know now, the answer is yes. Adding another person to the prison population costs about $30,000 per year but can be expected to yield benefits (in terms of crime prevention) of more than $50,000 per year. Although adding an officer to the police force has an expected cost of about $80,000 per year, that officer can be expected to produce crime-prevention benefits of almost $200,000. These numbers suggest that we can expect further increases in spending on crime prevention in the years to come and perhaps even more reductions in the crime rate.

DISCUSSION QUESTIONS

1. The analysis just presented seems to make the assumption that criminals act rationally. Does the fact they do not necessarily do so negate the analysis?

2. In many cases, murder is committed among people who know each other. Does this mean that raising the penalty for murder will not affect the number of murders committed?

3. Consider the following prescription for punishments: "Eye for eye, tooth for tooth, hand for hand, foot for foot." Suppose our laws followed this rule, and further suppose we spent enough money on law enforcement to apprehend everyone who broke the law. What would the crime rate be? (*Hint:* If the penalty for stealing $10 was $10, and if you were certain you would be caught, would there be any expected gain from the theft? Would there be an expected gain from the theft if the penalty were only, say, $1, or if the chance of being caught were only 10 percent?)

4. In recent years, the penalty for selling illegal drugs has been increased sharply. How does that affect the incentive to sell drugs? For the people who decide to sell drugs anyway, what do the higher penalties for dealing do to their incentive to commit other crimes (such as murder) while they are engaged in selling drugs?

CHAPTER TWENTY-FOUR

The Graying of America

America is aging. The 78 million baby boomers who pushed the Beatles and the Rolling Stones into stardom are well into middle age. In twenty years, almost 20 percent of all Americans will be sixty-five or older. Just as the post–World War II baby boom presented both obstacles and opportunities, so does the graying of America. Let's see why.

Two principal forces are behind America's "senior boom." First, we're living longer. Average life expectancy in 1900 was forty-seven years; today, it is seventy-eight and is likely to reach eighty within the next decade. Second, the birthrate is near record low levels. Today's mothers are having far fewer children than their mothers had. In short, the old are living longer, and the ranks of the young are growing too slowly to offset that fact. Together, these forces are pushing up the proportion of the population over age sixty-five; indeed, the population of seniors is growing at twice the rate of the rest of the population. In 1970, the **median age** in the United States—the age that divides the older half of the population from the younger half—was twenty-eight; it is now thirty-eight and rising. Compounding these factors, the average age at retirement has been declining as well, from sixty-five in 1963 to sixty-two currently. The result is more retirees relying on fewer workers to help ensure that their senior years are also golden years.

Why should a person who is, say, college age be concerned with the age of the rest of the population? Well, old people are expensive. In fact, people over sixty-five now consume over one-third of the federal government's budget. Social Security payments to retirees are the biggest item, now running over $500 billion a year. Medicare, which pays hospital and doctors' bills for the elderly, costs around $350 billion a year and is increasing rapidly. Moreover, fully a third of the $300 billion-a-year budget for Medicaid, which helps pay medical bills for the poor of all ages, goes to those over the age of sixty-five.

Under current law, the elderly will consume 40 percent of all federal spending within fifteen years: Medicare's share of the gross domestic product (GDP) will double, as will the number of very old—those over eighty-five and most in need of care. Within twenty-five years, probably *half* of the federal budget will go to the old. In a nutshell, senior citizens are the beneficiaries of an expensive and rapidly growing share of all federal spending. What are they getting for our dollars?

To begin with, today's elderly are already more prosperous than any previous generation. Indeed, the annual discretionary income of Americans over sixty-five averages 30 percent higher than the average discretionary income of all other age groups. Each year, inflation-adjusted Social Security benefits paid to new retirees are higher than the first-year benefits paid to people who retired the year before. In addition, for almost thirty-five years, cost-of-living adjustments have protected Social Security benefits from inflation. The impact of Social Security is evident even at the lower end of the income scale: The poverty rate for people over sixty-five is much lower than for the population as a whole. Retired people today collect Social Security benefits that are two to five times what they and their employers contributed in payroll taxes plus interest earned.

Not surprisingly, medical expenses are a major concern for many elderly. Perhaps reflecting that concern, each person under the age of sixty-five in America currently pays an average of more than $1,600 a year in federal taxes to subsidize medical care for the elderly. Indeed, no other country in the world goes to the lengths that America does to preserve life. Some 30 percent of Medicare's budget goes to patients in their last year of life. Coronary bypass operations, costing over $40,000 apiece, are routinely performed on Americans in their sixties and seventies. For those over sixty-five, Medicare picks up the tab. Even heart transplants are now performed on people in their sixties and paid for by Medicare for those over sixty-five. By contrast, the Japanese offer no organ transplants. Britain's National Health Service generally will not provide kidney dialysis for people over fifty-five. Yet Medicare subsidizes dialysis for more than one hundred thousand Americans, half of them over age sixty. The cost: More than $4 billion a year. Overall, the elderly receive Medicare benefits worth five to twenty times the payroll taxes (plus interest) they paid for this program.

The responsibility for the huge and growing bills for Social Security and Medicare falls squarely on current and future workers, because both programs are financed by payroll taxes. Thirty years ago, these programs were adequately financed with a payroll levy of less than 10 percent of the typical worker's earnings. Today, the tax rate exceeds 15 percent of median wages and is expected to grow rapidly.

By the year 2020, early baby boomers, born in the late 1940s and early 1950s, will have retired. Late baby boomers, born in the early 1960s, will be nearing retirement. Both groups will leave today's college students, and their children, a staggering bill to pay. For Social Security and Medicare to stay as they are, the payroll tax rate may have to rise to 25 percent of wages over the next fifteen years. And a payroll tax rate of 40 percent is not unlikely by the middle of the twenty-first century.

One way to think of the immense bill facing today's college students and their successors is to consider the number of retirees each worker must support. In 1946, the burden of one Social Security recipient was shared by forty-two workers. By 1960, nine workers had to foot the bill for each retiree's Social Security benefits. Today, roughly three workers pick up the tab for each retiree's Social Security and Medicare benefits. By 2030, only two workers will be available to pay the Social Security and Medicare benefits due each recipient. Thus a working couple will have to support not only themselves and their family but also someone outside the family who is receiving Social Security and Medicare benefits.

Paying all the bills presented by the twenty-first century's senior citizens will be made more difficult by another fact: Older workers are leaving the workplace in record numbers. We noted earlier that the average retirement age is down to sixty-two and declining. Only 30 percent of the people age fifty-five and over hold jobs today, compared with 45 percent in 1930. So even as the elderly are making increasing demands on the federal budget, fewer of them are staying around to help foot the bill.

Part of the exodus of the old from the workplace is due simply to their prosperity. Older people have higher disposable incomes than any other age group in the population and are using it to consume more leisure. Importantly, however, the changing work habits of older individuals have been prompted—perhaps inadvertently—by American businesses. Career advancement often slows after age forty—more than 60 percent of American corporations offer early retirement plans, whereas only about 5 percent offer inducements to delay retirement. Looking ahead to career dead-ends and hefty retirement checks, increasing numbers of older workers are opting for the golf course instead of the morning commute.

Recently, however, the private sector has begun to realize that the graying of America requires that we rethink the role of senior citizens in the workforce. Some firms are doing more than just thinking. For example, a major chain of home centers in California has begun vigorously recruiting senior citizens as salesclerks. The result has been a sharp increase in customer satisfaction: The older workers know the merchandise better and have more experience in dealing with people. Moreover, turnover and absenteeism have plummeted. People with gray hair, it seems, are immune to "surfer's throat," a malady that strikes younger Californians when sunny weekends are forecast.

Other firms have introduced retirement transition programs. Instead of early retirement at age fifty-five or sixty, for example, older workers are encouraged to simply cut back on their workweek while staying on the job. Often it is possible for workers to get the best of both worlds, collecting a retirement check even while working part-time at the same firm. Another strategy recognizes the importance of rewarding superior performance among older workers. At some firms, for example, senior technical managers are relieved of the drudgery of mundane management tasks and allowed to spend more time focusing on the technical side of their specialties. To sweeten the pot, a pay hike is often included in the package.

Congress and the executive branch have seemed unwilling to face the pitfalls and promises of an aging America. Although the age of retirement for Social Security purposes is legislatively mandated to rise to sixty-seven from sixty-five, the best that politicians in Washington, D.C., appear able to do is appoint commissions to "study" the problems we face. And what changes are our politicians willing to make? We got a sample of this in 2003, with new legislation promising taxpayer-funded prescription drug benefits for senior citizens. Even people in favor of the new program called it the largest expansion in **entitlement programs** in forty years. Before passage of the law, President Bush claimed it was going to cost $35 billion a year, but within a couple of months, that estimate had been hiked to over

$50 billion. In fact, the benefits of the program will be less than claimed, and the costs will be even higher, because more than three-quarters of senior citizens had privately funded prescription drug plans *before* the new law took effect. These private plans are already disappearing, leaving seniors with fewer choices and sticking you with a larger tax bill.

By now you may be wondering how we managed to commit ourselves to the huge budgetary burden of health and retirement benefits for senior citizens. There are three elements to the story. First, the cause is worthy: After all, who would want to deny the elderly decent medical care and a comfortable retirement? Second, the benefits of the programs are far more concentrated than the costs. A retired couple, for example, collects more than $20,000 per year in Social Security and consumes another $15,000 in subsidized medical benefits. In contrast, the typical working couple pays only about half of this each year in Social Security and Medicare taxes. Hence the retired couple has a stronger **incentive** to push for benefits than the working couple has to resist them. And finally, senior citizens vote at a far higher rate than members of any other age group, in no small part because they are retired and thus have fewer obligations on their time. They are thus much more likely to make it clear at the ballot box exactly how important their benefits are to them.

It is possible for government to responsibly address the crisis in funding programs for senior citizens. Chile, for example, faced a national pension system with even more severe problems than our Social Security system. Its response was to transform the system into one that is rapidly (and automatically, as time passes) converting itself into a completely private pension system. The result has been security for existing retirees, higher potential benefits for future retirees, and lower taxes for all workers. Americans could do exactly what the Chileans have done—if we chose to do so.

In the meantime, if Social Security and Medicare are kept on their current paths and older workers continue to leave the workforce, the future burden on today's college students is likely to be unbearable. If we are to avoid the social tensions and enormous costs of such an outcome, the willingness and ability of older individuals to retain more of their self-sufficiency must be recognized. To do otherwise is to invite a future in which the golden years are but memories of the past.

DISCUSSION QUESTIONS

1. How do the payroll taxes levied on the earnings of workers affect their decisions about how much leisure they consume?

2. When the government taxes younger people to pay benefits to older people, how does this affect the amount of assistance that younger people might voluntarily choose to offer older people?

3. When the government taxes younger people to pay benefits to older people, how does this affect the size of the bequests that older people are likely to leave to their children or grandchildren when they die?

4. In general, people who are more productive earn higher incomes and thus pay higher taxes. How would a change in the immigration laws that favored more highly educated and skilled individuals affect the future tax burden of today's American college students? Would the admission of better-educated immigrants tend to raise or lower the wages of American college graduates? On balance, would an overhaul of the immigration system benefit or harm today's college students?

CHAPTER TWENTY-FIVE
Heavenly Highway

If you've ever been caught in a rush-hour traffic jam, you understand what happens when a **scarce good** has a price of zero. In this case, the scarce good is highway travel, and when the money price of travel is zero, something else must be used to ration the quantity of the good demanded. During rush hour (and much of the rest of the day in places such as Los Angeles, New York, Seattle, and Atlanta), the "something" that rations travel demand is time—the time of the motorists caught in traffic.

Whenever a person drives a car, he or she generates a variety of costs. First are the **private costs** of driving: fuel, oil, vehicular wear and tear, and the value of the driver's time.[1] These are all borne by the driver, so when deciding whether and how much highway travel to consume, the driver weighs these costs against the benefits of that travel. If these were the only costs of driving—and on some roads at some times they are—this discussion would end here. Drivers would bear the full cost of their activities, just as the consumers of pizza do, and there would be no further issues to consider. But in most places in the world, during parts of most days, driving generates another cost—congestion—that is not borne by the individuals responsible for it.

On any road, after traffic volume reaches some level, additional cars entering the road slow the flow of traffic. Once this process of congestion occurs, every additional car slows traffic even more. Eventually, traffic may come to a complete halt. Under these circumstances, each driver is implicitly using, without paying for it, a valuable resource that belongs to other people—the time of other drivers. Unless drivers are made to bear the **congestion costs** they generate, we know two things

---

[1]Ideally, the excise taxes on fuel, as well as automobile licensing fees, are set to accurately reflect the costs of maintaining and policing the road system. Hence drivers pay not only for their vehicles and their time but also for roads and the police necessary to keep them safe.

must be true: first, the money price of traveling on the road is too low, and second, the value of motorists' time spent in traffic must be rationing the quantity of travel demanded.

Why do economists worry about congestion? Because its existence raises the possibility that the people using the road could actually be made better off if they were charged a money price for using the road. This money price would induce fewer motorists to drive because some would carpool, others would use public transit, and still others might telecommute rather than come into the office at all. The reduced driving would reduce congestion and so conserve the valuable time of those people who continued to drive. In fact, it is even possible that by charging drivers a monetary fee or toll to drive on a road, more people would succeed in reaching their destination in any given time period. It is easiest to see this when traffic is so bad that it comes to a halt. The toll would discourage some people from entering the road and so permit the remaining traffic to move and thus reach its destination. But the general principle holds true even when traffic is just greatly slowed down by the congestion: Road tolls can both improve traffic flow and make drivers better off—surely a heavenly combination for those sick of being stuck in traffic.

Why, then, do we not see more widespread use of tolls on highways? There are three reasons. First, toll collection is not free, and until recently, the costs were often large enough to offset many of the benefits. If you've ever traveled on older toll roads, such as the Pennsylvania or New Jersey turnpikes, you have some notion of these costs. The toll booths there must be constructed and then manned twenty-four hours a day, and traffic must come to a halt to pay the toll. The result is that the tolls are creating some of the congestion they are supposed to relieve.

But over the past couple of decades, electronic toll collection systems have been developed that reduce these costs substantially. Small, inexpensive electronic devices called transponders can be installed in cars that will be using the toll road. The transponders transmit identifying information to receivers at the toll stations, which are suspended above the roadway. (The toll stations are also equipped with cameras to record the license plate number of anyone passing through with a missing or malfunctioning transponder.) Cars need not even slow down from cruising speeds to have their identification recorded as they pass through. At the end of the month, each motorist receives a bill in the mail for the toll charges (or a ticket if the driver tried to avoid the toll).

Clearly, such a system is designed for roads or bridges heavily trafficked by regular commuters, but in these circumstances, such as on the bridges in the New York City area, electronic toll collection has drastically lowered the costs of using monetary prices to ration roadway use. The result has been reduced congestion and improved economic efficiency. Drivers are better off, and local governments have extra revenue to spend on other services.

California, Texas, and Minnesota all offer examples of how modern toll collection technology can be used to speed highway travel, even during the heaviest traffic periods. Along stretches of multilane roads in Orange County, San Diego, Houston, and Minneapolis, specified lanes are designated as high-occupancy toll (HOT) lanes. These are limited-access highway lanes that provide zero- or reduced-price access to qualifying high-occupancy vehicles (HOVs) and also provide access (at a price) to other vehicles not meeting passenger occupancy requirements. In San Diego, for example, a driver alone in a transponder-equipped car can pay a toll of 50 cents to $4.00 (depending on traffic conditions) to use the HOT lane on Interstate I-15. In doing so, the motorist can expect to travel at or near the speed limit even when traffic in adjacent lanes is bogged down during rush hour. In Orange County, California, the HOT lane charges on State Route 91 range from $1.15 in the middle of the night to $8.50 during the worst of the afternoon rush. As in other locations where HOT lanes are in use, the result is smooth sailing for a fee, even as drivers in the regular lanes spend their time playing stop-and-go. And it is not just the high-income crowd that gets to enjoy the trip. Surveys reveal that drivers at all points in the income distribution are users of the HOT lanes—because the value to them of the time saved is worth the added monetary cost.

Despite such successes, tolls are sometimes eschewed because pricing highway travel can yield radical and unpredictable consequences of changes in the cost of travel. Unlike a typical privately provided good, each road is part of a network of roads; a change in costs on one segment of the system can sometimes have striking and substantial consequences elsewhere—consequences that can largely or completely offset the benefits of the tolls.

The island nation of Singapore, for example, has some of the worst traffic in the world. As a result, its government has been experimenting with pricing roads since 1975, charging a special fee for vehicles entering the central business district during peak traffic periods. When combined with other traffic-control measures, the fee helped cut traffic in central Singapore by 45 percent during peak hours, enabling traffic speed to almost double, to about 22 miles per hour. But these positive effects in the central city between 7:30 and 9:30 A.M. were accompanied by deleterious effects elsewhere. For example, just outside the central city, traffic jams got worse as drivers sought routes they could use without paying. Moreover, on the roads leading into the central city, the drop in rush-hour traffic was nearly matched by a sharp increase in traffic just before 7:30 and after 9:30.

Tolls don't always have to have such adverse side effects, however, as illustrated by a successful implementation in London, England. Beginning in 2003, drivers entering the central area of London were charged a fee of £5 (about $10 at recent exchange rates), with fines ranging in excess of £200 if they failed to pay. The result has been a 20 percent reduction in traffic and about a 5 percent increase in average speeds—which doesn't sound like much until you realize that average traffic speeds in London actually *fell* during the twentieth century as cars first replaced horses and then simply got in each other's way. The big difference between Singapore and London seems to be the magnitude of the charge: London got it roughly right, but Singapore tried to charge too much—a point to which we shall return.

Perhaps the biggest impediment to efficient pricing of roads is that roads are typically operated by governments rather than by private-sector firms. Decisions to price roads must pass through the political process, which necessarily means that the efficiency concerns of the economist are often outweighed by political concerns over who shall pay how much for what. Public opinion polls from densely populated and heavily congested Hong Kong help us understand the consequences.

Although almost identical proportions of drivers and nondrivers in Hong Kong agree that traffic congestion is a serious problem (84.5 percent and 82.0 percent, respectively), they differ sharply on what they think should be done about it. Drivers favor new road construction, presumably because this would shift to taxpaying nondrivers part of the cost of relieving congestion. In contrast, nondrivers believe that financial disincentives to driving (such as tolls and licensing fees) should be given the top priority, presumably because this would shift more of the burden to drivers. These divergences of public opinion have slowed the use of private-sector remedies for the congestion on publicly owned roads, just as they have elsewhere in the world. The result is too many roads on which monetary prices are too low (or nonexistent) and congestion is correspondingly too high.

Japan offers us an illustration from the other end of the spectrum on the hazards of having politicians set prices. Unlike in the United States, where "freeways" are commonplace, all 4,350 miles of expressways in Japan's national highway system are toll roads. The nation began building the expressways in 1956 with loans from the World Bank, imposing tolls to pay off the loans. The loans are long-since paid off, but the tolls remain—generating $15 billion a year to help the national government pay off its $360 billion debt for other public-works projects. Yet the government is so addicted to tolls as a revenue source that many of its citizens think it has gone off the deep end. Tolls are so high that if you were to drive the length of Japan (a nation smaller than California), you would rack up $330 in tolls. Just making the ten-minute trip across Tokyo Bay from the airport will set you back $25, which is actually an improvement over the $42 that drivers used to pay. With fees like this, you can imagine the response: People buy airline tickets rather than drive when making trips of 200 miles, and trucking companies devise elaborate routing schemes for their trucks to keep toll costs down. And how's traffic? Well, along many of the pricier portions of the Japanese highway system, you may find yourself alone on the road.

The message is quite simple. For a variety of reasons, highways, unlike hamburgers, are tricky things to price correctly. But as the experiences of **congestion pricing** in central London and the HOT lanes in America attest, modern technology combined with political gumption can produce a heavenly trip. It is a lesson that could be profitably applied in many other locales.

DISCUSSION QUESTIONS

1. Rather than use tolls, some localities use other means to reduce congestion on major routes—for example, access-limiting traffic lights at freeway on-ramps. From an economist's perspective, what are the disadvantages of such a system?

2. If the purpose of a toll is to bring the private costs of a driver's actions into line with the **social costs,** should the size of the toll

depend on how many passengers are in the car? Should it depend on the size or weight of the car (or differ between cars, trucks, and buses)? Should it depend on the time of day that it is collected?

3. Suppose that when you ate a pizza, you had to pay only for the crust, not the toppings. What would happen to the number of pizzas you ate and the amount and quality of the toppings on each one? If you faced a price of zero for toppings, after you had fully adjusted to this new pricing, what would be the marginal value to you of the last topping consumed? (You can give an exact number.) Does this equal the marginal cost of the last topping, assuming that toppings are a scarce good? Are you consuming the efficient number of toppings? Of pizzas?

4. Can you think of a way to implement HOT lanes and other forms of congestion pricing more widely and yet ensure access by low-income individuals to roads covered by such pricing plans? (*Hint:* In America, food stamp **vouchers** are given to low-income individuals to make sure they can afford to purchase enough food to meet basic nutrition levels.)

Property Rights and the Environment

Introduction

You saw in Part Four that **monopoly** produces outcomes that differ significantly from the outcomes of **competition** and yields gains from trade that fall short of the competitive ideal. In Part Six, you will see that when **externalities** are present—that is, when there are discrepancies between the **private costs** of action and the **social costs** of action— the competitive outcome differs from the competitive ideal. Typically, the problem in the case of externalities is said to be *market failure,* but the diagnosis might just as well be termed *government failure.* For markets to work efficiently, **property rights** to **scarce goods** must be clearly defined, cheaply enforceable, and fully transferable, and it is generally the government that is believed to have a **comparative advantage** in ensuring that these conditions are satisfied. If the government fails to define, enforce, or make transferable property rights, the market will generally fail to produce socially efficient outcomes, and it becomes a moot point as to who is at fault. The real point is this: What might be done to improve things?

As population and per capita income both rise, consumption rises faster than either, for it responds to the combined impetus of both. With consumption comes the residue of consumption, also known as plain old garbage. Many of us have heard of landfills being closed because of fears of groundwater contamination or of homeless garbage scows wandering the high seas in search of a place to off-load; all of us have been bombarded with public service messages to recycle everything from aluminum cans to old newspapers. The United States, it seems, is becoming the garbage capital of the world. This is no doubt true, but it is also true that the United States is the professional football capital of the world—and yet pro football teams seem to have no problem finding cities across the country willing to welcome them with open arms. What is different about garbage? You are probably inclined to answer that football is enjoyable and garbage is not. True enough, but this is not why garbage sometimes piles up faster than anyone seems willing to dispose of it. Garbage becomes a problem only if it is not priced properly—that is, if the consumers and businesses that produce it are not charged enough for its removal and the landfills where it is deposited are not paid enough for its disposal. The message of Chapter 26, "The Trashman Cometh," is that garbage really is no different from the things we consume in the course of producing it. As long as the trashman is paid, he will come, and as long as we have to pay for his services, his burden will be bearable. We will still have garbage, but we will not have a garbage problem.

We noted earlier that the property rights to a scarce good or resource must be clearly defined, fully enforced, and readily transferable if that resource is to be used efficiently—that is, in the manner that yields the greatest net benefits. This is true whether the resource in question is space in a landfill, water in a stream, or as you will see in Chapter 27, "Bye-Bye, Bison," members of an animal species. If these conditions are satisfied, the resource will be used in the manner that benefits both its owner and society the most. If these conditions are not satisfied—as they were not for American bison on the hoof or passenger pigeons on the wing—the resource will generally not be used in the most efficient manner. And in the case of animal species that are competing with human beings, this sometimes means extinction. What should be done when a species becomes endangered? If our desire is to produce the greatest net benefit to humanity, the answer in general is not to protect the species at *any* possible cost, for this would be equivalent to assigning an infinite value to the species. Instead, the proper course of action is to devise rules that induce people to act as though the members of the species were private property. If such rules can be developed, we won't have to worry about spotted owls or African elephants becoming extinct any more than we currently worry about parakeets or cocker spaniels becoming extinct.

In Chapter 28, "Smog Merchants," property rights are again the focus of the discussion as we look at air pollution. We ordinarily think of the air around us as being something that we all own. The practical consequence of this is that we act as though the air is owned by none of us—for no one can exclude anyone else from using "our" air. As a result, we overuse the air in the sense that air pollution becomes a problem. This chapter shows that it is possible to define and enforce property rights to air, which the owners can then use as they see fit, which includes selling the rights to others. Once this is done, the users of clean air have the **incentive** to use it just as efficiently as they do all of the other resources (such as land, labor, and capital) used in the production process.

Air—or more generally, the atmosphere as a whole—reappears as the topic of Chapter 29, "Greenhouse Economics." Evidence is growing that human action is responsible for rising concentrations of so-called greenhouse gases in the earth's atmosphere and that left unchecked, this growth may produce costly increases in the average temperature of our planet. Given the nature of the problem—a **negative externality**— private action taken on the individual level will not yield the optimal outcome for society. Thus the potential gains from government action, in the form of environmental regulations or taxation, are substantial. The key word here is *potential,* for government action, no matter how well intentioned, does not automatically yield benefits that exceed the costs. As we seek solutions to the potential problems associated with greenhouse gases, we must be sure that the consequences of premature action are not worse than those of delaying action until the problem can be examined further. If we forget this message, greenhouse economics may turn into bad economics—and worse policy.

CHAPTER TWENTY SIX

The Trashman Cometh

Is garbage really different? To answer this question, let us consider a simple hypothetical situation. Suppose a city agreed to provide its residents with all the food they wished to consume, prepared in the manner they specified, and delivered to their homes for a flat, monthly fee that was independent of what or how much they ate. What are the likely consequences of this city food-delivery service? Most likely, people in the city would begin to eat more, because the size of their food bill would be independent of the amount they ate. They would also be more likely to consume lobster and filet mignon rather than fish sticks and hamburger because, again, the cost to them would be independent of their menu selections. Soon the city's food budget would be astronomical, and either the monthly fee or taxes would have to be increased. People from other communities might even begin moving (or at least making extended visits) to the city just to partake of this wonderful service. Within a short time, the city would face a food crisis as it sought to cope with providing an ever-increasing amount of food from a city budget that can no longer handle the financial burden.

If this story sounds silly to you, just change "food delivery" to "garbage pickup"; what we have just described is the way most cities in the country have historically operated their municipal garbage-collection services. The result during the 1990s was the appearance of a garbage crisis, with overflowing landfills, homeless garbage scows, and drinking-water wells said to be polluted with the runoff from trash heaps. This seeming crisis—to the extent it existed—was fundamentally no different from the food crisis just described. The problem was not that (1) almost nobody wants garbage or that (2) garbage can have adverse environmental effects or even that (3) we had too much garbage. The problem lay in that (1) we often do not put prices on garbage in the way we put prices on the goods that generate the garbage and (2) a strange assortment of bedfellows used a few smelly facts to make things seem worse than they were.

First things first. America produces plenty of garbage each year—about 250 million tons of household and commercial solid waste that has to be burned, buried, or recycled. (That works out to 1,600 pounds per person.) About 34 percent of this is paper; yard waste (such as grass trimmings) accounts for another 13 percent. Plastic accounts for about 20 percent of the volume of material that has to be disposed of, but because plastic is relatively light, it makes up only about 12 percent of the weight. More than 80 million tons of this trash is recycled.

Landfills are the final resting place for most of our garbage, although incineration is also widely used in some areas, particularly in the Northeast, where land values are high. Both methods began falling out of favor with people who lived near these facilities (or might eventually), as NIMBY ("not in my backyard") attitudes spread across the land. Federal, state, and local regulations also made it increasingly difficult to establish new waste disposal facilities or even to keep old ones operating. The cost to open a modern 100-acre landfill rose to an estimated $70 million or more, and the permit process needed to open a new disposal facility soared to seven years in some states. Meanwhile, environmental concerns forced the closure of many landfills throughout the country and prevented others from ever beginning operations. By the early 1990s, all but five states were exporting at least some of their garbage to other states. Today, most of the garbage from some densely populated states in the Northeast ends up in other people's backyards: New Jersey ships garbage to ten other states, and New York keeps landfill operators busy in thirteen different states. Across the country, some Americans have wondered where all of the garbage is going to go.

Although the failure of America's cities to price garbage appropriately led to an inefficient amount of the stuff, much of the appearance of a garbage crisis has been misleading. Rubbish first hit the headlines in 1987 when a garbage barge named *Mobro,* headed south with New York City trash, couldn't find a home for its load. As it turns out, the barge operator wanted to change his disposal contract after he sailed; when he tried to conduct negotiations over the radio while under way, operators of likely landfills (mistakenly) suspected he might be carrying toxic waste rather than routine trash. When adverse publicity forced the barge back to New York with its load, many people thought it was a lack of landfill space, rather than poor planning by the barge operator, that was the cause. This notion was reinforced by an odd combination of environmental groups, waste-management firms, and the Environmental Protection Agency (EPA).

The Environmental Defense Fund wanted to start a major campaign to push recycling, and the *Mobro* episode gave things the necessary push. As one official for the organization noted, "An advertising firm couldn't have designed a better vehicle than a garbage barge." Meanwhile, a number of farsighted waste-management companies had begun loading up on landfill space, taking advantage of new technologies that increased the efficient minimum size of a disposal facility. Looking to get firm contracts for filling this space, the trade group for the disposal industry started pushing the notion that America was running out of dump space. State and local officials who relied on the group's data quickly bought into the new landfills, paying premium prices to do so. The EPA, meanwhile, was studying the garbage problem but without accounting for the fact that its own regulations were causing the efficient scale of landfills to double and even quadruple in size. Thus the EPA merely counted landfills around the country and reported that they were shrinking in number. This was true enough, but what the EPA failed to report was that because landfills were getting bigger much faster than they were closing down, total disposal capacity was *growing* rapidly, not shrinking.

For a while, it seemed that recycling was going to take care of what appeared to be a growing trash problem. In 1987, for example, old newspapers were selling for as much as $100 per ton (in 2007 dollars), and many municipalities felt that the answer to their financial woes and garbage troubles was at hand. Yet as more communities began putting mandatory recycling laws into effect, the prices for recycled trash began to plummet. Over the next five years, 3,500 communities in more than half the states had some form of mandatory curbside recycling; the resulting increase in the supply of used newsprint meant that communities were soon having to pay to have the stuff carted away. For glass and plastics, the story is much the same. The market value of the used materials is below the cost of collecting and sorting it. Numerous states have acted to increase the demand for old newsprint by requiring locally published newspapers to have a minimum content of recycled newsprint. Because of these mandates, the recycling rate for newsprint has doubled over the past twenty years, but the current rate of 70 percent is thought by many experts to be about the practical maximum.

Recycling raises significant issues that were often ignored during the early rush to embrace the concept. For example, the production of 100 tons of de-inked fiber from old newsprint produces about 40 tons of sludge that must be disposed of somehow. Although the total volume of material is reduced, the concentrated form of what is left can make it more costly to dispose of properly. Similarly, recycling paper is unlikely to save trees, for most virgin newsprint is made from trees planted expressly for that purpose and harvested as a crop; if recycling increases, many of these trees simply will not be planted. In a study done for Resources for the Future, A. Clark Wiseman concluded, "The likely effect of [newsprint recycling] appears to be smaller, rather than larger, forest inventory." Moreover, most virgin newsprint is made in Canada, using clean hydroelectric power. Makers of newsprint in the United States (the primary customers for the recycled stuff) often use higher-polluting energy such as coal. Thus one potential side effect of recycling is the switch from hydroelectric power to fossil fuels.

Some analysts have argued that we should simply ban certain products. For example, Styrofoam cups have gotten a bad name because they take up more space in landfills than paper hot-drink cups and because Styrofoam remains in the landfill forever. Yet according to a widely cited study by Martin B. Hocking of the University of Victoria in British Columbia, Canada, the manufacture of a paper cup consumes 36 times as much electricity and generates 580 times as much wastewater as the manufacture of a Styrofoam cup. Moreover, as paper degrades underground, it releases methane, a greenhouse gas that contributes to global climate change. In a similar vein, consider disposable diapers, which have been trashed by their opponents because a week's worth generates 22.2 pounds of post-use waste, whereas a week's worth of reusable diapers generates only 4 ounces. Because disposable diapers already amount to 1 percent of the nation's solid waste, the edge clearly seems to go to reusable cloth diapers. Yet the use of reusable rather than disposable diapers consumes more than three times as many BTUs (British thermal units) of energy and generates ten times as much water pollution. It would seem that the trade-offs that are present when we talk about "goods" are just as prevalent when we discuss "bads" such as garbage.

It also appears that more government regulation of the garbage business is likely to make things worse rather than better, as may be illustrated by the tale of two states, New Jersey and Pennsylvania. A number of years ago, to stop what was described as price gouging by organized crime, New Jersey decided to regulate waste hauling and disposal as a public utility. Once the politicians got involved in the trash business, however, politics very nearly destroyed it. According to Paul

Kleindorfer of the University of Pennsylvania, political opposition to passing garbage-disposal costs along to consumers effectively ended investment in landfills. In 1972, there were 331 landfills operating in New Jersey; by 1991, the number had fallen to 50, because the state-regulated fees payable to landfill operators simply didn't cover the rising costs of operation. Half of the state's municipal solid waste is now exported to neighboring Pennsylvania, in part because only about twenty landfills remain open in New Jersey.

Pennsylvania's situation provides a sharp contrast. The state does not regulate the deals that communities make with landfill and incinerator operators; the market takes care of matters instead. For example, despite the state's hands-off policy, tipping fees (the charges for disposing of garbage in landfills) are below the national average in Pennsylvania, effectively limited by competition between disposal facilities. The market seems to be providing the right **incentives;** in one recent year, there were thirty-one pending applications to open landfills in Pennsylvania but only two in New Jersey, despite the fact that New Jersey residents are paying the highest disposal rates in the country to ship garbage as far away as Michigan, Illinois, Missouri, and Alabama.

Ultimately, two issues must be solved when it comes to trash. First, what do we do with it once we have it? Second, how do we reduce the amount of it that we have? As hinted at by the Pennsylvania story and illustrated further by developments elsewhere in the country, the market mechanism can answer both questions. The fact of the matter is that in many areas of the country, population densities are high and land is expensive. Hence a large amount of trash is produced, and it is expensive to dispose of locally. In contrast, there are some areas of the country where there are relatively few people around to produce garbage, where land for disposal facilities is cheap, and where wide-open spaces minimize the potential air-pollution hazards associated with incinerators. The sensible thing to do, it would seem, is to have the states that produce most of the trash ship it to states where it can be most efficiently disposed of—for a price, of course. This is already being done to an extent, but residents of potential recipient states are (not surprisingly) concerned, lest they end up being the garbage capitals of the nation. Yet Wisconsin, which imports garbage from as far away as New Jersey, is demonstrating that it is possible to get rid of the trash without trashing the neighborhood. Landfill operators in Wisconsin are now required to send water-table monitoring reports to neighbors and to maintain the landfills for forty years after closure. Operators also have guaranteed the value of neighboring homes to gain the permission of nearby residents and in some cases have purchased homes to quiet neighbors' objections. These features all add to the cost of operating landfills, but as long as prospective customers are willing to pay the price and neighboring residents are satisfied with their protections—and so far these conditions appear to have been met—it would seem tough to argue with the outcome.

Some people might still argue that it does not seem right for one community to be able to dump its trash elsewhere. Yet the flip side is this: Is it right to prevent communities from accepting trash if that is what they want? Consider Gilliam County, Oregon (population 1,950), which wanted Seattle's garbage so badly that it fought Oregon state legislators' attempts to tax out-of-state trash coming into Oregon. Seattle's decision to use the Gilliam County landfill generated $1 million per year for the little community—some 25 percent of its annual budget and enough to finance the operations of the county's largest school.

Faced with the prospect of paying to dispose of its garbage, Seattle had to confront the problem of reducing the amount of trash its residents were generating. Its solution was to charge householders according to the amount they put out. Seattle began charging $16.55 per month for each can picked up weekly. Yard waste that has been separated for composting costs $5.00 per month, and paper, glass, and metal separated for recycling are hauled away at no charge. In the first year that per-can charges were imposed, the total tonnage that had to be buried fell by 22 percent. Voluntary recycling rose from 24 percent of waste to 36 percent—a rate almost triple the national average at the time. The "Seattle stomp" (used to fit more trash into a can) became a regular source of exercise, and the city had trouble exporting enough garbage to fulfill its contract with Gilliam County.

The Seattle experience is paralleled by a similar program in Charlottesville, Virginia. A few years ago, this university town of forty thousand began charging 80 cents per 32-gallon bag or can of residential garbage collected at the curb. The results of the city's new policy suggest that people respond to garbage prices just as they do to all other prices: When an activity becomes more expensive, people engage in less of it. In fact, after controlling for other factors, the introduction of this unit-pricing plan induced people to reduce the volume of garbage presented for collection by 37 percent.

Where did all of the garbage go? Well, some of it didn't go anywhere because many residents began practicing their own version of the Seattle stomp, compacting garbage into fewer bags. Even so, the total weight of Charlottesville's residential garbage dropped by 14 percent in response to unit pricing. Not all of this represented a reduction in garbage production because some residents resorted to "midnight dumping"—tossing their trash into commercial Dumpsters or their neighbors' cans late at night. This sort of behavior is much like the rise in gasoline thefts that occurred in the 1970s when gas prices jumped to the equivalent of over $3 per gallon. But just as locking gas caps ended most gas thefts, there may be a simple way to prevent most midnight dumping. Economists who have studied the Charlottesville program in detail suggest that property taxes or monthly fees could be used to cover the cost of one bag per household each week, with a price per bag applied only to additional bags. According to these estimates, a one-bag allowance would stop all midnight dumping by most one-person households and stop almost half the dumping by a hypothetical three-person household. Moreover, such a scheme would retain most of the environmental benefits of the garbage-pricing program.

The message beginning to emerge across the country, then, is that garbage is no different from the things we consume in the course of producing it. As long as the trashman is paid, he will come, and as long as we must pay for his services, his burden will be bearable.

DISCUSSION QUESTIONS

1. How do deposits on bottles and cans affect the incentives of individuals to recycle these products?

2. Why do many communities mandate recycling? Is it possible to induce people to recycle more without requiring that all residents recycle?

3. How do hefty per-can garbage pickup fees influence the decisions people make about what goods they will consume?

4. A community planning on charging a fee for trash pickup might structure the fee in any of several ways. It might, for example, charge a fixed amount per can, an amount per pound of garbage, or a flat fee per month without regard to amount of garbage. How would each of these affect the amount and type of garbage produced? Which system would lead to an increase in the use of trash compactors? Which would lead to the most garbage?

CHAPTER TWENTY-SEVEN

Bye-Bye, Bison

The destruction of animal species by humans is nothing new. For example, the arrival of human beings in North America about twelve thousand years ago is tied to the extinction of most of the megafauna (very large animals) that then existed. The famous La Brea Tar Pits of Southern California yielded the remains of twenty-four mammals and twenty-two birds that no longer exist. Among these are the saber-toothed tiger, the giant llama, the 20-foot ground sloth, and a bison that stood 7 feet at the hump and had 6-foot-wide horns.

Although many experts believe that human hunting was responsible for the demise of these species and that hunting and habitat destruction by humans have led to the extinction of many other species, the link is not always as clear as it might seem at first glance. For example, it is estimated that only about 0.02 percent (1 in 5,000) of all species that have ever existed are currently extant. Most of the others (including the dinosaurs) disappeared long before humans ever made an appearance. The simple fact is that all species compete for the limited resources available, and most species have been outcompeted, with or without the help of *Homo sapiens.* Just as important is that basic economic principles can help explain why various species are more or less prone to meet their demise at the hands of humans and what humans might do if they want to delay the extinction of any particular species.[1]

Let's begin with the passenger pigeon, which provides the most famous example of the role of human beings in the extinction of a species. At one time, these birds were the most numerous species of birds in North America and perhaps in the world. They nested and migrated in huge flocks and probably numbered in the billions. When flocks passed overhead, the sky would be dark with pigeons for days at

---

[1]We say "delay" rather than "prevent" extinction because there is no evidence to date that any species—*Homo sapiens* included—has any claim on immortality.

a time. The famous naturalist John James Audubon measured one roost at 40 miles long and 3 miles wide, with birds stacked from treetop down to nearly ground level. Although the Native Americans had long hunted these birds, the demise of the passenger pigeon is usually tied to the arrival of the Europeans, who increased the **demand** for pigeons as a source of food and sport. The birds were shot and netted in vast numbers; by the end of the nineteenth century, an animal species that had been looked on as almost indestructible because of its enormous numbers had almost completely disappeared. The last known passenger pigeon died in the Cincinnati Zoo in 1914.

The American bison only narrowly escaped the same fate. The vast herds that roamed the plains were easy targets for hunters; with the advent of the railroad and the need to feed crews of workers as the transcontinental railroads were built, hunters such as Buffalo Bill Cody killed bison by the thousands. As the demand for bison hides increased, the animals became the target of more hunting. Like the passenger pigeon, the bison had appeared to be indestructible because of its huge numbers, but the species was soon on the road to extinction. Despite the outcries of the Native Americans who found their major food source being decimated, it was not until late in the nineteenth century that any efforts were made to protect the bison.[2]

These two episodes, particularly that of the bison, are generally viewed as classic examples of humans' inhumanity to our fellow species, as well as to our fellow humans, for many Native American tribes were ultimately devastated by the near demise of the bison. A closer look reveals more than simply wasteful slaughter; it discloses exactly why events progressed as they did and how we can learn from them to improve modern efforts to protect species threatened by human neighbors.

Native Americans had hunted the bison for many years before the arrival of Europeans and are generally portrayed as both carefully husbanding their prey and generously sharing the meat among tribal members. Yet the braves who rode their horses into the thundering herds marked their arrows so that it would be clear who had killed each bison. The marked arrows gave the shooter rights to the best parts of the

---

[2] For the bison's cousin, the eastern buffalo—which stood 7 feet tall at the shoulder, was 12 feet long, and weighed more than a ton—the efforts came too late. The last known members of the species, a cow and her calf, were killed in 1825 in the Allegheny Mountains.

animal. Tribal members who specialized in butchering the kill also received a share as payment for processing the meat. Indeed, the Native American hunting parties were organized remarkably like the parties of the Europeans who followed: Once an animal was killed, its ownership was clearly defined, fully enforced, and readily transferable. Moreover, the rewards were distributed in accordance with the contribution that each person had made to the overall success of the hunt.

Matters were different when it came to the ownership rights to living bison. Native Americans, like the white hunters and settlers who came later, had no economically practical way to fence in the herds. The bison could (and did) migrate freely from one tribe's territory into the territory of other tribes. If the members of one tribe economized on their kill, their conservation efforts would chiefly provide more meat for another tribe, who might well be their mortal enemies. This fact induced Native Americans to exploit the bison, so that the herds disappeared from some traditional territories on the Great Plains by 1840—before Buffalo Bill was even born.

Two factors made the efforts of the railroad hunters more destructive, hastening the disappearance of the bison herds. First, the white population (and thus the demand for the meat and hides) became much larger than the Native American population. Second, white hunters used firearms—a technological revolution that increased the killing capacity of a given hunter by a factor of 20 or more, compared to the bow and arrow. Nevertheless, the fundamental problem was the same for whites and Native Americans alike: The **property rights** to live bison could not be cheaply established and enforced. To own a bison, one had to kill it, and so too many bison were killed.

The property rights to a **scarce good** or **resource** must be clearly defined, fully enforced, and readily transferable if that resource is to be used efficiently—that is, in the manner that yields the greatest net benefits. This is true whether the resource in question is the American bison, the water in a stream, or a pepperoni pizza. If these conditions are satisfied, the resource will be used in the manner that best benefits both its owner and society.[3] If they are not satisfied—as they were not for bison on the hoof or passenger pigeons on the wing—the resource will generally

---

[3]This does not mean that all species will be permanently protected from extinction, for reasons that are suggested in Chapter 3, "Flying the Friendly Skies?" It does mean that extinction will be permitted to occur only if the benefits of letting it occur exceed the costs.

not be used in the most efficient manner. In the case of animal species that are competing with human beings, this sometimes means extinction.

In modern times, the government has attempted to limit hunting and fishing seasons and the number of animals that may be taken by imposing state and federal regulations. In effect, a rationing system (other than prices) is being used in an attempt to induce hunters and fishermen to act as though the rights to animals were clearly defined, fully enforced, and readily transferable. The results have been at least partially successful. It is likely, for example, that there are more deer in North America today than there were at the time of the colonists—a fact that is not entirely good news for people whose gardens are sometimes the target of hungry herds.

The threatened status of many species of whales illustrates that the problem is far from resolved. The pattern of harvesting whales has been the subject of international discussion ever since World War II, for migratory whales are like nineteenth-century bison: To own them, one must kill them. It was readily apparent that without some form of restraint, many species of whales were in danger of extinction. The result was the founding in 1948 of the International Whaling Commission (IWC), which attempted to regulate international whaling. But the IWC was virtually doomed from the start, for its members had the right to veto any regulation they considered too restrictive, and the commission had no enforcement powers in the event that a member nation chose to disregard the rules. Moreover, some whaling nations (such as Chile and Peru) refused to join the IWC, so commission quotas had little effect on them. Some IWC members have used nonmember flagships to circumvent agreed quotas, while others have claimed that they were killing the whales solely for exempt "research" purposes.

The story of the decimation of a species is well told in the events surrounding blue whales, which are believed to migrate thousands of miles each year. A blue whale, which can weigh almost 100 tons, is difficult to kill even with the most modern equipment; nevertheless, intensive hunting gradually reduced the stock from somewhere between 300,000 and 1 million to, at present, somewhere between 600 and 3,000. In the 1930–1931 winter season, almost 30,000 blue whales were taken, a number far in excess of the species' ability to replenish through reproduction. Continued intense harvesting brought the catch down to fewer than 10,000 by 1945–1946, and in the late 1950s, the yearly harvest was down to around 1,500 per year. By 1964–1965, whalers managed to find and kill only 20 blue whales. Despite a 1965 ban by the IWC, the hunting of blues continued by nonmembers such as Brazil, Chile, and Peru.

Humpback whales have suffered a similar fate. From an original population estimated at three hundred thousand, there remain fewer than five thousand today. Like the blues, humpbacks are now under a hunting ban, but the lack of monitoring and enforcement capacity on the part of the IWC makes it likely that some harvesting is still taking place. IWC conservation attempts designed to protect finbacks, minke whales, and sperm whales have also been circumvented, most notably by the Russians and the Japanese, who simply announced their own unilateral quotas.

Whales are not the only seagoing creatures to suffer from an absence of clearly defined, cheaply enforceable, and transferable property rights. Codfish off the New England and eastern Canadian coasts were once so abundant, it was said, that a person could walk across the sea on their backs. The fish grew into 6-foot-long, 200-pound giants, and generations of families from coastal communities knew they could count on the fish for a prosperous livelihood. The problem was that the fish had to be hauled from the sea before rights to it could be established. The result was overfishing, which led to declining yields and shrinking fish. Over the past thirty years alone, the catch has dropped more than 75 percent, and the typical fish caught these days weighs but 20 pounds. As a result, the Canadians have virtually closed down their cod fishery, and the American fleet is a ghost of its former self.

The cod is not alone in its demise. In the northeastern Atlantic, haddock, mackerel, and herring are all in serious trouble. Along the West Coast of the United States, lingcod, rockfish, and bocaccio are threatened as well. Worldwide, 30 percent of fish stocks, including orange roughy, shark, swordfish, and tuna, are declining due to overfishing, and another 40 percent or more of the commercial stocks are on the verge of trouble.

A number of nations have taken legislative action in the hope of stemming the decline. Beginning in 1996, for example, the U.S. National Maritime Fisheries Service was required to begin working with eight regional fishing councils around the country to come up with plans to stem the demise of traditional fish stocks. Yet not all the councils are actually following the plans they have laid out, so the overfishing continues. A more promising approach may be seen in Britain, where under the terms of European Union rules, catches of all major fish stocks are limited by quotas, which specify the amount of fish that may legally be taken. The British innovation has been to make those quotas transferable—that is, the right to catch specific numbers of fish can be purchased and sold, just like any other good. The quotas assign rights to fish, and their transferability ensures that the lowest-cost, most sensible means of taking those fish will be used. With quotas set at levels consistent with the long-term survival of the fish and the elimination of the pressure to "catch it or lose it," fish stocks in the affected areas have begun a turnaround.

The Canadian province of British Columbia has started a similar program covering its halibut fishery, with equally promising results. Since 1923, management of the Pacific halibut fishery has been regulated jointly by the United States and Canada. Yet despite stringent controls, which included limits on the number of vessels that could fish and reductions in the length of the season, the halibut stock showed signs of collapse by the late 1980s.

Joint efforts by fishers and the Canadian Department of Fisheries and Oceans led to the creation of a system of individual vessel quotas (IVQs) in 1991. Existing license holders now own a percentage of the total allowable catch. In effect, each vessel owner has secure property rights to a specified poundage of fish each year, and the result has been to change their incentives and behavior drastically.

The allocation of individual vessel quotas eliminated the need for a short fishing season, originally created in a futile effort to halt overfishing. Prior to IVQs, the short season forced the fishers into the same prime areas at the same time, resulting in damaged and lost fishing gear and "ghost fishing," in which lost fishing gear continued to catch fish. From six days in 1990, the season has been lengthened to 245 days, with fishers allowed to choose when they will take the catch that belongs to them. Vessels no longer conflict with one another, preventing substantial losses of gear and fish each season. Moreover, before the individual quotas, vessels had extra crew on board to ensure the most rapid possible harvesting of fish. Under IVQs, the total number of crew members in the fleet quickly dropped by about 20 percent.

Before quotas, vessel owners felt compelled to fish regardless of weather conditions, because the loss of even a day of fishing could make the difference between profit and loss for the season. Now that pressure has been eliminated, greatly enhancing the safety of the fishers. The longer fishing season also has enabled fishers to sell higher-quality and fresher fish. Prior to IVQs, only about half the catch could be sold as fresh fish, which are more valuable; now nearly all of it is sold fresh, yielding a better product for consumers and higher profits for producers.

The IVQs are transferable (with some restrictions), and transferability has added to the benefits of the system. For example, the number of vessels has been reduced because smaller, less efficient fishers have sold or leased their licenses to more efficient operators. This has decreased capital costs and helped reduce total crew in the fleet. Similarly, average vessel size has risen, increasing the safety of the crews. Transferability also gets the quotas into the hands of the "highliners," the skippers who are best at finding the fish and harvesting them in the lowest-cost manner. Finally, the best news of all is reserved for the halibut themselves. Since the introduction of IVQs, fishers no longer need to harvest the halibut to establish rights to them, so they no longer have an incentive to overfish. As a result, halibut stocks in the Pacific fishery have begun to grow rapidly—one more illustration that the clear assignment of enforceable, transferable property rights remains the most effective way we know to protect other species from the depredations of *Homo sapiens*.

DISCUSSION QUESTIONS

1. Has there ever been a problem with the extinction of dogs, cats, or cattle? Why not?

2. Some people argue that the only way to save rare species is to set up private game reserves to which wealthy hunters can travel. How could this help save endangered species?

3. Is government *ownership* of animals needed to protect species from extinction?

4. In the United States, most fishing streams are public property, with access available to all. In Britain, most fishing streams are privately owned, with access restricted to those who are willing to pay for the right to fish. Anglers agree that over the past thirty years, the quality of fishing in the United States has declined, while the quality of fishing in Britain has risen. Can you suggest why?

CHAPTER TWENTY-EIGHT

Smog Merchants

Pollution is undesirable, almost by definition. Most of us use the term so commonly it suggests we all know, without question, what it means. Yet there is an important sense in which "pollution is what pollution does." Consider, for example, ozone (O_3), an unstable collection of oxygen atoms. At upper levels of the atmosphere, it is a naturally occurring substance that plays an essential role in protecting life from the harmful effects of ultraviolet radiation. Without the ozone layer, skin cancer would likely become a leading cause of death, and spending a day at the beach would be as harmful as snuggling up to an open barrel of radioactive waste. At lower levels of the atmosphere, however, ozone occurs as a byproduct of a chemical reaction between unburned hydrocarbons (as from petroleum products), nitrogen oxides, and sunlight.[1] In this form, it is a major component of smog, and breathing it can cause coughing, asthma attacks, chest pain, and possibly long-term lung-function impairment.

Consider also polychlorinated biphenyls (PCBs), molecules that exist only in synthetic form. Because they are chemically quite stable, PCBs are useful in a variety of industrial applications, including insulation in large electrical transformers. Without PCBs, electricity generation would be more expensive, as would the thousands of other goods that depend on electricity for their production and distribution. Yet PCBs are also highly toxic; acute exposure (as from ingestion) can result in rapid death. Chronic (long-term) exposure is suspected to cause some forms of cancer. Illegal dumping of PCBs into streams and lakes has caused massive fish kills and is generally regarded as a threat to drinking-water supplies. And because PCBs are chemically stable (that is, they decompose very slowly), once they are released into the environment, they remain a potential threat for generations.

---

[1]Ozone is also produced as a by-product of lightning strikes and other electrical discharges. Wherever and however it occurs, it has a distinctive metallic taste.

As these examples suggest, the notion of pollution is highly sensitive to context. Even crude oil, so essential as a source of energy, can become pollution when it washes up on Alaska's pristine shores. Despite this fact, we shall assume in what follows that (1) we all know what pollution is when we see, smell, taste, or even read about it, and (2) holding other things constant, less of it is preferable to more.

There are numerous ways to reduce or avoid pollution. Laws can be passed banning production processes that emit pollutants into the air and water or specifying minimum air- and water-quality levels or the maximum amount of pollution allowable. Firms would then be responsible for developing the technology and for paying the price to satisfy such standards. Or the law could specify the particular type of production technology to be used and the type of pollution-abatement equipment required in order to produce legally. Finally, subsidies could be paid to firms that reduce pollution emission, or taxes could be imposed on firms that engage in pollution emission.

No matter which methods are used to reduce pollution, costs will be incurred and problems will arise. For example, setting physical limits on the amount of pollution permitted discourages firms from developing the technology that will reduce pollution beyond those limits. The alternative of subsidizing firms that reduce pollution levels may seem a strange use of taxpayers' dollars. The latest solution to the air-pollution problem—selling or trading the rights to pollute—may seem even stranger. Nevertheless, this approach is now being used around the nation, especially in Los Angeles, the smog capital of the country.

Under the plan that operates in the Los Angeles area, pollution allowances have been established for 390 of the area's largest polluters. Both nitrous oxide (NO_x) and sulfur dioxide (SO_2), the two main ingredients of Southern California's brown haze, are covered. Prior to the plan, which went into effect in 1994, the government told companies such as power plants and oil refineries what techniques they had to use to reduce pollutants. Under the new rules, companies are simply told how much they must reduce emissions each year, and they are then allowed to use whatever means they see fit to meet the standards. Over the initial ten years of the plan, firms had their baseline emissions limits cut by 5 to 8 percent a year. Emissions of NO_x from these sources are down by 75 percent, and SO_2 emissions have been cut by 60 percent.

The key element in the program is that the companies are allowed to buy and sell pollution rights. A firm that is successful in reducing pollutants below the levels to which it is entitled receives emission reduction credits for doing so. The firm can sell those credits to other firms, enabling the latter to exceed their baseline emissions by the amount of credits they purchase.

Presumably, firms that can cut pollutants in the lowest-cost manner will do so, selling some of their credits to firms that find it more costly to meet the standards. Because the total level of emissions is determined ahead of time by the area's air-quality management district, the trading scheme will meet the requisite air-quality standards. Yet because most of the emissions reductions will be made by firms that are the most efficient at doing so, the standards will be met at the lowest cost to society.

A similar market-based plan covering SO_2 has been adopted by the Environmental Protection Agency (EPA) on a nationwide level. Each emission allowance issued under this plan permits a power utility to emit one ton of SO_2 into the air. Based on their past records, utilities have been given rights to emit SO_2 into the air at a declining rate into the future. Companies can either use their allowances to comply with the clean-air regulations, or they can beat the standards and sell their unused allowances to other utilities.

There are also EPA-initiated trading programs for the emissions produced by heavy-duty on-highway engines (such as found in large trucks) and for NO_x emissions from power plants in the eastern United States. Although data for the recently begun power plant program are limited, reliable patterns have begun to emerge for the other emission-trading plans. In particular, the private markets in tradable allowances seem to be quite efficient at doing what they are designed to do—move allowances to their highest-valued locations, permit equalization of control costs across sources, and generate information about the costs of reducing emissions.

Because firms can freely choose between either abating or releasing a given amount of emissions, they will pay no more for an allowance than it will save them in abatement costs. Equivalently, a company will pay no more for abatement than it would pay for an allowance to emit the pollutant. Thus the existence of a common price for allowances assures us that the cost per ton of cutting emissions must be at that same level. If the price of a permit to emit a ton of SO_2 is $400, for example, then the costs of abating SO_2 emissions must be running about $400 per ton.

According to the U.S. Council of Economic Advisers, the tradable-permit plans have not only helped contribute to substantial cuts from major sources but have also reduced the costs of achieving this environmental improvement. It also appears that the **transaction costs** of trading allowances are quite low—about 2 percent of the prevailing price—and that the prices at which trade takes place at any point in time are all quite close together. Hence this market is not only doing what it is supposed to be doing, but it is accomplishing this at low costs.

Perhaps not surprisingly, the notion of selling the right to pollute has been controversial, particularly among environmental organizations. The activist group Greenpeace, for example, claims that selling pollution allowances "is like giving a pack of cigarettes to a person dying of lung cancer." Nonetheless, other environmental groups have chosen to buy some of the allowances and retire them unused. One such group was the Cleveland-based National Healthy Air License Exchange, whose president said, "It is our intent . . . to have a real effect on this market and on the quality of air."

Some observers have been disappointed that the government has taken so long to approve emission-trading schemes. There appear to be two key reasons why progress has been so slow. First, many environmentalists have been vigorously opposed to the very concept of tradable emissions, arguing that it amounts to putting a price on what has traditionally been considered a "priceless" resource—the environment. Because most of the cost savings that stem from tradable-emissions rights accrue to the polluters and their customers, government agencies have proceeded carefully, to avoid charges that they are somehow selling out to polluters.

Ironically, the second reason for the delay in developing markets for tradable pollution rights has been the reluctance on the part of industry to push harder for them. Similar programs in the past involved emissions credits that could be saved up (banked) by a firm for later use or bartered on a limited basis among firms. Under these earlier programs, environmental regulators would periodically wipe out emissions credits that firms thought they owned, on the ground that doing so provided a convenient means of preventing future environmental damage.

Not surprisingly, some companies believe that any credits purchased under a tradable-rights plan might be subject to the same sort of confiscation. Under such circumstances, these firms have been understandably reluctant to support a program that might not prove to be of real value.[2] Indeed, even under the tradable-emissions plan adopted for Los Angeles, the regulators have explicitly stated that the emissions credits are *not* property rights and that they can be revoked at any time. Sadly, unless obstacles such as these can be removed, achieving environmental improvement at the lowest **social cost** is likely to remain a goal rather than an accomplishment.

DISCUSSION QUESTIONS

1. Does marketing the right to pollute mean that we are allowing too much destruction of our environment?

2. Who implicitly has property rights to the air when the EPA sells SO_2 permits? Does your answer depend on who gets the revenue raised by the sale?

3. Some environmental groups have opposed tradable pollution rights on the grounds that this puts a price on the environment when in fact the environment is a priceless resource. Does this reasoning imply that we should be willing to give up *anything* (and therefore everything) to protect the environment? Does environmental quality have an infinite value? If not, how should we place a value on it?

4. Environmental regulations that prohibit emissions beyond some point implicitly allow firms and individuals to pollute up to that point at no charge. Don't such regulations amount to giving away environmental quality at no charge? Would it be better to charge a price via emissions taxes, for example, for the initial amount of pollutants? Would doing so reduce the amount of pollution?

---

[2]One can imagine the enthusiasm people would feel toward, say, the market for automobiles if the government announced that because cars were a source of pollution, the property rights to them might be revoked at any time, for any reason.

CHAPTER TWENTY-NINE

Greenhouse Economics

The sky may not be falling, but it is getting warmer—maybe. The consequences will not be catastrophic, but they will be costly—maybe. We can reverse the process but should not spend very much to do so right now—maybe. Such is the state of the debate over the greenhouse effect—the apparent tendency of carbon dioxide (CO_2) and other gases to accumulate in the atmosphere, acting like a blanket that traps radiated heat, thereby increasing the earth's temperature. Before turning to the economics of the problem, let's take a brief look at the physical processes involved.

Certain gases in the atmosphere, chiefly water vapor and CO_2, trap heat radiating from the earth's surface. If they did not, the earth's average temperature would be roughly 0°F instead of just over 59°F, and everything would be frozen solid. Human activity helps create some so-called greenhouse gases, including CO_2 (mainly from combustion of fossil fuels), methane (from landfills and livestock), and chlorofluoro-carbons (CFCs, from aerosol sprays, air conditioners, and refrigerators). We have the potential, unmatched in any other species, to profoundly alter our ecosystem.

There seems little doubt that humankind has been producing these gases at a record rate and that they are steadily accumulating in the atmosphere. Airborne concentrations of CO_2, for example, are increasing at the rate of about 0.5 percent per year; over the past fifty years, the amount of CO_2 in the atmosphere has risen a total of about 25 percent. Laboratory analysis of glacial ice dating back at least 160,000 years indicates that global temperatures and CO_2 levels in the atmosphere do, in fact, tend to move together, suggesting that the impact of today's rising CO_2 levels may be higher global temperatures in the future. Indeed, the National Academy of Sciences (NAS) has suggested that by the middle of the twenty-first century, greenhouse gases could be double the levels they were in 1860 and that global temperatures could rise by 2°F to 9°F.[1] The possible consequences of such a temperature increase include a rise in the average sea level, inundating coastal areas, including much of Florida; the spread of algal blooms capable of deoxygenating major bodies of water, such as Chesapeake Bay; and the conversion of much of the midwestern wheat and corn belt into a hot, arid dust bowl.

When an individual drives a car, heats a house, or uses an aerosol hair spray, greenhouse gases are produced. In economic terms, this creates a classic **negative externality.** Most of the costs (in this case, those arising from global warming) are borne by individuals *other than* the one making the decision about how many miles to drive or how much hair spray to use. Because the driver (or sprayer) enjoys all the benefits of the activity but suffers only a part of the cost, that individual engages in more than the economically efficient amount of the activity. In this sense, the problem of greenhouse gases parallels the problem that occurs when someone smokes a cigarette in an enclosed space or litters the countryside with fast-food wrappers. If we are to get individuals to reduce production of greenhouse gases to the efficient rate, we must somehow induce them to act *as though* they bear all the costs of their actions. The two most widely accepted means of doing this are government regulation and taxation, both of which have been proposed to deal with greenhouse gases.

The 1988 Toronto Conference on the Changing Atmosphere, attended by representatives from forty-eight nations, favored the regulation route. The conference recommended a mandatory cut in CO_2 emissions by 2005 to 80 percent of their 1988 level—a move that would have required a major reduction in worldwide economic output. The 1997 Kyoto conference on climate change, attended by representatives from 160 nations, made more specific but also more modest proposals. Overall, attendees agreed that by 2012, thirty-eight developed nations should cut greenhouse emissions by 5 percent relative to 1990 levels. Developing nations, including China and India (the two most populous nations in the world), would be exempt from emissions cuts. On the taxation front, one prominent U.S. politician has proposed a tax of $100 per ton on the carbon emitted by fuels. It is estimated that such a tax

---

[1]This may not sound like much, but it does not take much to alter the world as we know it. The global average temperature at the height of the last ice age eighteen thousand years ago—when Canada and most of Europe were covered with ice—was 51°F, a mere 8°F or so cooler than today.

would raise the price of coal by $70 per ton (about 300 percent) and elevate the price of oil by $8 per barrel, or about 13 percent. These proposals, and others like them, clearly have the potential to reduce the buildup of greenhouse gases but only at substantial costs. It thus makes some sense to ask, what are we likely to get for our money?

Perhaps surprisingly, the answer to this question is not obvious. Consider the raw facts of the matter. On average over the past century, greenhouse gases have been rising, and so has the average global temperature. Yet most of the temperature rise occurred before 1940, whereas most of the increase in greenhouse gases occurred after 1940. In fact, global average temperatures fell about 0.5°F between 1940 and 1970; this cooling actually led a number of prominent scientists during the 1970s to forecast a coming ice age!

Over the past three decades, the upward march of global temperatures has resumed, accompanied by rising concentrations of greenhouse gases. At the same time, however, sunspot and other solar activity has risen considerably, and the sun is brighter than it has been in a thousand years. Many scientists believe that the sun has thus contributed significantly to the earth's apparent warming. Debate remains, however, over how big this contribution has been.

Let us suppose for the moment that barring a significant reduction in greenhouse gas emissions, global warming is under way and that more is on the way. What can we expect? According to the most comprehensive study yet of this issue, by the NAS, the answer is a "good news, bad news" story.

The bad news is this: The likely rise in sea level by 1 to 3 feet will inundate significant portions of our existing coastline; the expected decline in precipitation will necessitate more widespread use of irrigation; the higher average temperatures will compel more widespread use of air conditioning, along with the associated higher consumption of energy to power it; and the blazing heat in southern latitudes may make these areas too uncomfortable for all but the most heat-loving souls. The good news is that the technology for coping with changes such as these is well known and the costs of coping surprisingly small (on a scale measured in hundreds of billions of dollars, of course). Moreover, many of the impacts that loom large at the individual level will represent much smaller costs at a societal level. For example, although higher average temperatures could prove disastrous for farmers in southern climes, the extra warmth could be an enormous windfall farther north, where year-round farming might become feasible. Similarly, the loss of shoreline due to rising sea levels would partly just be a migration of coastline inland—current beachfront property owners would suffer, but their inland neighbors would gain.[2]

None of these changes are free, of course, and there remain significant uncertainties about how global warming might affect species other than *Homo sapiens*. It is estimated, for example, that temperate forests can "migrate" only at a rate of about 100 kilometers per century, not fast enough to match the speed at which warming is expected to occur. Similarly, the anticipated rise in the sea level could wipe out between 30 and 70 percent of today's coastal wetlands. Whether new wetlands would develop along our new coastline and what might happen to species that occupy existing wetlands are questions that have not yet been resolved.

Yet the very uncertainties that surround the possible warming of the planet suggest that policy prescriptions of the sort that have been proposed—such as the cut in worldwide CO_2 emissions agreed to at Kyoto—may be too much, too soon. Indeed, the NAS recommended that we learn more before we leap too far. Caution seems particularly wise, because the exclusion of China, India, and other developing nations from any emissions cuts could result in huge costs for developed nations but little or no reduction in worldwide greenhouse gases. Some sense of the damage that can be wrought by ignoring such counsel and rushing into a politically popular response to a complex environmental issue is well illustrated by another atmospheric problem: smog.

Although gasoline is a major source of the hydrocarbons in urban air, its contribution to smog is plummeting because new cars are far cleaner than their predecessors. In the 1970s, cars spewed about 9 grams of hydrocarbons per mile; emissions controls brought this down to about 1.5 grams per mile by 1995. The cost of this reduction is estimated to be approximately $1,000 for each ton of hydrocarbon emissions prevented—a number that many experts believe to be well below the benefits of the cleaner air that resulted. Despite the improvements in air quality, smog is still a significant problem in many major cities. Additional federal regulations aimed primarily at the nine smoggiest urban areas, including New York, Chicago, and Los Angeles, went

---

[2]There would be a net loss of land area and thus a net economic loss. Nevertheless, the net loss of land would be chiefly in the form of less valuable inland property.

into effect in 1995. Meeting these standards meant that gasoline had to be reformulated at a cost of about 6 cents per gallon. This brought the cost of removing each additional ton of hydrocarbons to about $10,000—ten times the per-ton cost of removing the first 95 percent from urban air.

Over the past ten years, new Environmental Protection Agency (EPA) rules for reformulated gasoline (RFG) have added even more to the cost of gasoline and have had other (presumably unintended) adverse consequences. For example, initially, the RFG standards could be met only with the addition to gasoline of ethanol or methyl tertiary butyl ether (MTBE). Because ethanol was considerably more expensive than MTBE, refiners used MTBE. But after a few years, it appeared that leakage of MTBE from storage tanks was contaminating groundwater and that the substance was highly carcinogenic. Numerous states banned its use on the grounds that whatever it did to improve air quality, its adverse effects elsewhere were likely far more damaging. (The EPA has since allowed refiners more flexibility in meeting the RFG standards.)

Overall, EPA rules on RFG have led to a "patchwork quilt" of regulations across the country: Some dirty-air locales must use one type of gas, while other locales, with cleaner air, can use different gas. The presence of multiple EPA standards across the country has left supplies of gasoline vulnerable to disruption, because fuel often cannot be transshipped from one area to another to meet temporary shortages. This fact has contributed substantially to large spikes in the price of gasoline in major midwestern cities, such as Milwaukee and Chicago, every time there has been even a minor supply disruption.

Overall, the costs of EPA-mandated gasoline reformulation are huge, even though the EPA has never shown that RFG is necessary to meet its air-quality standards. The potential benefits of RFG appear to be small compared to the costs, yet we are stuck with this EPA mandate because few politicians want to be accused of being in favor of smog.

There is no doubt that atmospheric concentrations of greenhouse gases are rising and that human actions are the cause. It is probable that as a result, the global average temperature is rising. If temperatures rise significantly, the costs will be large, but the consequences are likely to be manageable. Given the nature of the problem, private action, taken on the individual level, will not yield the optimal outcome for society.

Thus the potential gains from government action, in the form of environmental regulations or taxation, are substantial. But the key word here is *potential* because government action, no matter how well intentioned, does not automatically yield benefits that exceed the costs. As we seek solutions to the potential problems associated with greenhouse gases, we must be sure that the consequences of action are not worse than those of first examining the problem further. If we forget this message, greenhouse economics may turn into bad economics—and worse policy.

DISCUSSION QUESTIONS

1. Why will voluntary actions, undertaken at the individual level, be unlikely to bring about significant reductions in greenhouse gases such as CO_2?

2. Does the fact that the CO_2 produced in one nation results in adverse effects on other nations have any bearing on the likelihood that CO_2 emissions will be reduced to the optimal level? Would the problem be easier to solve if all the costs and benefits were concentrated within a single country? Within a single elevator or office?

3. The policy approach to greenhouse gases will almost certainly involve limits on emissions rather than taxes on emissions. Can you suggest why limits rather than taxes are likely to be used?

4. It costs about $80,000 per acre to create wetlands. How reasonable is this number as an estimate of what wetlands are worth?

International Trade and Economic Prosperity

Introduction

Many of the key public issues of our day transcend national borders or affect the entirety of our $13 trillion economy. The rapid developments in information processing, communications, and transportation over the past thirty years are gradually knitting the economies of the world closer together. Political developments, most notably the demise of the Iron Curtain and the dissolution of the Soviet Union, have contributed to this growing economic integration, as have reductions in long-standing barriers to international trade. Moreover, the past decade was a period of growing awareness that the economic vitality of individual markets was importantly determined by decisions made in Washington, D.C.

The passage of the North American Free Trade Agreement (NAFTA) and the creation of the **World Trade Organization (WTO)** have substantially reduced the barriers to trade between the United States and most of the rest of the world. If we take advantage of these lower trade barriers, we have the opportunity to make ourselves far better off by specializing in activities in which we have a **comparative advantage** and then trading the fruits of our efforts with other nations. Yet voluntary exchange also often redistributes wealth, in addition to creating it, so there will always be some individuals who oppose free trade. There are many smoke screens behind which the self-interested opposition to free trade is hidden, as we see in Chapter 30, "Free Trade, Less Trade, or No Trade?" Nevertheless, although **protectionism**—the creation of **trade barriers** such as **tariffs** and **quotas**—often sounds sensible, it is in fact a surefire way to reduce rather than enhance our wealth. If we ignore the value of free trade, we do so only at our peril.

To illustrate the tremendous damages that can be wrought when protectionism gains the upper hand, Chapter 31, "The $750,000 Steelworker," examines what happens when tariffs and quotas are imposed in an effort to "save" U.S. jobs from foreign **competition.** The facts are that in the long run, it is almost impossible to effectively protect U.S. workers from foreign competition, and efforts to do so not only reduce Americans' overall living standards but also end up costing the jobs of other Americans. The moral of our story is that competition is just as beneficial on the international scene as it is on the domestic front.

For decades, Americans have worried about competition from cheap labor in China. As you will see in Chapter 32, "The Lion, the Dragon, and the Future," China has been adopting capitalist **institutions** over the past thirty years and has reaped the rewards, most notably in the form of a rapidly rising standard of living for its people. But accompanying this has been the emergence of China as a major player in world markets. Indeed, China is now America's number two trading partner (after Canada) and may even have risen to number one by the time you read this. The growing volume of trade between the United States and China has created enormous wealth for people in both nations, albeit not without costly adjustments for some individuals. India, too, is becoming an important player in world markets, although its relatively late entry into global competition makes it less significant than China—for the moment. When discussing trade with any nation, however, the crucial fact to keep in mind is that international trade is fundamentally no different from interstate trade or interpersonal trade: As long as it is voluntary, the result is a higher standard of living for all participants.

CHAPTER THIRTY

Free Trade, Less Trade, or No Trade?

The past fifteen years have been a time of great change for international trade. The North American Free Trade Agreement (NAFTA), for example, substantially reduced the barriers to trade among citizens of Canada, the United States, and Mexico. On a global scale, the Uruguay round of the General Agreement on Tariffs and Trade (GATT) was ratified by 117 nations, including the United States. Under the terms of this agreement, GATT was replaced by the **World Trade Organization (WTO)**, whose membership now numbers about 150, and **tariffs** were cut worldwide. Agricultural **subsidies** were reduced, patent protections were extended, and the WTO established a set of arbitration boards to settle international disputes over trade issues.

Many economists believe that both NAFTA and the agreements reached during the Uruguay round were victories not only for free trade but also for the citizens of the participating nations. Nevertheless, many noneconomists, particularly politicians, opposed these agreements, so it is important that we understand what is beneficial about NAFTA, the Uruguay round, and free trade in general.

Voluntary trade creates new wealth. In voluntary trade, both parties in an exchange gain. They give up something of lesser value in return for something of greater value. In this sense, exchanges are always unequal. But it is this unequal nature of exchange that is the source of the increased **productivity** and higher wealth that occurs whenever trade takes place. When we engage in exchange, what we give up is worth less than what we get—for if this were not true, we would not have traded. And what is true for us is also true for our trading partner, meaning that partner is better off, too.

Free trade encourages individuals to use their talents and abilities in the most productive manner possible and to exchange the fruits of their efforts. The **gains from trade** lie in one of the most fundamental ideas in economics: A nation gains from doing what it can do best *relative to other nations,* that is, by specializing in endeavors in which it has a **comparative advantage.** Trade encourages individuals and nations to discover ways to specialize so they can become more productive and enjoy higher incomes. Increased productivity and the subsequent increase in economic growth are exactly what the signatories of the Uruguay round and NAFTA sought—and are obtaining—by reducing trade barriers.

Despite these gains from exchange, free trade is routinely opposed by some (and sometimes many) people, particularly in the case of international trade. There are many excuses offered for this opposition, but they all basically come down to one issue. When our borders are open to trade with other nations, some individuals and businesses within our nation face more competition. As you saw in Chapter 20, most firms and workers hate competition, and who can blame them? After all, if a firm can keep the competition out, **profits** are sure to rise. And if workers can prevent competition from other sources, they can enjoy higher wages and greater selection among jobs. So the real source of most opposition to international trade is that the opponents to trade dislike the competition that comes with it. There is nothing immoral or unethical about this—but there is nothing altruistic or noble about this, either. It is self-interest, pure and simple.

Opposition to free trade is nothing new. One of the most famous examples of such opposition led to the Smoot-Hawley Tariff of 1930. This major federal statute was a classic example of **protectionism**—an effort to protect a subset of American producers at the expense of consumers and other producers. It included tariff schedules for more than twenty thousand products, raising taxes on affected imports by an average of 52 percent.

The Smoot-Hawley Tariff encouraged beggar-thy-neighbor policies by the rest of the world. Such policies represent an attempt to improve (a portion of) one's domestic economy at the expense of foreign countries' economies. In this case, tariffs were imposed to discourage **imports** so that domestic import-competing industries would benefit. The beggar-thy-neighbor policy at the heart of Smoot-Hawley was soon adopted by the United Kingdom, France, the Netherlands, and Switzerland. The result was a massive reduction in international trade that likely worsened the worldwide depression of the 1930s.

Opponents of free trade sometimes claim that beggar-thy-neighbor policies benefit the United States by protecting import-competing industries. In general, this claim is not correct. It is true that some Americans benefit from such policies, but two large groups of Americans lose. First, there are the purchasers of imports and import-competing goods. They suffer from higher prices and reduced selection of goods and suppliers caused by tariffs and import **quotas.** Second, the decline in imports caused by protectionism also causes a decline in **exports,** thereby harming firms and employees in these industries. This follows directly from one of the most fundamental propositions in international trade: *In the long run, imports are paid for by exports.* This proposition simply states that when one country buys goods and services from the rest of the world (imports), the rest of the world eventually wants goods from that country (exports) in exchange. Given this fundamental proposition, a corollary becomes obvious: *Any restriction on imports leads to a reduction in exports.* Thus any business for import-competing industries gained as a result of tariffs or quotas means at least as much business *lost* for exporting industries.

Opponents of free trade raise a variety of objections in their efforts to restrict it. For example, it is sometimes said that foreign companies engage in dumping, that is, selling their goods in America below cost. The first question to ask is, below *whose* cost? Clearly, if the foreign firm is selling in America, it must be offering the good for sale at a price that is at or below the cost of American firms, or else it could not induce Americans to buy it. But the ability of individuals or firms to get goods at lower cost is one of the *benefits* of free trade, not one of its negatives.

What about claims that import sales are taking place at prices below the foreign company's costs? This amounts to arguing that the owners of the foreign company are voluntarily giving some of their wealth to us, namely, the difference between their costs and the lower price they charge us. It is possible, though unlikely, that they might wish to do this as a way of getting us to try a product that we would not otherwise purchase. But if so, why would we want to refuse this gift? As a nation, we are richer if we accept it. Moreover, it is a gift that will be offered only for a short while, for there is no point in selling below one's cost unless one hopes soon to raise price profitably above cost!

Another argument sometimes raised against international trade is that the goods are produced abroad using unfair labor practices (such as the use of child labor) or using production processes that do not meet American environmental standards. Such charges are sometimes correct. But we must remember two things here. First, although we may find the use of child labor (or perhaps sixty-hour weeks with no over-time pay) objectionable, such practices were at one time commonplace in the United States. They used to be engaged in here for the same reason they are currently practiced abroad: The people involved were (or are) too poor to do otherwise. Some families in developing nations literally cannot survive unless all members of the family contribute. As unfortunate as this is, if we insist on imposing our tastes and attitudes—shaped in part by our great wealth—on peoples whose wealth is far smaller than ours, we run the risk of making them worse off even as we think we are helping them.

Similar considerations apply to environmental standards.[1] It is well established that individuals' and nations' willingness to pay for environmental quality is very much shaped by their wealth: Environmental quality is a **luxury good;** that is, people who are rich (such as Americans) want to consume much more of it per capita than people who are poor. Insisting that other nations meet environmental standards that we find acceptable is much like insisting that they wear the clothes we wear, use the modes of transportation we prefer, and consume the foods we like. The few people who manage to afford it will indeed be living in the style to which we are accustomed, but most people will not be able to afford much of anything.

Our point is not that foreign labor or environmental standards are, or should be, irrelevant to Americans. Our point instead is that achieving high standards of either is costly, and trade restrictions are unlikely to be the most efficient or most effective way to achieve them. Just as important, labor standards and environmental standards are all too often raised as smoke screens to hide the real motive: keeping the competition out.

If it is true that free trade is beneficial and that restrictions on trade are generally harmful, we must surely raise the question, how does

---

[1]There is one important exception to this argument. In the case of foreign air or water pollution generated near enough to our borders (for example, with Mexico or Canada) to cause harm to Americans, good public policy presumably dictates that we seek to treat such pollution as though it were being generated inside our borders.

legislation like the Smoot-Hawley Tariff (or any other trade restriction) ever get passed? As Mark Twain noted many years ago, the reason the free traders win the arguments and the protectionists win the votes is this: Foreign competition often clearly affects a narrow and specific import-competing industry such as textiles, shoes, or automobiles, and thus trade restrictions benefit a narrow, well-defined group of economic agents. For example, restrictions on imports of Japanese automobiles in the 1980s chiefly benefited the Big Three automakers in this country: General Motors, Ford, and Chrysler. Similarly, long-standing quotas on the imports of sugar benefit a handful of large American sugar producers. And when tariffs of up to 30 percent were slapped on many steel imports in 2002, an even smaller number of American steelmakers and their employees benefited. Because of the concentrated benefits that accrue when Congress votes in favor of trade restrictions, sufficient funds can be raised in those industries to convince members of Congress to impose those restrictions.

The eventual reduction in exports that must follow is normally spread in small doses throughout all export industries. Thus no specific group of workers, managers, or shareholders in export industries will feel that it should contribute money to convince Congress to reduce international trade restrictions. Furthermore, although consumers of imports and import-competing goods lose due to trade restrictions, they too are typically a diffuse group of individuals, none of whom individually will be affected a great deal because of any single import restriction. It is the simultaneous existence of concentrated benefits and diffuse costs that led to Mark Twain's conclusion that the protectionists would often win the votes. (Concentrated benefits and dispersed costs are at the heart of Chapter 2, "Ethanol Madness," and Chapter 21, "Raising Less Corn and More Hell," in explaining some U.S. domestic policies.)

Of course, the protectionists don't win all the votes—after all, about one-seventh of the U.S. economy is based on international trade. Despite the opposition to free trade that comes from many quarters, its benefits to the economy as a whole are so great that it is unthinkable that we might do away with international trade altogether. Thus when we think about developments such as NAFTA and the WTO, it is clear that both economic theory and empirical evidence indicate that Americans will be better off after—and because of—the move to freer trade.

DISCUSSION QUESTIONS

1. During the late 1980s and early 1990s, American automobile manufacturers greatly increased the quality of the cars they produced relative to the quality of the cars produced in other nations. What effect do you think this had on American imports of Japanese cars, on Japanese imports of American cars, and on American exports of goods and services other than automobiles?

2. Over the past twenty years, some Japanese automakers have opened plants in the United States so that they could produce (and sell) "Japanese" cars here. What effect do you think this had on American imports of Japanese cars, on Japanese imports of American cars, and on American exports of goods and services other than automobiles?

3. For a number of years, Japanese carmakers voluntarily limited the number of cars they exported to the United States. What effect do you think this had on Japanese imports of American cars and on American exports of goods and services other than automobiles?

4. Until recently, American cars exported to Japan had driver controls on the left side (as in the United States), even though the Japanese drive on the left side of the road and Japanese cars sold in Japan had driver controls on the right side. Suppose the Japanese tried to sell their cars in the United States with the driver controls on the right side. What impact would this likely have on their sales in this country? Do you think the unwillingness of American carmakers to put the driver controls on the correct side for exports to Japan had any effect on their sales of cars in that country?

The $750,000 Steelworker

In even-numbered years, particularly years evenly divisible by 4, politicians are apt to give speeches about the need to protect U.S. jobs from the evils of foreign **competition.** We are thus encouraged to buy American. If further encouragement is needed, we are told that if we do not voluntarily reduce the amount of imported goods we purchase, the government will impose (or make more onerous) either **tariffs** (taxes) on imported goods or **quotas** (quantity restrictions) that physically limit **imports.** The objective is to save U.S. jobs.

Unlike black rhinos or blue whales, U.S. jobs are in no danger of becoming extinct. There are an infinite number of potential jobs in the American economy, and there always will be. Some of these jobs are not very pleasant, and many others do not pay very well, but there will always be employment of some sort as long as there is **scarcity.** Thus when a steelworker making $72,000 per year says that imports of foreign steel should be reduced to save his job, what he really means is this: He wants to be protected from competition so he can continue his present employment at the same or higher salary rather than move to a different employment that has less desirable working conditions or pays a lower salary. There is nothing wrong with the steelworker's goal (better working conditions and higher pay), but it has nothing to do with saving jobs.

In any discussion of the consequences of restrictions on international trade, it is essential to remember two facts. First, *we pay for imports with **exports.*** It is true that in the short run, we can sell off assets or borrow from abroad if we happen to import more goods and services than we export. But we have only a finite amount of assets to sell, and foreigners do not want to wait forever before we pay our bills. Ultimately, our accounts can be settled only if we provide (export) goods and services to the trading partners from whom we purchase (import) goods and services. Trade, after all, involves *quid pro quo* (literally, something for something). The second point to remember is that *voluntary trade is mutually beneficial to the trading partners.* If we restrict international trade, we reduce those benefits, both for our trading partners and for ourselves. One way these reduced benefits are manifested is in the form of curtailed employment opportunities for workers. In a nutshell, even though tariffs and quotas enhance job opportunities in import-competing industries, they also cost us jobs in export industries; the net effect seems to be *reduced* employment overall.

What is true for the United States is also true for other countries: They will buy our goods only if they can market theirs, because they too have to export goods to pay for their imports. Thus any U.S. restrictions on imports—via tariffs, quotas, or other means—ultimately cause a reduction in our exports, because other countries will be unable to pay for our goods. Hence import restrictions must inevitably decrease the size of our export sector. So imposing trade restrictions to save jobs in import-competing industries has the effect of costing jobs in export industries.

Import restrictions also impose costs on U.S. consumers. By reducing competition from abroad, quotas, tariffs, and other trade restraints push up the prices of foreign goods and enable U.S. producers to hike their own prices. Perhaps the best-documented example of this is the automobile industry.

Due in part to the enhanced quality of imported cars, sales of domestically produced automobiles fell from 9 million units in 1978 to an average of 6 million units per year between 1980 and 1982. **Profits** for U.S. automobile manufacturers plummeted as well, turning into substantial losses for some of them. U.S. automakers and autoworkers' unions demanded protection from import competition. They were joined in their cries by politicians from automobile-producing states. The result was a voluntary agreement by Japanese car companies (the most important competitors of U.S. firms) that restricted U.S. sales of Japanese cars to 1.68 million units per year. This agreement—which amounted to a quota even though it never officially bore that name— began in April 1981 and continued into the 1990s in various forms.

Robert W. Crandall, an economist with the Brookings Institution, has estimated how much this voluntary trade restriction has cost U.S. consumers in terms of higher car prices. According to his estimates, the reduced supply of Japanese cars pushed their prices up by $1,600 apiece, measured in 2005 dollars. The higher price of Japanese imports in turn enabled domestic producers to hike their prices an average of $640 per car. The total tab in the first full year of the program was about $7 billion. Crandall also estimated the number of jobs in automobile-related industries that were saved by the voluntary import restrictions at about 26,000. Dividing $7 billion by 26,000 jobs yields a cost to consumers of about $275,000 per year for every job saved in the automobile industry. U.S. consumers could have saved over $2 billion on their car purchases each year if instead of implicitly agreeing to import restrictions, they had simply given $75,000 to every autoworker whose job was preserved by the voluntary import restraints.

The same types of calculations have been made for other industries. Tariffs in the apparel industry were increased between 1977 and 1981, saving the jobs of about 116,000 U.S. apparel workers at a cost of $45,000 per job each year. At about the same time, the producers of citizens band radios also managed to get tariffs raised. Approximately six hundred workers in the industry kept their jobs as a result, at an annual cost to consumers of over $85,000 per job.

The cost of protectionism has been even higher in other industries. Jobs preserved in the glassware industry due to trade restrictions cost $200,000 apiece each year. In the maritime industry, the yearly cost of trade protection is $270,000 per job. In the steel industry, the cost of preserving a job has been estimated at an astounding $750,000 per year. If free trade were permitted, each worker losing a job could be given a cash payment of half that amount each year, and consumers would still save a lot of money.

Even so, this is not the full story. None of these studies estimating the cost to consumers of saving jobs in import-competing industries have attempted to estimate the ultimate impact of import restrictions on the flow of exports, the number of jobs lost in the export sector, and thus the total number of jobs gained or lost.

When imports to the United States are restricted, our trading partners can afford to buy less of what we produce. The resulting decline in export sales means fewer jobs in exporting industries. And the total reduction in trade leads to fewer jobs for workers such as stevedores (who unload ships) and truck drivers (who carry goods to and from ports). On both counts—the overall cut in trade and the accompanying decline in exports—**protectionism** leads to job losses that might not be obvious immediately.

Several years ago, Congress tried to pass a domestic content bill for automobiles. In effect, the legislation would have required that cars sold in the United States have a minimum percentage of their components manufactured and assembled in this country. Proponents of the legislation argued that it would have protected three hundred thousand jobs in the U.S. automobile manufacturing and auto parts supply industries. Yet the legislation's supporters failed to recognize the negative impact of the bill on trade in general and its ultimate impact on U.S. export industries. A U.S. Department of Labor study did recognize these impacts, estimating that the domestic content legislation would actually cost more jobs in trade-related and export industries than it protected in import-competing businesses. Congress ultimately decided not to impose a domestic content requirement for cars sold in the United States.

More recently, when President Bush decided in 2002 to impose tariffs of up to 30 percent on steel imports, the adverse effects on the economy were substantial and soon apparent. To take but one example, prior to the tariffs, the Port of New Orleans relied on steel imports for more than 40 percent of its revenues, in part because once steel coming into the port is offloaded, the ships are cleaned and refilled with U.S. grain for export. By reducing imports, the tariffs slashed economic activity at the port and cut U.S. grain exports. Businesses and farms all up and down the Mississippi River were adversely affected. More broadly, the higher costs of imported steel produced a decline in employment in U.S. industries that use steel as an input. Indeed, one study estimated that due to the tariffs, some two hundred thousand people lost their jobs in 2002 in these industries alone—a number that exceeded the total number of people actually employed by the steel manufacturing firms protected by the tariff.

In principle, trade restrictions are imposed to provide economic help to specific industries and to increase employment in those industries. Ironically, the long-term effects may be just the opposite. Researchers at the **World Trade Organization (WTO)** examined employment in three industries that have been heavily protected throughout the world: textiles, clothing, and iron and steel. Despite stringent trade protection for these industries, employment *declined* during the period of protection, in some cases dramatically. In textiles, employment fell 22 percent in the United States and 46 percent in the European Union. The clothing industry had employment losses ranging from 18 percent in the United States to 56 percent in Sweden. Declines in employment in the iron and steel industry ranged anywhere from 10 percent in Canada to 54 percent in the United States. In short, restrictions on free trade are no guarantee against job losses, even in the industries supposedly being protected.

The evidence seems clear: The cost of protecting jobs in the short run is huge. And in the long run, it appears that jobs cannot be protected, especially if one considers all aspects of protectionism. Free trade is a tough platform on which to run for office. But it is the one that yields the most general benefits if implemented. Of course, this does not mean that politicians will embrace it, and so we end up "saving" jobs at a cost of $750,000 each.

DISCUSSION QUESTIONS

1. Who gains and who loses from import restrictions?

2. What motivates politicians to impose trade restrictions?

3. If it would be cheaper to give each steelworker $375,000 per year in cash than impose restrictions on imports of steel, why do we have the import restrictions rather than the cash payments?

4. Most U.S. imports and exports travel through our seaports at some point. How do you predict that members of Congress from coastal states would vote on proposals to restrict international trade? What other information would you want to know when making such a prediction?

CHAPTER THIRTY-TWO

The Lion, the Dragon, and the Future

In the 1980s, a select group of economies in Asia came to be known as the "Asian tigers" because of their aggressive approach to economic growth. Among the tigers were Singapore, Malaysia, Thailand, and Indonesia. All took the view that a combination of low wages and high **export** sales represented the fast track to economic growth and prosperity. Now these tigers are being overtaken by the "dragon" of Asia—China— which is following the same path, with perhaps even more success.

For decades after the Communists' rise to power in 1949, China was best known for poverty and repression, and its aggression came mostly on the military front. But in recent years, *economic* aggression has become the byword. Although both poverty and repression are still the norm, both are changing for the better. China, it seems, is trying to learn from capitalism, even if not converting to it.

China's economic offensive began almost thirty years ago in its southeastern province of Guangdong. The Chinese leadership decided to use this province as a test case, to see if capitalist **direct foreign investment** could stimulate **economic growth** in a way that could be politically controlled. The experience was deemed a success— economic growth soared amid political stability. What the government learned from the experience helped it smooth the 1997 transition of Hong Kong from British to Chinese control. Most important in terms of China's long-term economic aspirations, many foreign investors came to view the Guangdong experiment as solid evidence that they could invest in China without fear that the Communist government would confiscate their capital. Beginning about 1992, foreign investment in China began to soar. The annual rate of such investment is more than ten times greater than it was at the beginning of the 1990s.

There are two powerful forces that are attracting economic investment to China: **demand** and **supply.** On the demand side, 1.3 billion people live there, some 20 percent of the world's population. Although **per capita income** is still low by world standards, it has been increasing by more than 6 percent per year, after adjusting for inflation. At that rate, the standard of living for the Chinese people—and hence their **purchasing power** in world markets—is doubling every decade or so. China is already the world's largest cell-phone market, with 200 million customers. Within a few years, it is estimated, China will account for 25 percent of the world's purchases of personal computers. Indeed, China now spends over $60 billion per year on information technology and services, and this amount is growing at a rate of nearly 30 percent per year. By 2030, the Chinese economy will likely have replaced the economy of the United States as the world's largest.

With its population of 1.3 billion, China also offers attractions on the supply side. Highly skilled workers have been plentiful in the Chinese labor market. China's universities produce more than 450,000 engineering graduates each year, including 50,000 in computer science. (By comparison, there are about 30,000 new computer science graduates each year in the United States.) In many cities, the fact that the Chinese workforce is generally well educated and often English-speaking has helped make the country attractive to foreign employers. Collaborative scientific ventures between Chinese researchers and U.S. firms are becoming increasingly common. A research team at Beijing University played a role in deciphering the genetic makeup of rice, for example. American computer hardware and software firms Intel, IBM, Oracle, and Microsoft have shifted some key components of their research to China in recent years. American firms are even setting up customer-service call centers in China. Microsoft customers from the United States who call for help may well find themselves talking with one of that company's four hundred engineers who are located in Shanghai.

Malaysia, Thailand, and Singapore are increasingly concerned by the growing competition they face from their neighbor to the north. Chinese medium- and high-tech industries are starting to cut into the **market share** of the very sectors that have helped fuel the growth of the Asian tigers in recent decades. The situation is even more critical in Japan, where wages are much higher than in China but whose technological lead over China is gradually eroding. "Are we to become a vassal of the Chinese dynasty again?" asked one Japanese official, clearly concerned that his nation's manufacturing firms were having trouble competing with Chinese firms. Eventually, Japan and China's other neighbors will adjust to the growing economic presence of China, but the transition may be unpleasant.

Most Americans, however, are more concerned about the likely impact on the U.S. economy of China's capitalist ambitions. Will the dragon consume American firms and jobs as it grows? The short answer is no. The long answer has two elements. To this point, a key element of China's competitiveness has been the low wages there. Even though American and European firms operating in China choose to pay their workers more than state-owned enterprises pay, this has still yielded considerable savings. As recently as five years ago, unskilled and semiskilled labor in China cost only 25 percent as much as in Europe. Moreover, foreign firms have been able to hire engineers for salaries that are only 10 to 20 percent of the cost of hiring engineers in the West.

Labor markets in China are changing rapidly, however. Average wages are rising at 6 to 8 percent per year, with bigger increases among higher-skilled workers, and migration into the cities has slowed due to a sharp cut in agricultural taxes. Many firms have been unable to hire as many workers as they would like, and most firms have had to upgrade their fringe benefits and other on-the-job amenities just to retain existing workers. Even so, turnover has soared as firms compete for a pool of talent that is no longer growing. Wages are still well below American and European levels, but the gap is closing steadily, thereby cutting the competitive advantage of many Chinese firms.

Rising wages in China will also translate into higher demand for goods produced by American and European firms. China, like all nations, must in the long run import goods equal in value to those it exports (unless China intends to give its exports away, which so far no one is claiming). This means that just as China has become a potent supplier of many goods and services, it is at the same time becoming a potent demander of still other goods and services.

Thus far, the Chinese demand for goods has not been as visible in American markets because American firms tend to produce goods and services designed for higher-income consumers, and China has, as yet, relatively few of those. In the meantime, the demand-side influence of the Chinese economy is already showing up, albeit in odd places. To take one example, right now China's most important import from the United States is trash. Ranging from used newspapers to scrap steel, Chinese companies buy billions of dollars' worth of the stuff every year to use as raw materials in the goods they produce. In addition to yielding profits (and employment) in these U.S. export industries, this exportation of U.S. trash reduces the burden on U.S. landfills and, by pushing up the prices of recyclable scrap, encourages more recycling in the United States.

Eventually, of course, we'd like to be sending China more than our rubbish, and that time is coming. As China's economy grows, so will the number of affluent Chinese, and with 1.3 billion potential candidates, that ultimately means *plenty* of consumers for America's high-end goods. Thus the long-run effects of China's growth will mean a different American economy—we'll be producing and consuming different mixes of goods and services—but America will also be a richer nation. Voluntary exchange, after all, creates wealth, and the Chinese dragon is big enough to create a lot of wealth.

Just to China's southwest, another giant is stirring. Around 1990, the lion of India began to throw off the self-imposed shackles of nearly a half-century of markets largely closed to international competition. The central government, for example, began opening many of its state-owned companies to competition from private-sector rivals. FedEx and United Parcel Service (UPS) have made huge inroads on the Indian postal service, and numerous foreign firms are now competing with the state-owned telephone service, which had long been a complete **monopoly.**

Entry into the Indian market brought familiarity with its workforce, many of whose members are fluent in English. The technical capabilities of graduates of top Indian universities, combined with their English skills and low wages, made them perfect staffers for a proliferation of call centers that have opened throughout India. Tens of thousands of technical and customer-relations jobs that used to go to Middle America are now held by the growing middle class in India. As we discussed in Chapter 14, "A Farewell to Jobs," it was in many respects this very movement that brought **outsourcing** to the forefront of the American consciousness.

But India, too, is struggling with growth. The talent pool at the top is thin: Only a dozen or so of India's seventeen thousand universities and colleges can compete with America's best, and the wages of graduates of these top schools are soaring. Moreover, India suffers from overwhelming infrastructure problems: Much of its road system is either overcrowded or in disrepair, and its port facilities are in desperate need of modernization. For the time being, such transportation problems are likely to keep India from becoming a major manufacturing powerhouse. India has also been hampered by its huge and seemingly permanent government bureaucracy. For example, despite the fact that the postal service there has lost more than half of its business to newcomers such as FedEx and UPS, none of the 550,000 postal service employees can be fired.

At least India is a democracy, and its legal system, inherited from the British, who ruled there for so long, is in close conformity with the legal systems of most developed nations. Matters are rather different in China. As noted in Chapter 4, "The Mystery of Wealth," political and legal **institutions** are crucial foundations for sustained economic growth. Despite the advances China has made over the past thirty years, its wealth-creating future may be clouded unless it can successfully deal with two crucial institutional issues.

First, there is the matter of resolving the tension inherent when a Communist dictatorship tries to use capitalism as the engine of economic growth. Capitalism thrives best in an environment of freedom and itself creates an awareness of and appreciation for the benefits of that freedom. Yet freedom is antithetical to the ideological and political tenets of the Communist government of China. Will the government be tempted to confiscate the fruits of capitalist success to support itself? Or will growing pressure for more political freedom force the government to repress the capitalist system to protect itself? Either route would likely bring economic growth in China to a swift halt.

The second potential long-run problem faced by China lies in that nation's cultural attitude toward **intellectual property.** In a land in which imitation is viewed as the sincerest form of flattery, it is routine to use the ideas of others in one's own pursuits. As a result, patent and copyright laws in China are far weaker than in Western nations. Moreover, actions elsewhere considered to be commercial theft (such as software piracy) are largely tolerated in China. If foreign firms find that they cannot protect their economic assets in the Chinese market, foreign investment will suffer accordingly, and so will the growing dragon that depends on it so heavily.

DISCUSSION QUESTIONS

1. Currently, AIDS is spreading rapidly in China and India. If the governments of these nations fail to stop the spread of AIDS, what are the likely consequences for future economic growth in China and India?

2. In 1989, a massive protest against political repression in China was halted by the government's massacre of more than 150 individuals at Tiananmen Square in Beijing. What impact do you think that episode had on foreign investment and growth in China during the years immediately thereafter?

3. Most of the advances in institutions in China have come in the cities rather than in the countryside. Indeed, local officials in farming villages actively redistribute wealth among villagers to keep the distribution of income among local farmers roughly equal. Thus a farmer's success or failure with his crops has little impact on his family's standard of living. Given these facts, where do you think the economic growth in China has occurred over the past thirty years, in the cities or on the farms? Explain.

4. Explain how the following factors will influence India's ability to compete in a highly competitive, rapidly changing global marketplace: (a) an educational system that is largely state-operated and that emphasizes job security for teachers and professors; (b) a transportation infrastructure that is largely antiquated and in disrepair; and (c) a political system that is adept at protecting favored constituents from competition and handing out favors that have concentrated benefits and widely dispersed costs.

Glossary

Absolute advantage: The ability to produce more of a good, without regard for the costs of forgone output of other goods.

Acreage-restriction program: A federal government limit on the number of acres that a farmer can plant with a particular crop.

Biofuels: Fuels made from once-living organisms or their by-products.

Capital stock: The collection of productive assets that can be combined with other inputs, such as labor, to produce goods and services.

Cartel: A group of independent businesses, often on an international scale, that agree to restrict trade, to their mutual benefit.

Civil law system: A legal system in which statutes passed by legislatures and executive decrees, rather than judicial decisions based on precedent, form the basis for most legal rules.

Common law system: A legal system in which judicial decisions based on precedent, rather than executive decrees or statutes passed by legislatures, form the basis for most legal rules.

Comparative advantage: The ability to produce a good at a lower opportunity cost than others. The principle of comparative advantage implies that individuals, firms, and nations will specialize in producing goods for which they have the lowest opportunity cost compared to other entities.

Compensating differential: Additional pay given to workers employed in particularly hazardous or unpleasant jobs.

Competition: Rivalry among buyers or sellers of outputs or among buyers or sellers of inputs.

Congestion costs: Costs (such as excess travel time) caused by too many users attempting simultaneously to access a facility such as a highway or a computer network.

Congestion pricing: Adjusting prices to counteract the fact that use of a resource by one consumer reduces its value for other consumers or raises their costs of using it; examples are road tolls that vary by the amount of traffic on the road.

Constant-dollar price: Price corrected for changes in the purchasing power of the dollar, taking inflation and deflation into account.

Cost: The highest-valued (best) forgone alternative; the most valuable option that is sacrificed when a choice is made.

Demand: The willingness and ability to purchase goods.

Demand curve: A graphic representation of demand: a negatively sloped line showing the inverse relationship between the price and the quantity demanded.

Demand schedule: A set of prices and the quantity demanded at each price. This schedule shows the rate of planned purchases per time period at different prices of the good.

Direct foreign investment: Resources provided to individuals and firms in a nation by individuals or firms located in other countries, often taking the form of foreign subsidiary or branch operations of a parent company.

Economic good: Any good or service that is scarce.

Economic growth: Sustained increases over time in real per capita income.

Economic profits: Profits in excess of competitive profits, which are the minimum necessary to keep resources employed in an industry.

Economies of scale: Cost structure for the firm that has the characteristic that the average costs of production decline as the level of output increases. *See also* Increasing returns.

Elastic demand: Characteristic of a demand curve in which a given percentage change in price will result in a larger inverse percentage change in quantity demanded. Total revenues and price are inversely related in the elastic portion of the demand curve.

Elasticity: A measure of the responsiveness of one variable to changes in the value of another variable, calculated as the percentage change in the dependent variable divided by the percentage change in the independent variable.

Elasticity of demand: Responsiveness of the quantity of a commodity demanded to a change in its price per unit. *See also* Price elasticity of demand.

Elasticity of supply: Responsiveness of the quantity of a commodity supplied to a change in its price per unit. *See also* Price elasticity of supply.

Entitlement program: A government program that guarantees a certain level of benefits to persons who meet the requirements set by law.

Equilibrium price: Price that clears the market when there is no excess quantity demanded or supplied; the price at which the demand curve intersects the supply curve. *Also called* Market-clearing price.

Exports: Sales of goods or services to a foreign country.

Externalities: Benefits or costs of an economic activity that spill over to a third party. Pollution is a negative spillover or externality.

Fixed exchange rates: A system of legally fixed prices (rates) at which two or more national currencies trade (exchange) for one another.

Free good: Any good or service available in larger quantities than desired at a zero price.

Full cost: The combined measure of all of the things that must be given up to undertake an activity; includes both the money price (other goods that must be sacrificed) and the value of the time that must be sacrificed.

Gains from trade: The extent to which individuals, firms, or nations benefit by engaging in exchange.

Human capital: The accumulated training, education, and knowledge of workers.

Imports: Purchases of goods or services from a foreign country.

Import tariff: A tax applied specifically to imports of goods or services from another nation.

Incentives: Perceived consequences of actions or decisions; they may be positive or negative and monetary or nonmonetary.

Incentive structure: The set of costs and benefits facing decision makers.

Income elasticity of demand: A measure of the responsiveness of demand to changes in income, calculated as the percentage change in demand for a good divided by the percentage change in consumer income.

Income mobility: The tendency of individuals to move around in the income distribution over time.

Increasing returns: Cost structure for the firm that has the characteristic that the average costs of production decline as the level of output increases. *See also* Economies of scale.

Inelastic demand: Characteristic of a demand curve in which a given change in price will result in a less than proportionate inverse change in the quantity demanded. Total revenue and price are directly related in the inelastic region of the demand curve.

In-kind transfers: Grants of goods and services, rather than cash to recipients who meet certain criteria. Examples include Medicare, Medicaid, subsidized housing, food stamps, and school lunches.

Institutions: The basic rules, customs, and practices of society.

Intellectual property: Creative ideas and expressions of the human mind that have commercial value and receive the legal protection of a property right, as through the issuance of a patent, copyright, or trademark.

Labor force participation rate: The sum of all people who are working or are available for and looking for work, divided by the population; both numerator and denominator are generally restricted to persons age sixteen and above.

Law of demand: Law stating that quantity demanded and price are inversely related—more is bought at a lower price and less at a higher price (other things being equal).

Law of supply: Law stating that a direct relationship exists between price and quantity supplied (other things being equal).

Luxury good: A good for which the income elasticity of demand is greater than 1, meaning that people spend an increasing proportion of their income on the good as they get richer.

Marginal analysis: Analysis of what happens when small changes take place relative to the status quo.

Marginal benefits: Additional benefits associated with one more unit of a good or action; the change in total benefits due to the addition of one more unit of production.

Marginal costs: Changes in total costs due to a change in one unit of production.

Market-clearing price: *See* Equilibrium price.

Market share: The proportion of total sales in an industry accounted for by the sales of a specific firm or group of firms in that industry.

Market supply: Total quantities of a good offered for sale by suppliers at various prices.

Median age: Age that exactly separates the younger half of the population from the older half.

Merger: The joining together into common ownership of two or more formerly independent companies.

Minimum wage: The lowest hourly wage that firms may legally pay their workers.

Models, or theories: Simplified representations of the real world used to make predictions or to better understand the real world.

Monitoring costs: Costs that must be incurred to observe the behavior of a politician or other agent to whom responsibilities have been delegated.

Monopolistic competition: The situation that exists when producers and sellers offer for sale similar products with slight variations in features or quality; although the products are priced above their average minimum cost, competition among firms reduces long-run economic profits to zero.

Monopoly: A single supplier; a firm that faces a downward-sloping demand curve for its output and therefore can choose the price at which it will sell the good; an example of a *price searcher.*

Monopoly power: The ability of a company to charge a price for its product that is in excess of the marginal cost of producing the product.

Monopsonist: A firm operating as a monopsony.

Monopsony: A single buyer; a firm that faces an upward-sloping supply curve for its input and therefore can choose the price at which it will buy the good; an example of a *price searcher.*

Natural monopoly: A monopoly that arises when there are large economies of scale relative to the industry's demand.

Natural-resource endowments: The collection of naturally occurring minerals (such as oil and iron ore) and living things (such as forests and fish stocks) that can be used to produce goods and services.

Negative externality: A cost associated with an economic activity that is paid by third parties. Pollution is a negative externality because, for example, someone other than the driver of an automobile bears part of the cost of the car's exhaust emissions.

Network effect: Change in the benefit that an agent derives from a good when the number of other agents consuming (or using) the same kind of good changes.

Nominal prices: Prices expressed in terms of current dollars rather than in terms of inflation-adjusted dollars.

Nonprice competition: Offering additional services or higher product quality to attract business instead of cutting prices to do so.

Oligopoly: A firm that is one of very few sellers (or buyers) in a market; in such a case, each firm reacts to changes in the prices and quantities of its rivals.

Opportunity cost: The highest-valued alternative that must be sacrificed to attain something or to satisfy a want.

Outsourcing: The practice of having workers located in foreign lands perform tasks (typically services) that have traditionally been performed by domestic workers.

Per capita income: Average income per person.

Perfectly elastic: Characterized by an infinite value for the ratio of the percentage change in quantity over the percentage change in price, measured along a demand or supply curve; visually, a perfectly elastic curve appears horizontal.

Physical capital: Nonhuman productive resources.

Political economy: The use of economics to study the causes and consequences of political decision making.

Positive-sum game: Process or setting in which more than one participant gains. Voluntary exchange is said to be a positive-sum game because both parties are simultaneously made better off.

Price discrimination: Selling at prices that do not reflect differences in marginal costs; different prices with the same marginal costs, for example, or the same prices with different marginal costs.

Price elasticity of demand: The percentage change in quantity demanded divided by the percentage change in price. *See also* Elasticity of demand.

Price elasticity of supply: The percentage change in quantity supplied divided by the percentage change in price. *See also* Elasticity of supply.

Price searcher: A firm that must search for the profit-maximizing price because it faces a downward-sloping demand curve (if it is a seller) or an upward-sloping supply curve (if it is a buyer); often used as a synonym for *monopoly* or *monopsony*.

Price-support program: A government program that mandates minimum prices for crops.

Price taker: Any economic agent that takes the market price as given; often used as a synonym for a firm operating in a market characterized by *pure competition*.

Private costs: Costs incurred by the relevant decision maker.

Product differentiation: Distinguishing products by brand name, color, and other minor attributes.

Productivity: Output produced per unit of input.

Profit: Income generated by selling something for a higher price than was paid for it. In production, the income generated is the difference between total revenues received from consumers who purchase the goods and the total cost of producing those goods.

Property and contract rights: Legal rules governing the use and exchange of property, and the enforceable agreements between people or businesses.

Property rights: Set of rules specifying how a good may be used and exchanged.

Protectionism: The imposition of rules designed to protect certain individuals or firms from competition, usually competition from imported goods.

Proven reserves: Estimated quantities of oil and gas that geological and engineering data demonstrate with reasonable certainty to be recoverable in future years from known reservoirs under existing economic and operating conditions.

Purchasing power: Ability or means to acquire goods and services.

Pure competition: A market structure in which participants individually have no influence over market prices; all act as *price takers.*

Quality-constant price: The price of a good adjusted upward or downward to reflect the higher- or lower-than-average quality of that good.

Quota: A limit on the amount of a good or an activity; often used in international trade to limit the amount of some foreign good that may be imported into a country.

Rate of return: The net benefit, in percentage terms, of engaging in an activity. For example, if the investment of $1.00 yields a gross return of $1.20, the net benefit is $0.20 and the rate of return is $0.20/$1.00 = 20$ percent.

Rational ignorance: A state in which knowledge is incomplete because obtaining perfect information is too costly.

Real per capita income: Gross domestic product (GDP) corrected for inflation and divided by population.

Real price: A price that is adjusted for inflation and thus is expressed in terms of some base year.

Regulated monopoly: A price searcher whose key business decisions, such as the price at which it sells its output, are regulated by a government agency.

Rent control: A system in which the government tells building owners how much they can charge for rent.

Resource: Any input used in the production of desired goods and services.

Rule of law: The principle that relations between individuals, businesses, and the government are governed by clearly enumerated rules that apply to everyone in society.

Scarce good: Any good that commands a positive price.

Scarcity: State of nature in which resources are limited even though wants are unlimited. Scarcity means that nature does not freely provide as much of everything as people want.

Shortage: Situation in which an excess quantity is demanded or an insufficient quantity is supplied; the difference between the quantity demanded and the quantity supplied at a specific price below the market-clearing price.

Social cost: The full cost that society bears when a resource-using action occurs. For example, the social cost of driving a car is equal to all private costs plus any additional cost that other members of society bear (such as air pollution and traffic congestion).

Stock: The quantity of something at a particular point in time. An inventory of goods is a stock. A bank account at a point in time is a stock. Stocks are defined independent of time, although they are assessed at a point in time.

Subsidies: Government payments for the production of specific goods, generally designed to raise the profits of the firms receiving the subsidies and often intended to increase the output of the subsidized goods.

Supply: The willingness and ability to sell goods.

Supply curve: A graphic representation of supply, which slopes upward (has a positive slope) showing the positive relationship between price and quantity supplied.

Supply schedule: A set of prices and the quantity supplied at each price; a schedule showing the rate of planned production at each relative price for a specified time period.

Support price: The minimum price that farmers are guaranteed to receive for their crop, as set by the federal government. If the market price falls below the support price, the government purchases enough of the crop to bring the market price up to the support price.

Surplus: Excess quantity supplied or an insufficient quantity demanded; the difference between the quantity supplied and the quantity demanded at a price above the market-clearing price. As applied to the government budget, an excess of tax receipts over expenditures.

Tangible assets: Assets that have a physical presence, such as cars, buildings, and jets, as contrasted with intangible assets such as copyrights, patents, bonds, and stocks.

Target price: The minimum price that farmers are guaranteed to receive for their crop, as set by the federal government. If the market price falls below the target price, farmers receive a payment equal to the difference between the two (multiplied by their production of the crop).

Tariff: A tax levied on imports.

Technological change: A change in the set of feasible production possibilities, typically the result of the productive implementation of new knowledge.

Trade barriers: Any rules having the effect of reducing the amount of international exchange. *Tariffs* and *quotas* are trade barriers.

Trade-off: Term relating to opportunity cost. In order to get a desired economic good, it is necessary to trade off (give up) some other desired economic good in a situation of scarcity. A trade-off involves making a sacrifice in order to obtain something.

Transaction costs: *Costs* of conducting exchanges of goods.

Type I error: An error of commission, such as might arise when an unsafe drug is mistakenly permitted to be sold.

Type II error: An error of omission, such as might arise if a beneficial drug is mistakenly prevented from reaching the market.

Voucher: A document that authorizes a person to receive a specified dollar amount of services at no charge.

White-collar jobs: Employment in which workers rely chiefly on their intellect and knowledge rather than their physical skills.

World Trade Organization (WTO): An association of more than 145 nations that helps reduce trade barriers among its members and settles international trade disputes among them.

Zone pricing: Setting different retail prices in different geographical areas, depending on the characteristics of customers in those areas; a practice of major oil companies.

Selected References

Chapter 1—Death by Bureaucrat

Kazman, Sam. "Deadly Overcaution: FDA's Drug Approval Process." *Journal of Regulation and Social Cost* 1, no. 1 (1990): 35–54.

Peltzman, Sam. "An Evaluation of Consumer Protection Legislation: The 1962 Drug Amendments." *Journal of Political Economy* 81, no. 1 (1973): 1049–1091.

Walker, Steven. "S.O.S. to the FDA." *Wall Street Journal Online,* August 26, 2003. (http://online.wsj.com/article/SB106185410295150100-search.html)

Chapter 2—Ethanol Madness

Barrionuevo, Alexei. "Boom in Ethanol Reshapes Economy of Heartland." *New York Times,* June 25, 2006, p.1.

Environmental Protection Agency. *Regulatory Announcement: Removal of Reformulated Gasoline Oxygen Content Requirement and Revision of Commingling Prohibition to Address Non-Oxygenated Reformulated Gasoline.* Document no. EPA420-F-06–020. Washington, D.C.: Environmental Protection Agency, February 2006.

Tokgoz, Simla. "Policy and Competitiveness of U.S. and Brazilian Ethanol." *Iowa Ag Review Online,* Spring 2006. (www.card.iastate.edu/iowa_ag_review/spring_06/article3.aspx)

www.eia.doe.gov. Official Web site of the Energy Information Administration.

Chapter 3—Flying the Friendly Skies?

Mitchell, Mark L., and Michael T. Maloney. "Crisis in the Cockpit? The Role of Market Forces in Promoting Air Travel Safety." *Journal of Law and Economics* 32, no. 2 (1989): 139–184.

www.airsafe.com. Statistics on airline safety.

www1.faa.gov. Official Web site of the Federal Aviation Administration.

Chapter 4—The Mystery of Wealth

Easterly, William, and Ross Levine. "Tropics, Germs, and Crops: How Endowments Influence Economic Development." *Journal of Monetary Economics* 50, no. 1 (2003): 3–39.

Mahoney, Paul G. "The Common Law and Economic Growth: Hayek Might Be Right." *Journal of Legal Studies* 30, no. 3 (2001): 503–525.

Chapter 5—Sex, Booze, and Drugs

Becker, Gary, Kevin M. Murphy, and Michael Grossman. "The Market for Illegal Goods: The Case of Drugs." *Journal of Political Economy* 114, no. 1 (2006): 38–60.

Benjamin, Daniel K., and Roger LeRoy Miller. *Undoing Drugs: Beyond Legalization.* New York: Basic Books, 1993.

Hardy, Quentin. "Inside Dope." *Forbes,* November 10, 2003, pp. 146–154.

Miron, Jeffrey A., and Jeffrey Zwiebel. "Alcohol Consumption during Prohibition." *American Economic Review* 81, no. 2 (1991): 242–247.

Chapter 6—Expanding Waistlines

Chou, Shin-Y., Michael Grossman, and Henry Saffer. *An Economic Analysis of Adult Obesity: Results from the Behavioral Risk Factor Surveillance System.* NBER Working Paper no. 9247. Boston: National Bureau of Economic Research, 2002.

Cutler, D. M., E. L. Glaeser, and J. M. Shapiro. *Why Have Americans Become More Obese?* Cambridge, Mass.: Harvard University Department of Economics, 2003.

Lakdawalla, D., and T. Philipson. *The Growth of Obesity and Technological Change: A Theoretical and Empirical Analysis.* NBER Working Paper no. 8946. Boston: National Bureau of Economic Research, 2002.

Thorpe, Kenneth E., and David H. Howard. "The Rise in Spending among Medicare Beneficiaries: The Role of Chronic Disease Prevalence and Changes in Treatment Intensity." *Health Affairs* 25, no. 5 (2006): W328–W388.

Chapter 7—Is Water Different?

Anderson, Terry, and Pamela S. Snyder. *Water Markets: Priming the Invisible Pump.* Washington, D.C.: Cato Institute, 1997.

Hanke, Steve. "Demand for Water under Dynamic Conditions." *Water Resources Research* 6, no. 5 (1970): 1253–1261.

Chapter 8—Slave Redemption in Sudan

Miniter, Richard. "The False Promise of Slave Redemption." *Atlantic Monthly*, January 1999, pp. 63–70.

Vick, Karl. "Ripping Off Slave 'Redeemers.'" *Washington Post,* February 26, 2002, p. A1.

Walsh, Declan. "Fake Slaves Con Aid Agency in Sudanese Liberation Scam." *Scotsman,* February 24, 2002. (scotlandonsunday.scotsman.com/index.cfm?id=212232002)

Chapter 9—Smoking and Smuggling

Bartlett, Bruce. "Cigarette Smuggling." National Center for Policy Analysis, October 30, 2002. (www.ncpa.org/pub/ba/ba423)

Benjamin, Daniel K., and William R. Dougan. "Efficient Excise Taxation: The Evidence from Cigarettes." *Journal of Law and Economics* 40, no. 1 (1997): 113–136.

Yurekli, Ayda A., and Ping Zhang. "The Impact of Clean Indoor-Air Laws and Cigarette Smuggling on Demand for Cigarettes: An Empirical Model." *Health Economics* 9, no. 1 (2000): 159–170.

Chapter 10—Bankrupt Landlords, from Sea to Shining Sea

Downs, Anthony. *Residential Rent Controls: An Evaluation.* Washington, D.C.: Urban Land Institute, 1988.

Glaeser, Edward L., and Erzo F. P. Luttmer. "The Misallocation of Housing under Rent Control." *American Economic Review* 93, no. 4 (2003): 1027–1046.

Chapter 11—(Why) Are Women Paid Less?

Becker, Elizabeth, and Cotton M. Lindsay. "The Limits of the Wage Impact of Discrimination." *Managerial and Decision Economics* 26 (2005): 513–525.

Becker, Gary. *The Economics of Discrimination.* Chicago: University of Chicago Press, 1957.

Heckman, James J. "Detecting Discrimination." *Journal of Economic Perspectives* 12, no. 1 (1998): 101–116.

Chapter 12—The Effects of the Minimum Wage

Baker, Michael, Dwayne Benjamin, and Shuchita Stanger. "The Highs and Lows of the Minimum Wage Effects: A Time-Series Cross-Section Study of the Canadian Law." *Journal of Labor Economics* 17, no. 2 (1999): 318–350.

Card, David, and Alan Krueger. "Minimum Wages and Employment: A Case Study of the Fast-Food Industry in New Jersey and Pennsylvania." *American Economic Review* 84, no. 3 (1994): 772–793.

Neumark, David, and William Wascher. "Minimum Wages and Employment: A Case Study of the Fast-Food Industry in New Jersey and Pennsylvania: Comment." *American Economic Review* 90, no. 5 (2000): 1362–1396.

Rottenberg, Simon (ed.). *The Economics of Legal Minimum Wages.* Washington, D.C.: American Enterprise Institute, 1981.

Chapter 13—Immigration, Superstars, and Poverty in America

Borjas, George. *Heaven's Door: Immigration Policy and the American Economy.* Princeton, N.J.: Princeton University Press, 2001.

Rosen, Sherwin. "The Economics of Superstars." *American Economic Review* 71, no. 5 (1981): 845–858.

U.S. Bureau of the Census. "The Effects of Government Taxes and Transfers on Income and Poverty, 2004." April 27, 2006. (www.census.gov/hhes/www/poverty/effect2004/effect2004.html)

Chapter 14—A Farewell to Jobs

Browning, Lynnley. "Outsourcing Abroad Applies to Tax Returns, Too." *New York Times,* February 15, 2004, p. 12.

Federal Reserve Bank of Dallas. *The Fruits of Free Trade.* Annual Report. Dallas, Tex.: Federal Reserve Bank, 2002.

Madigan, Kathleen. "Outsourcing Jobs: Is It Bad?" *Business Week,* August 25, 2003, pp. 36–38.

Chapter 15—Monopsony and Competition in Health Care

Anderson, Gerard F., Uwe E. Reinhardt, Peter S. Hussey, and Varduhi Petrosyan. "It's the Prices, Stupid: Why the United States Is So Different from Other Countries." *Health Affairs* 22, no. 3 (2003): 89–105.

Finkelstein, Amy. "The Aggregate Effects of Health Insurance: Evidence from the Introduction of Medicare." *Quarterly Journal of Economics* 122, no. 1 (2007): pp. 1–37.

Reinhardt, Uwe E., Peter S. Hussey, and Gerard F. Anderson. "U.S. Health Care Spending in an International Context." *Health Affairs* 23, no. 3 (2004): 10–17.

Thomassen, Melissa. "Health Insurance in the United States." *EH.Net Encyclopedia*, ed. Robert Whaples, April 18, 2003. (en.net/encyclopedia/article/thomassen.insurance.health.us)

Chapter 16—Big Oil, Big Oil Prices?

Edmonds.com Editors. "Torch My Ride: Arson for Hire." CNN.com.autos, June 11, 2006. www.edmunds.com/apps/vdpcontainers/do/vdp/articleId=115584/pageNumber=1.

Maugeri, Leonardo. "Oil, Oil Everywhere." *Forbes*, July 24, 2005, p. 42.

"A Survey of Oil." *Economist*, April 30, 2005, pp. 3–9, 25–26.

www.eia.doe.gov/oil_gas/petroleum/data_publications/wrgp/mogas_history. html. A useful source for weekly gasoline prices around the country.

Chapter 17—Contracts, Combinations, and Conspiracies

Kanfer, Steven. *The Last Empire: DeBeers, Diamonds, and the World.* New York: Farrar, Straus & Giroux, 1993.

www.eia.doe.gov. Official Web site of the Energy Information Administration.

Zimbalist, Andrew. *Unpaid Professionals: Commercialism and Conflict in Big-Time College Sports.* Princeton, N.J.: Princeton University Press, 2001.

Chapter 18—Coffee, Tea, or Tuition-Free?

Chevalier, Judith, and Austan Goolsbee. "Measuring Prices and Price Competition Online: Amazon.com versus BarnesandNoble.com." *Quantitative Marketing and Economics* 1, no. 2 (2003): 203–222.

Odlyzko, Andrew. "Privacy, Economics, and Price Discrimination on the Internet." St. Paul: University of Minnesota, Digital Technology Center, 2003.

"They're Watching You." *Economist,* October 18, 2003, p. 77.

Chapter 19—College Costs (. . . and Costs and Costs)

Ehrenberg, Ronald G. *Tuition Rising: Why Colleges Cost So Much.* Cambridge, Mass.: Harvard University Press, 2002.

U.S. News & World Report Staff. *U.S. News Ultimate College Guide, 2006.* New York: Source Books, 2006.

Vedder, Richard. "Why Does College Cost So Much?" *Wall Street Journal,* August 23, 2005, p. 9.

Chapter 20—Keeping the Competition Out

Lipton, Eric. "Finding the Intersection of Supply and Demand." *New York Times,* November 23, 2003, p. 31.

www.schallerconsult.com/taxi/topics.htm. Facts on the New York City taxicab and taxi medallion markets.

Chapter 21—Raising More Hell and Less Corn

Becker, Elizabeth. "U.S. Corn Subsidies Said to Damage Mexico: Study Finds Farmers Lose Livelihoods." *New York Times,* August 27, 2003, p. C4.

Edwards, Chris, and Dan DeHaven. *Save the Farms—End the Subsidies.* Washington, D.C.: Cato Institute, 2002.

Fackler, Martin. "Japanese Farmers Losing Clout." *Wall Street Journal,* February 20, 2004, p. A10.

Chapter 22—Killer Cars and the Rise of the SUV

Crandall, Robert W., and John D. Graham. "The Effect of Fuel Economy Standards on Automobile Safety." *Journal of Law and Economics* 32, no. 1 (1989): 97–120.

Godek, Paul. "The Regulation of Fuel Economy and the Demand for 'Light Trucks.'" *Journal of Law and Economics* 40, no. 2 (1997): 495–517.

White, Michelle J. 2004. "The 'Arms Race' on American Roads: The Effect of Sport Utility Vehicles and Pickup Trucks on Traffic Safety." *Journal of Law and Economics* 47, no. 2 (2004): 333–355.

Chapter 23—Crime and Punishment

Levitt, Stephen. "The Effect of Prison Population Size on Crime Rates: Evidence from Prison Overcrowding Litigation." *Quarterly Journal of Economics* 111, no. 2 (1996): 319–351.

Levitt, Stephen. "Using Electoral Cycles in Police Hiring to Estimate the Effect of Police on Crime." *American Economic Review* 87, no. 3 (1997): 270–290.

Levitt, Stephen. "Juvenile Crime and Punishment." *Journal of Political Economy* 106, no. 6 (1998): 1156–1185.

Chapter 24—The Graying of America

Council of Economic Advisers. "Restoring Solvency to Social Security," *Economic Report of the President.* Washington, D.C.: Government Printing Office, 2004, ch. 6.

Miron, Jeffrey A., and David N. Weil. "The Genesis and Evolution of Social Security." In Michael D. Bordo, Claudia Goldin, and Eugene N. White (eds.), *The Defining Moment: The Great Depression and the American Economy in the Twentieth Century.* Chicago: University of Chicago Press, 1998, pp. 297–322.

Chapter 25—Heavenly Highway

Singer, Jason. "Lonesome Highways: Japan's Hefty Tolls Drive Cars Away." *Wall Street Journal,* September 15, 2003, p. A1.

Wheatley, Malcolm. "How IT Fixed London's Traffic Woes." *CIO Magazine,* July 15, 2003. (www.cio.com/archive/071503/london.html)

Chapter 26—The Trashman Cometh

Benjamin, Daniel K. *Eight Great Myths of Recycling.* Policy Series no. PS-28. Bozeman, MT: Property and Environment Research Center, 2003.

Fullerton, Don, and Thomas C. Kinnaman. "Household Responses to Pricing Garbage by the Bag." *American Economic Review* 88, no. 2 (1996): 971–984.

Hocking, Martin B. "Paper versus Polystyrene: A Complex Choice." *Science,* February 1991, pp. 504–505.

Hocking, Martin B. "Disposable Cups Have Eco-Merit." *Nature,* May 1994, p. 107.

Rathje, William, and Cullen Murphy. *Rubbish: The Archeology of Garbage.* New York: HarperCollins, 1992.

Chapter 27—Bye-Bye, Bison

Adler, Jonathan. "Bad for Your Land, Bad for the Critters." *Wall Street Journal,* December 31, 2003, p. A8.

Anderson, Terry L., and Peter J. Hill. *The Not So Wild, Wild West: Property Rights on the Frontier.* Stanford, Calif.: Stanford University Press, 2004.

Coase, Ronald. "The Problem of Social Cost." *Journal of Law and Economics* 3, no. 2 (1960): 1–40.

Grafton, R. Quentin, Dale Squires, and Kevin J. Fox. "Private Property and Economic Efficiency: A Study of a Common-Pool Resource." *Journal of Law and Economics* 43, no. 2 (2000): 679–713.

Lueck, Dean, and Jeffrey A. Michael. "Preemptive Habitat Destruction under the Endangered Species Act." *Journal of Law and Economics* 46, no. 1 (2003): 27–60.

Chapter 28—Smog Merchants

Foster, Vivien, and Robert W. Hahn. "Designing More Efficient Markets: Lessons from Los Angeles Smog Control." *Journal of Law and Economics* 38, no. 1 (1995): 19–48.

Joskow, Paul L., Richard Schmalensee, and Elizabeth M. Bailey. "The Market for Sulfur Dioxide Emissions." *American Economic Review* 88, no. 5 (1998): 669–685.

www.epa.gov/airmarkets/trading. EPA Web site for tradable emissions.

Chapter 29—Greenhouse Economics

Bradsher, Keith. "China's Boom Adds to Global Warming Problem." *New York Times,* October 22, 2003, p. A1.

Castles, Ian, and David Henderson. "The IPCC Emission Scenarios: An Economic-Statistical Critique." *Energy and Environment* 14, nos. 2, 3 (2003).

Lomborg, Bjorn. *The Skeptical Environmentalist.* New York: Cambridge University Press, 2001.

Sohngen, Brent, and Robert Mendelsohn. "Valuing the Impact of Large-Scale Ecological Change in a Market: The Effect of Climate Change on U.S. Timber." *American Economic Review* 89, no. 4 (1999): 686–710.

Chapter 30—Free Trade, Less Trade, or No Trade?

Eichengreen, Barry. "The Political Economy of the Smoot-Hawley Tariff." *Research in Economic History* 12, no. 1 (1989): 1–43.

Federal Reserve Bank of Dallas. *The Fruits of Free Trade.* Annual Report. Dallas, Tex.: Federal Reserve Bank, 2002.

Irwin, Douglas A. "From Smoot-Hawley to Reciprocal Trade Agreements: Changing the Course of U.S. Trade Policy in the 1930s." In Michael D. Bordo, Claudia Goldin, and Eugene N. White (eds.), *The Defining Moment: The Great Depression and the American Economy in the Twentieth Century.* Chicago: University of Chicago Press, 1998, pp. 325–352.

Chapter 31—The $750,000 Steelworker

Berry, Steven, James Levinsohn, and Ariel Pakes. "Voluntary Export Restraints on Automobiles: Evaluating a Trade Policy." *American Economic Review* 89, no. 3 (1999): 400–430.

Crandall, Robert W. "The Effects of U.S. Trade Protection for Autos and Steel." *Brookings Papers on Economic Activity,* vol. 1987, no. 1 (1987): 271–288.

Chapter 32—The Lion, the Dragon, and the Future

Eckholm, Erik, and Joseph Kahn. "China's Power Worries Neighbors." *New York Times,* December 1, 2002, p. 7.

Goodman, Peter S. "China Takes Pivotal Role in High-Tech Production." *International Herald Tribune,* December 5, 2002, p. 2.

Restall, Hugo. "New Property Rights for Chinese Farmers?" *Wall Street Journal Europe,* October 3–5, 2003, p. A7.

Index